Changing Eyes

Leanne Antaya

To my daughter, Mekenzi,
your patience, love, friendship, humour,
and willingness to let me cry a million tears while
we relived Travis's life was invaluable.
Few people are lucky enough to work so closely
with their best friend, soul mate and
daughter all rolled into one special blessing.

*****

FOREWORD

I am not a doctor or an expert on drug addiction, and I don't have a PHD in substance abuse or behavioral science. I can't claim to know the reasons why addiction is presently the nation's biggest health problem and that it's impossible to predict who's vulnerable to eventual dependence and abuse of drugs.

I know that the physical and mental repercussions of addiction are incomprehensible. The numbers and statistics are staggering. "Opioid crisis" We hear these words often, but we don't listen to them because we are numb and detached. Experts compare living with a loved one addicted to drugs or alcohol to being a prisoner of war, living in constant fear of what will happen today and every day after that.

I am familiar, however, with the challenges, suffering and heartache that accompanies addiction. After searching for my son for a week, I feared the worst. His drinking had become life-threatening. I found him in a motel room surrounded by empty vodka bottles and the smell of death. I sought out people familiar with his problem, but I mentally prepared myself for a funeral. The helplessness I felt as a parent contradicted the protection I was supposed to provide. I suffered with him. My family suffered with him. It was all or nothing when he drank, and I wasn't sure he could stop. He did and survived. So far.

My name is Mike O'Connor; my friends call me Okie. I have known Leanne Antaya for 45 years and her husband Marc forever. I grew up with him across the same street, where his father taught us the value of hard work and how to swing a hammer at a young age. I loved his Italian mother like my own. We hung out, had fun, got into trouble. We played football in college together. He was the brother I never had, and when he left for California, I knew he wasn't coming back. It was destiny.

He met and married a beautiful girl with a contagious laugh where they created a west coast life filled with a stunning mountain home, four beautiful children and a thriving high-end construction business. They were my family in the West, and I loved them all.

When I heard about their son Travis, I called Marc. His panicked words remain etched in my mind. "Welcome to my nightmare, Okie".

Leanne Antaya's story exposes the nightmare and makes it personal. She has opened up her heart and soul and spilt out her family's tale of drugs and addiction without holding back. It is an unbelievable journey into the addiction abyss, an emotional roller coaster that evokes tears, laughter, and inspiration. Leanne has brought the anguish of addiction up-close and personal. As a loving mother, wife, businesswoman, and caregiver, she has gifted us with a story from the point of view that only a mother could present. Her devotion and dogged persistence in her pursuit of healing opens our eyes to addiction and brings it home. Her writings will inspire and establish hope for anyone experiencing their nightmare. It is a how-to book on mending, healing and accepting the scars of trauma. Leanne has exposed to us a dark world shattered by crisis, and how with the help of her family and faith, she painstakingly puts the pieces back together. Through her example and determination, she shows us how to live life after a tragedy and how to thrive. Leanne succeeds in not just holding her family together but bringing them closer through constant, unconditional devotion and love. I asked her how she found strength while writing and persevered while reliving the suffering and pain. She answered that her tears slowed her down but never stopped her and then stoically said, "I never want to hear another mother cry."

She shows us that no one is safe and that we all need to be aware of drugs' grip on our neighbors and communities. We need to remove the stigma surrounding drug abuse and addiction and bring our stories to the forefront. Leanne makes it clear just how fragile our world is. How, in the blink of an eye, our lives can be altered by drugs and or alcohol forever. Here is her story of survival, the survival of a family.

Preface

ALL OF MY ATTEMPTS TO HELP TREY HAD BEEN IN VAIN.

No one understood, especially the doctors and counsellors, that Trey never wanted help. He didn't feel the need to survive and didn't care about death. He was ruining his life, but that didn't concern him. For years, I painfully watched him with a mother's sorrowful heart turn to the world of drugs. He believed that he would never achieve the success he hungered for without them.

His intense belief brought hazy green eyes, wild with a fierce craving for more creativity. All I could do was hope that the day I dreaded would not come, but it did. Trey's insatiable drug habit abruptly ended when he overdosed, died and then survived.

With little hope and many doctor's doubts, I started the journey to defy all odds. A journal and pen were all that I needed as I found time to write every day. The words *"He's getting better"* were written repeatedly in different words but with the same meaning. I watched my now "CLEAN" son relearn all that he knew before the overdose, and with hope in my heart, I pleaded that no one else would experience what I had.

The memories will live inside me forever, with the hope I never hear another mother cry.

Table of Contents

"The eyes are the window to your soul."

William Shakespeare

Chapter 1

AN INTENSE SILENCE ENSURED BEFORE I'M awakened from my dreams by the ringing telephone near my bed. *Damn it. It must be three in the morning! Who could be calling at this time?* I sit up, confused in the darkness, as I reach for the telephone. I pick it up and put it to my ear. Lisa fights for her breath as she tries to formulate a thought. Her voice is scared and panicked as she stutters to find the right words. She is hysterical as she speaks. "Oh, my God, Leigh, he's not going to make it!" She cries as she wipes her black mascara tears from her face. "He's not going to make it . . . I found him on the bathroom floor."

I remain stiffly seated as the unbelievable heartache consumes me as I silently pray to God that Trey will be okay. *Please, God, let him be okay. Please.* The paralyzing hurt runs through my body as I feel my hands tremble. My fearful thoughts surround me as I cling to the telephone, wishing it hadn't rung. As time creeps by, I hold the phone to my ear, desperately trying to hear what is happening in the hotel's bathroom. I knew this day would come, and now it's here, and I don't know how to react. I close my eyes and try to stay calm. *All right, I need to go to the emergency room. Trey has overdosed.* I repeat the words. *I need to go.* I drop the telephone and grab my head while my eyes bleed tears.

"He'll be alright." Marco reaches for me. I notice his hands are cold and clammy as he tries to hide his fear.

We climb into the family car for the indescribably sad and depressing ride to the hospital, remembering how many times we've grieved before. The drugs have taken him away, piece by piece, throughout the years while he fought with drug addiction and the demons surrounding him.

Chapter 2

IT WAS BACK IN 1977 WHEN MARCO, AGED sixteen, rushed down the street covered in broken concrete due to the overgrown maple trees. They lined the narrow roads in a small town near Boston where two-family homes were crammed together near the graveyards in the neighbourhood. A deep recession was evident in Marco's home town as for-sale signs yelled out for buyers, and the old industrial building had to close its doors at the end of the street. Marco's uncle, who once worked there, found himself unemployed along with many others.

"Mangia! Mangia!" A short, red-haired, big-bosomed Italian woman stood flat-footed as she stirred spaghetti sauce in a large cast-iron pot. Beatrice often spoke in her native tongue about her childhood in Italy and the family she left behind. She wore an old and worn-out apron with her favourite crucifix hanging between her breasts as she heated leftovers on her overly used stove. Pastries filled the large Italian bowl which sat on the rarely used dishwasher pushed up against the screened porch door. She preferred to wash her favourite dishes by hand. Statues of Saint Teresa and Padre Pio, whom Beatrice prayed to diligently, decorated her kitchen. When a coral-coloured rose presented itself in her garden, she claimed the Saints had answered her prayers. Overlapping prints of Van Gogh hanging by carpenter nails borrowed from Marco's dad's construction bags covered the walls. Her hands were tired yet strong as she ruled her family with solid morals and principles.

She shouted from an open window to Marco, carrying a handful of books. "Dinner's getting cold! Where have you been? I've been praying all day for your safe return. Mangiamo!" Beatrice was Marco's mother and Trey's grandmother.

Marco's father, Ray, was a carpenter with a long heritage of the skills he learned from his forefathers in Canada. Penny pincher was the proper term for him. He wasn't poor, but they sure lived like they were. Ray kept a small diary of every expenditure, no matter how insignificant it was. He built their modest two-story home in Massachusetts years before Marco was born, and he planned to stay there until his last day. Marco carried on the family trade with pride as he dreamed of a better life in California.

At twenty-three, Marco could no longer take the harsh New England winters. The biting cold chilled his fingers into frozen numbness. His hand was frostbitten as he reached for his hammer and realized how burned out he was. He glanced at his smashed finger and then remembered how it hadn't bled due to the below-average temperatures. The cold seeped into his toes and spread painfully throughout his feet. His toes felt like they were on the icy snow rather than in his work boots. His lips turned a bluish hue, and his teeth chattered. The frigid wind wrapped itself around him. He knew nothing was friendly about the storm that blinded everyone who lived there.

With his friend Jack, they drove west after anticipating the cold winter that was already here. A drop of holy water wrapped in a scapular hung to the visor of his red Datsun pickup truck. The token of devotion was there to ensure a safe trip and as a small reminder that his mother awaited his return. After a gruelling trip across the country, they eventually landed in California, the Golden State, a week later. A carpenter all his life, work came quickly to Marco in the booming construction fields in California. There, in the office of my father's construction company was where I first heard about him.

*****

"Have you met your dad's new employee yet?" In my mother's voice, I could hear that she was excited and impatient for me to settle down and have a family as she continued. "He's a nice-looking guy, and with your good looks, you two would make a perfect couple. Be sure to stay in the office until he comes in today, so you don't miss him. I can't wait to hear what you think."

"I know, I know. You've already told me about our new employee. I promise I will meet him today." I reached into my purse to find my Ombre Red-Orange lipstick. I knew he would come into the office to collect his paycheck in the afternoon, so I hiked up my skirt, exposing my long tan legs. The freckles that splattered across them were difficult to cover, so an extra handful of self-tanning lotion was added to my daily shower routine, making my skin glow in true California fashion.

He entered through the front door with his long curly black hair held back with a red bandana, perfectly shaped white teeth that flashed with every smile, and irresistible charm. My bright green eyes jumped out at him as I greeted him at my desk. I hadn't forgotten about my hiked-up skirt as I watched his eyes go in search of it.

"Hi, Marco. You must be the new guy I've heard about." My voice sounded nervous as I tried to hide my apparent interest.

"Yes. I'm glad I finally got to meet you. You are as pretty as the other guys say you are!" I tried not to blush.

"How do you like California?" I wanted desperately to change the subject.

"It's great here. I like the people, and the weather couldn't be better." As he spoke, I admired his strong, muscular frame.

"Do you have time to go out for a drink after you finish up here today? We can go over to the bar on the corner if you want." He naively pointed over to Mr Michael's, a local gay bar.

"Sure." I suppressed a giggle knowing of the neighbourhood secret. About an hour later, we walked across the street, and as we entered the bar, we found a table for two, snuggled into the corner of the dimly lit room. Smoky mirrors behind the bar reflected the gleaming colours of the extensive selections of alcohol, wine, and beer.

"What would you like to drink?" Marco asked politely. I glanced over to the bar then noticed the strong and handsome male bartender leaning over and kissing an older gentleman. I was reminded of a night in Hollywood several months ago.

It started as a fluke as my gay hairdresser talked about his West Hollywood fun and suggested we go together. "Hey, we should go tonight! We would have so much fun!" He giggled as he thought about how straight I was.

"Don't think I won't go!" I replied as I noticed how blonde my hair had become. "My God, Ronnie, what have you done to my hair?"

"Oh, you know you love it!" he said with a sarcastic smile. We left later that evening and arrived at the popular Robertshaw just in time for their spotlight dance. It started at 10:30 p.m. as the lights began to dim and the Love Machine began. In the club's dark, all I could see was Ronnie's high cheekbones and mischievous eyes. The music excited him as he jumped onto the dance floor. He jived and boogied like no one was watching, but of course, they all were. He just didn't care. He knew he could do anything as he wiggled and shook. The other men on the floor kept a close eye on the single dancer as they moved in closer. Being the only female in the club, I sat and watched and knew there was no chance of anyone being interested in me. I finally motioned it was time to go after noticing Ronnie locked eyes with someone sitting in a dark corner.

I told Marco white wine might taste good. He ordered our drinks, "I'll have a Jack and Coke, the lady a glass of Kendall Jackson Chardonnay." *Wow, this bandana-wearing hic sure knows his wine.*

The small talk ended when he politely said he needed to use the men's room. There I sat waiting, with my blood boiling, over fifteen minutes for his return. Something finally clicked. That jerk wasn't coming back. I picked up the check, stormed out, and couldn't wait to call my dad.

"You've got to fire that asshole! I hate him!" I screeched at my dad over the phone while he continued to refuse my request.

"Leigh, calm down, he's one of the best carpenters I have, and I don't want to lose him."

"I don't give a goddamn about him! You have to get rid of him, or you will be sorry!"

I was furious.

"Your mother is smiling, Leigh. She says you have finally met your match." He chuckled as I slammed down the phone. *I will show them! I will quit in the morning, so I never have to see that bastard again.*

I pulled into the parking lot behind the office the next day, where I saw Marco waiting in his truck. *Oh shit!* I tried to look away, but he caught my eye as he approached my car. "I'm sorry, Leigh. Some gay man tried to hit on me, and it pissed me off. I wanted to bash his head in, so I decided it best to leave. I'm sorry." As I gazed into Marco's eyes, he seemed sincere as he apologized, and I must say boy, did he look sexy. I forgave him, *not that I had a choice,* and made a date for the following Friday night.

As the days passed, I found myself waiting later in the day to close the office. I'd hoped Marco would drop in unexpectedly, so I waited, hoping not to miss him. I hadn't seen or heard from him as our date was drawing near and wondered if he'd forgotten. *Should I call him?* I waited until he finally showed up at the office Friday afternoon after work.

"Hey, I've got tickets to see the Rolling Stones at the Forum tonight. Mike can't go. You want to?" *Are you kidding? Tonight? What happened to our date? Mike? Me?*

"Okay, I'd love to go. What time will you be by to pick me up?" I was annoyed, and it was evident in my voice.

"Everyone is meeting at my apartment, so I thought maybe you could meet me there." He glanced at his watch. I seethed inside. *He wants me to drive twenty minutes over to his apartment? Who does he think he is? What an asshole!*

"Okay, what time?" I bit my lip.

I drove over to the apartment to find five guys waiting to go. Marco was in the shower as I arrived. I wore my skin-tight, bell-bottom blue jeans and a black velvet bustier with eighteen tiny clasps holding it together in the front. My boobs pushed up, front and centre. The slim spaghetti straps in the back added so much sex appeal that it was, by far, my most favourite top to wear on a first date. My feet ached in the black high heels that squeezed my toes together as I thought about the parking lot at the Los Angeles Forum, which I knew was quite a hike from the grand stage.

I began to feel cosy with the other guys as I waited for Marco. Their laughter and jokes made me feel comfortable and welcomed as Marco walked out of his bedroom wearing that same red bandana he wore the last time I saw him. *I wonder if he sleeps in the silly thing.* He looked pleased as he studied my appearance then handed me my concert ticket. Three rows from the centre stage. *Wow!*

As we arrived at the concert and took our seats, the energy filled the stadium. There were hordes of concertgoers looking for their places to sit as Marco excused himself and left for some libation. I patiently waited for his return. The concert began with Mick Jagger's lips hugging the microphone as people left their seats and rushed the stage. Hundreds of people pushing and shoving their way closer to the grandstand surrounded Marco and me as he returned with our drinks. I suddenly felt his arm around my waist as he leaned over.

"Let's get out of here!"

We downed our drinks, then pushed through the crowd and found peace in the nosebleed section of the massive stadium. There I felt safe as Marco placed his arm over my shoulder, and we enjoyed the concert together. As I sat there surrounded by this gorgeous man, I felt a rush of satisfaction and warmth. I might have fallen in love with him right then and there.

I didn't hear from him after that for two weeks, as I fought myself not to call. *I can't believe that I fell for that asshole!* I heard from a few of the other employees that his only interest was sleeping with the boss's daughter and nothing else. He was working to earn enough money to pay for a one-way ticket home. The weeks flew by as I tried to get him out of my mind and date other guys. I tried not to think about him, but I slipped many times. The pain of not hearing from him was getting more manageable, but I was starting to feel numb. The wise thing would be to run away from this potentially destructive and certainly mentally unstable man, but I knew I couldn't. Seconds passed while I tried to sort things out, and then a voice in my head answered. MAKE UP YOUR MIND! CALL HIM! I obeyed and picked up the phone.

"Why haven't you called me?"

"I've been busy. I'm heading down to Ocean Pier tonight with a few buddies. Do you want to go?" He sounded distracted as his voice faded. I wondered if he wanted me to go as I clung to the phone.

"What time are you going?" I was distracted by my thoughts of being too aggressive.

"We're going down at eight. Maybe you can meet me there?" He seemed distant and arrogant. *I mean, who does he think he is?*

"Okay. I might make it, but don't count on it." I had to play hard to get, so I put the phone down while I struggled with the idea and fought the strings that pulled at my heart. Our conversation rang in my head for the next few minutes while I tried to figure this guy out. *Should I go? I ask myself over and over. Should I give in and call my girlfriend to see if she had plans for the night?* I gave in.

"There's a bunch of guys going down to the pier tonight. I know a few of them, and some of them are cute!" I found myself wanting to go. *Bad!*

She was free, so we decided to meet him there. The hour drive to the pier flew by as I found myself bitching and complaining about him to this unsuspecting girlfriend.

"He's a real asshole, but for some reason, I like him. I can't be with someone who plays so many games. If he truly wanted me to go, he would have picked me up! I don't like it this way, so I'm going to stop dating him! It's over after tonight, but I'm so attracted to him. I'll give him one more chance. It is time for me to walk away." My one-sided conversation lasted until we got there.

Once there, I noticed he was nowhere. I waited until I spotted his roommate casting a fishing line over the side of the pier. I fluffed my hair, reapplied my lipstick, and walked over to him. "Catching anything?" I winked at him and noticed that his fishing line was dangling in the air too short of hitting the water. "Fishing for flying fish?" I smiled as he looked at me, then at his line, and broke out laughing. I noticed Marco watched from afar, so I poured it on while cosying up to his buddy. He finally made his way over, intentionally breaking up the fun and taking my hand.

"Let's go for a walk." We walked down the pier as he opened up to me. "I've tried to forget you. I've tried to get you off my mind, but I can't. I'm supposed to head home next week, but something keeps stopping me. I think it's you." He stopped and kissed me as my heart stopped beating for a moment. It was fate.

Whatever it was that had happened that night, and whether it was the adrenaline or the attraction to this guy that was responsible, it had woken me up. For the first time in a long time, I didn't know what to expect next.

*****

The following year, many power struggles followed as Marco and I fought to get to know one another. Our strong desire to control each other led to many fights, followed by hot and passionate sex. Between the arguments and lovemaking, I found myself living with Marco and his friends, which made things even more difficult. We differed in many areas, especially where we saw our relationship heading. I wanted to marry; he remained non-committal. I couldn't understand and didn't want to waste my time on someone who might never take the next step, so I packed an overnight bag and headed over to my mom's house.

"What's wrong?" My mom opened the door, surprised to see me.

"Everything is wrong. I'm tired of waiting for a commitment from Marco. We've been together nonstop and haven't made any progress towards marriage. I'm living with him and his buddies, and he seems happy with that kind of relationship. I can't wait any longer. I want to get married and have a family, so I'm going to break up with him." I wept and went to the back bedroom. Sad and alone, I fell asleep.

When I awoke, I overheard whispers coming from the kitchen. It was Marco and my mom. "I'm not sure what she wants. We spend all of our spare time together. I take her wherever she wants to go. I'm constantly spending money on her. I'm faithful to her, and I always tell her how much I love her. I don't think I could treat her any better." Marco sounded confused.

"I know Marco, but you better be careful. Once Leigh puts her mind to something, she won't change it. I fear if you don't ask her to marry you, you will lose her." My mother was persuasive.

Marco surprised me with an engagement ring, it was small, but I adored it.

*****

Two quick years passed when I found myself dressed in a white lace-covered gown with long sleeves and a neckline that made me choke as I stood in front of the floor-length mirror. My mother smiled and watched. "I am so proud of you! This day is so special!" I glanced into my memory a few years ago.

My younger sister found herself pregnant as a junior during high school, so my parents were forced to throw together a shotgun wedding. Many doubts formed as the bride and groom-to-be made it known they didn't want to marry but knew there were no other choices. As her maid-of-honour, I stood beside my pregnant sister at the altar and watched my mother disguise her hidden shame in the small Catholic parish. She was a proud woman with strict morals, and pregnancy before marriage was unforgivable. She felt it pointed directly at her for poor parenting. I knew it was my responsibility to do it the right way. A large wedding for me would satisfy my mother's dreams and wishes.

It could have been one hundred and six degrees in the small Catholic church as beads of sweat formed on my face forcing my near-perfect makeup to run. Wearing a gown that wasn't my first choice, I stood in the small room with my bridesmaids surrounding me. My budget was ninety-nine dollars due to my dad's sloppy bookkeeping and a craving for spending money. I

13

enjoyed many years of my dad's self-gratification, as he spent every penny he earned on boats, vacations, and motorhomes. Those memories of my high school days seem like yesterday.

In those days, my high school class revered me as a spoiled rich kid because of my extravagant house. My dad's plans to impress his bride had worked when he bought her the house of her dreams. My mom loved everything about our grand home, but as the years passed and the money began to disappear, it all ended in bankruptcy, and the house was for sale. We were heartbroken and embarrassed.

My dad scrambled, knowing a plan was never put into place for his retirement or any other future expenses, as he struggled to find a way to pay for my wedding and reception. Marco and I finally exchanged our vows in August of 1980 in a small Catholic church. An intimate wedding reception immediately followed in a rented flower store where a room in the back was large enough to accommodate a minuscule number of guests. As Marco led me through the front door to the reception area, the store came alive with flower arrangements made for other patrons. Exotic fragrances danced through the air, and the flowers somehow expressed our love for each other. There was something about their beauty that brought the party together. We loved it.

Chapter 3

IN THE LATE SPRING AND AFTER A NATURAL labor and easy delivery, we welcomed a baby boy, Russell. The early days of caring for my first baby were easy, while Marco worked hard to provide us with our needed things. Life was simple as we dreamed of having a large family and were grateful that we'd started it.

My breath caught for just a moment in my throat as my OB told me the news that I was pregnant again as Russell approached nine months. Our next child was due in the autumn of 1983, the season of Pink Floyd, the Moody Blues, and David Bowie.

For nine months, I anticipated another calm birth as we'd had with Russell due to no morning sickness or other craziness during that timeframe but found myself dead wrong.

On a warm evening in October, I lay in bed and felt my first hard contraction begin. I choked back the building scream. I had to keep things under control, but the pain was unbearable.

And then a familiar, husky voice called from the dark. "Leigh!" it sounded worried. "What is happening?"

I needed two seconds to shake off the pain before I could move. "The pain, I'm in labour!" Marco was clinging precariously to my already-packed suitcase as I awkwardly climbed into the car. My hands pressed deep into the headliner of the roof of the vehicle as I let out another blood-curdling scream. A popping sound and the cramping sensation grasped me from inside as my water broke and gushed all over the car seat.

"My water just broke; this is going too fast." I panted in excitement as I looked over at Marco.

"Your water just broke all over our new sheepskin seat covers?"

He barked as he rushed back into the house to fetch a towel. *Are you kidding? I'm in excruciating pain, and you're worried about the damn sheepskin covers?* My next contraction came hard, and as Marco was climbing into the car, I was in hard labour and pushing uncontrollably to get the baby out.

"Leigh, please don't push! I can't do this by myself." Marco's screams were louder than mine as he pressed the gas pedal harder. I couldn't control the urge to push as I felt the tiny head crowning between my legs. Beads of sweat dripped from my brow as I glanced over to see the speedometer reaching eighty miles per hour. We sped to the hospital as if no one else were on the road until a black-and-white cruiser came from behind and pulled us over. An obvious ticket was due and expected as Marco peered into his rearview mirror. Upon hearing screams from the car and seeing the terrified look on Marco's face, the police went in the opposite direction as we slowly pulled back out onto the dark highway.

We parked at the hospital. Marco lifted me into his arms and grunted into the medical centre and onto the elevator. "I'm trying to keep", he huffed, shifting his weight onto his other leg, "my promise to stay calm!" I blinked my wet blurry eyes, suddenly sure that I was dreaming.

"When did you ever promise to stay calm?" I yelled. He snorted, unamused and terrified, as I stooped frozen in the elevator corner, trying not to give birth to our second baby.

"Leigh, please get up so we can get you into the delivery room. I don't know what I am going to do if you don't!" Marco hysterically cried as the elevator doors flung open.

"Anyone, please, someone must help me!" He lifted and placed me onto a sheet-draped gurney just outside the elevator door, then yanked my jogging pants down as an off-duty nurse came running around the corner. He could see the tiny babies head crowning as he screamed one more time for help.

"Oh, my God, what is happening?" The terrified nurse froze as I gave my final push.

Marco looked at her then held the ever-so-small baby between his hands.

"What do I do?" He quivered as he looked at me and then again at the wet slippery child.

"Hand the baby to me." I softly whispered as he laid our newborn on my chest. Marco's eyes were glistening, and in a broken voice, he told me that we had a new son. We both burst into tears of joy and relief while the young baby's cries filled the maternity ward. I smiled but hardly hid the trauma as my body bounced on the gurney in shock.

"From the time her water broke, he was born in eighteen minutes," Marco proudly told the nurse as he checked his watch.

"I can't take his screaming and crying anymore." I failed as a mother at age thirty. Trey was a problematic infant from the moment he was born. "He cries all day, and I just can't do this any longer." Tears poured down my face. Marco had a long day at work and was tired of being greeted with tears.

After a frustrating pause, he impatiently asked, "Did you call the doctor yet?"

Prolonged bouts of colic made Trey cry as I watched his poor little body fold with stomach cramps. I held him close as I watched his tiny hands clutch my shirt. I sat in silence, struggling with what to do next as his howls of misery worsened. The pain he experienced came in waves, one of calm followed by the next in pure torture. At my wit's end, I decided to take Trey to the doctors who diagnosed a food allergy. *I should have nursed him.* I cried inside from guilt, my hands soaked with tears streaming down my face.

I fed him every type of baby formula, trying to find something that agreed with him, but nothing helped. Vivonex to stem the oncoming pain was the last resort. The yellowish, watery substance smelled like vomit and was gross, but he tolerated it, and that was all that mattered to me. Spit-up stains on his newborn "onesies" finally decreased as he adjusted to his newfound diet, and my life miraculously became easier.

I remained quiet, knowing Russell was safe in the bedroom next door as I rocked Trey in an old wooden chair and comforted him as he snuggled in a warm blanket. It seemed like a waste of time as his eyes remained open and alert. *Damn it! Go to sleep!* I rubbed his back while he lay in his crib until his eyes slowly started to close. I backed away, one small step at a time, only one step at a time, only to hear screams before I could shut the door.

"Make him cry it out." Dr Bake lectured me as if he believed listening to a crying baby was an easy thing to do. I couldn't. I never wanted him to feel alone and abandoned, so I sat night after night, rocking him to sleep while Marco breathed deeply to the rhythmic sound of the chair. I rocked back and forth through endless nights as I thought about the family that Marco and I created, and of the tiny baby I held in my arms.

As I sat in the darkness of the night clutching my baby tightly, I noticed a reflection on the wall. As I glanced over, above the night-light, I saw a beautiful picture, painted by my mother, of a woman holding an infant. It was saintly, I thought, as I stared into the woman's face and began to reflect on my childhood.

My parents, Pharis and Annamae, were very busy while I was growing up. Their dreams and creativity moulded our family of five into a close and artsy clan. My mother painted dozens of pictures ranging from landscapes to portraits. Her most well-known artwork came to be called the Boob Woman, *a shot of a topless young woman sitting cross-legged while weaving a basket. My mom used to joke, saying, "I painted this self-portrait while looking in the mirror." She admired the perfectly shaped breasts as she laughed. The naked woman called to the neighbourhood boys who came for a glimpse of her. My mother would open the front door, watch the boys' eyes pop, then smile as she watched them leave. Their giggles echoing through the trees made her laugh. She knew they left satisfied that they'd seen the epitome of porn.*

Next to the Boob Woman *hung a mosaic of a juggling court jester dressed in an orange clown outfit that my dad created. He patiently coloured and cut each tile to fit perfectly together as he grouted each joint after dinner. After watching my parents' artwork evolve, I began to pick up some of their creativity and started including oil paint sets and brushes onto my Christmas lists. Years later, amateur artwork, painted by me, leaned against our home's walls waiting for their perfect resting place.*

The long lonely nights ended when Trey turned nine months, started walking, and tolerated different types of food.

My third pregnancy was no surprise, as I read the positive test I had taken earlier in the morning. "Marco, I saw the doctor today who did the sonogram." He had just gotten home from work.

"Oh, yea, do we know what we're having?" He set his keys down and gave both Russell and Trey a kiss.

"Yes, another boy!" I handed him the results while I watched his eyes gleam, and I tried to hide my disappointment.

The pregnancy went fast as I studied every possible method to ensure safe and peaceful delivery. In my third trimester, Dr Fox informed me that inducement was necessary due to the incredible pace of my ability to deliver. Reluctantly, the date in the middle part of April was scheduled, two weeks before my due date.

Everything advanced smoothly as the day of inducement arrived. My mother stayed with Russell and Trey while Marco and I were at the hospital. I felt comfortable leaving them with her, although I knew they were quite a handful.

We were cautious not to risk another birth like Trey's, so we checked into the nearby hospital two hours early. As we waited, I prepared myself with my planned breathing exercises. Marco was excited as we sat in the newly decorated private birthing room while I was hooked up to an intravenous drip delivering Pitocin.

Dr Fox checked in with us before noon. "Looks like you're in good hands, and everything is going as planned. I'm going to have lunch in the cafeteria and will check back afterwards." He turned to leave.

"Don't worry, as you know; I've done this before." My excited grin stretched wide across my face, and my bright white teeth stood in vivid contrast to the rosy colour of my skin. I laughed and watched him leave through the door. It wasn't ten minutes before my first hard contraction began, and I wished Dr Fox were still with me. I vowed to stay calm as I followed my contractions on the graph displaying the highs and lows. The cramps stayed steady, and I remained still, having peaceful labour and delivery. Marco stayed close by in his powder-blue scrubs as I delivered Cameron in just forty minutes.

*****

The boys finished a small lunch of peanut butter and jelly sandwiches and then off to nap time. I enjoyed peace for two hours as a daily routine with Trey and Russell in their separate rooms and Cameron in mine. My mom and I sat whispering while I occasionally checked on the boys.

Russell was fast asleep, wrapped in a knitted powder-blue blanket. Cameron, too, was content as he finally greeted the Sandman. I expected to find Trey sound asleep, but I found him awake as I opened his door. I saw him sitting in the middle of his room, playing with his toy truck as I peered in. I suddenly noticed three different colours of crayon marks covering the better half of the blank white wall on the far side of his room. I controlled my temper and frustration, remembering Russell and Cameron were asleep in the rooms next door. I remained quiet as I bit my lip and stormed out. I looked over at my mother with disgust and reached under the kitchen cabinet for cleaning liquid and paper towels.

I returned to a little boy who looked up at me and said, "Saw we." His brown eyes showed regret, my heart melted, and my eyes teared as I wrapped my arms around him. I cherished those little boys and, in my heart, knew that they could do no wrong.

Trey's insufficient rest didn't cause him to act out because he didn't need much sleep to function. I excused him from his nap time and then heard faint noises in the back bedrooms. I found both Russell and Cameron awake after a peaceful nap and led the three of them to the kitchen, where they had a glass of apple juice and a snack.

The years slipped away while the days seemed shorter as I got to know each of my boys and the differences in their personalities and looks. Russell, the clear leader, bossed Trey around as they shared the patio in our backyard. As I watched them play, I noticed Russell's eyes, an intelligent blue-green, held a shade of green that resembled a mixture of the sky and the grass.

They provided a sharp contrast to his brother's, Trey, co-gnac-coloured eyes, which had an earthy and autumnal hue with a sense of richness and luxury. Trey was adventurous as he continually played in the dirt, and Cameron, my baby, snuggled up to me at every chance with eyes as blue as the sky. My three boys and our family dog were all I needed to satisfy my every wants or wish in life. As they grew past their toddler stage into preschool years, I enjoyed every moment.

I was tired and burned out after chasing the boys when my phone rang. It was my mother. *Oh shit! How will I tell her that Marco and I have decided not to have any more kids?* I knew this would meet my mother, who always dreamed of having a girl, with disappointment. After a brief conversation, I finally found the courage. "Marco and I have decided to take precautions against having more kids. Marco's worried we might have another boy if we try for a girl. I'm tired and worn out during the day."

"You have to go for the girl. You'll be so sorry if you don't because girls stay close to their mothers while boys follow their wives. Please don't stop before you get your girl." With my mother's pleas ringing through my mind, I took it up with Marco.

"Marco, we need to try for a girl. I promise I will set up an appointment right after the baby is born and have my tubes tied, whether it's a boy or a girl." He reluctantly agreed.

Chapter 4

IT'S FOUR IN THE MORNING! WHO WOULD CALL AT this time?

She drank in silence, hoping the answer lay at the bottom of the bottle. Mary fumbled with the phone and spoke a few slurred words as the night dragged on. "No, you don't get it!" Mary yelled over the phone. "I've been doing just fine-fine by myself for years!" She fell unconscious.

I thought about Mary. Sick as she was, she was still beautiful. There was something pure and good about her face. I met her during a class in high school and ran into her during Friday night parties. It'd been years since we graduated, and she had attended USC. Her parents had a lot of money. Money meant next to nothing to Mary or the rest of her family. It was just something that accumulated when you had unlimited time on your hands and an aunt who had an uncanny ability to predict trends in the stock market. That is what put Mary through school and a career in pharmaceutical sales.

"Who was that?" Marco sat up.

"Oh, it was Mary again. I'll have to go to her house in the morning to be sure she is okay." I fell back to sleep quickly as I knew the kids would be up early.

My mom came to watch the boys, so I left the house and drove toward Mary's apartment. I'd remembered how her father blamed her for her mother's death in high school. "If it weren't for you, your mother would still be alive!" Those words she never forgot, and the guilt was like gasoline in her stomach. Her insides died slowly in the toxicity, needing no more than a spark to set it ablaze. The fire burned her so badly there was nothing left but a shell. She tried very hard to make up for something that was never her fault. And yet, she had to work so hard to be good. That is when she found alcohol. It was the only thing that dulled and numbed her pain. It made her forget. As I drove, I lost myself to my thoughts and wondered how she could survive the words she had heard so often.

As I pulled into the parking lot and locked the car, I noticed how dark the morning was. I wondered what I would find as I opened Mary's unlocked front door. A man with a smile greeted me and explained he was there to clean her carpets. I went in search of Mary as the cleaning man finished up. I peered into her bedroom, and there she lay, naked and stretched across her bed. Her hair was tousled, and in her hand was a flask of Scope, a bottle of mouthwash that contained alcohol. I covered her with a thin sheet and then wandered into the kitchen to find two empty vodka vessels covered in the newspaper in the trash. She had tried to hide them. I went in search of more to protect her from herself. There was nothing in her refrigerator, cupboards, or anywhere else. She had drunk it all. I felt sad as I left after I ensured she was warm, safe, and the carpet-cleaning man was gone.

Once I got home, I spoke to my mom regarding Mary's problem and concerns about her being around the boys. "She gets drunk so often. I don't trust her. I need to tell her I don't want her around the kids. Maybe she'll stop calling." I felt depressed.

*****

Time began to trip along much more quickly than before. The kids, the house, and Marco, not necessarily in that order, created a neat and effortless pattern to follow.

I couldn't wait for Marco to return home from work after calling earlier and saying he had some exciting news. I wondered what could make him so enthusiastic as he burst through the door. "Mr Henry is selling his house for two hundred and ten thousand dollars! He offered it to me, but I told him I'd have to talk to you first!" I threw my arms around him instinctively, wrapping them around his waist and pressing my face against his.

My interest piqued as I remembered the neighbourhood in Lacana as an upscale community with high-priced homes and a place where I always wanted to live. Marco quickly continued.

"It's on Lion's Peak Avenue. It has two bedrooms and two bathrooms. It needs some fixing up, but I can easily do it in my spare time. For that price, it has significant potential! I can't wait for you to see it tomorrow." Marco was so excited he barely took a breath.

We packed up the kids in the old station wagon in the morning and drove over to the house. We parked on the street in front of Mr Henry's house. Marco and I viewed the small, single-story cabin surrounded by multi-million-dollar homes. The house sat on an impressive corner lot with tall trees and beautifully manicured grounds. The original design and layout offered Marco plenty to work with while he dreamed of expanding its size from 1800 to 4500 square feet.

The siding on the front of the house was old, needed replacing, and the wood was cracking. The flat roof had plenty of apparent leaks and needed some much-needed repair. An abandoned guest house sat behind the main quarters, and overgrown avocado trees surrounded it. We deemed we were up to the challenge and could squeeze our family of five into this tiny cabin. With Marco's expertise in building and mine in decorating, we looked forward to buying this home to remodel and sell.

Escrow opened and closed within thirty days. After only a few weeks, we were knee-deep in construction. Marco knocked down the walls and removed the flat roof. Marco's keen eye spotted areas where the moisture from outside could get in, so he covered those areas with Visqueen. It was a mess to deal with as the kids ran through the mounds of broken drywall. We spent countless nights prepping and painting walls as we blasted the Rolling Stones.

*****

The magic moment came when Dr Fox made the phone call. "You'll be happy to know that you are pregnant again and this time with a girl!" His lips formed a half-circle as he spoke of the great news.

Marco's dreams of having a daughter came true, and I found contentment that our family would finally be complete. Days of chasing the boys were old, and I was tired and already uncomfortable. A pregnancy carrying a girl was a whole new experience as she kicked and punched me from a breech position.

I desperately needed help and a break, so we brought in another family member, Adriana.

She was a young, dark-eyed girl from Peru who illegally came into the United States across the Mexican border. After reaching the United States, her father paid for and set up the transfer while making no other plans for her. Adriana's brother abandoned her once they were on American ground, leaving her alone and penniless.

She contemplated getting into line at the employment office when Marco saw her, alone and scared. After working in the construction industry in Southern California for years, he knew enough Spanish to offer her a job. An offer of a position in the family at forty dollars a week plus a pillow under her head was all she needed. She was a mere seventeen years old when Madison was born.

*****

It was Friday night when Marco and I decided to take an evening off, away from the kids and out for a romantic dinner. We dressed up, told our dark-eyed nanny to give the kids dinner, bathe them, and put them to bed. The simple request was all we asked of her. "You kids better behave tonight while we are gone." A hint of anxiety formed in my eyes. We headed out the door and left to enjoy our Italian meal. A pianist serenaded us at the piano bar while we stopped thinking of the kids and what they were doing. We finished our nightcaps, satisfied, fortified, and headed home.

We found the boys running wild through the house with toys scattered everywhere upon returning home. Telephones were unplugged, and the kids were on the loose for quite some time from the looks of things.

"What the hell? Where is Adriana?" I demanded an answer as feelings of being unnerved formed. "Where is Adriana?" I hissed, and my voice was a bit stronger. The boys stood there with dumb looks on their faces with nothing to say. There was nothing but crickets. Marco looked at me.

"Did you hear that?" He had an awkward look in his eyes as he heard strange sounds coming from a locked closet door. He paused, listened and then walked over, opened the door, and there was Adriana, who, we found, had spent most of the evening there with Madison.

"Who's watching who?" My voice showed anger but knowing she didn't speak much English; I reworded my question. "Were you watching the kids?" I knew she couldn't have been if she had been in the closet for most of the night. Adriana nodded once, her face calm. She made a brief comment in an unfamiliar, liquid language. I could only be positive that it wasn't in French or English, but I guessed it was some form of Spanish. I took a deep breath. She was too embarrassed to make eye contact with me as she turned and went to her room. As I thought about the crazy kids and knew they could get pretty wild, I apologised the following day. In what language, I wasn't sure.

*****

Clutching his small, yellow lunch pail in his tiny hand, Trey headed into his kindergarten classroom with a swollen black eye and a bump the size of a newly-laid egg on his forehead after colliding with Cameron in the hallway at home. The narrow corridor did not accommodate two rowdy little boys chasing after one another, nor did it care if anyone got hurt. I rubbed his forehead while he cried. "You're all right," I said while showing little sympathy and maybe deep down inside, felt as though he deserved it as he sucked it up and started chasing Cameron again. The boys were noisy as I yelled, "You're going to get hurt again." I shook my head in disbelief and screamed the words once again. Trey had gotten the worst end of the crash, and his teacher mistakenly wondered if child abuse might be in our home.

"Trey!" Mrs Beasley was crouching over him anxiously. "Trey, are you alright?"

"I'm great." Trey enthused. He flexed his arms and legs. Everything seemed to be working correctly except for the egg that continued to turn blue.

"I don't think so." Mrs Beasley sounded worried. "I think I'd better call your mom."

Mrs Beasley instantly headed to the office to make a call and insist on getting more details on Trey's injury. She was optimistic that this must be coming from home and demanded to meet me in person.

Without a brief introduction to our meeting, she went right to the point with a scowl on her face.

"Mrs Morelli? Is it possible that someone is mistreating Trey at home? He has come to school for the last few days with bruises and scratches all over him. He mentioned that he had gone camping with his dad over the weekend." As I watched her speak, I could see the genuine concern on her face. She was not that old, but her body had aged past her years. I studied the lifeless, grey mane that limply framed her frumpy, round face. Her forehead was deeply wrinkled, caused by years of constant scowling. Silver-rimmed glasses surrounded her squinty-blue eyes, which harboured a disrespectful glare. She seemed drained of any signs of joy and amusement but instead displayed a look of regular displeasure.

"Mrs Beasley, you know, he has two brothers, and they are tough little guys. You must have misunderstood Trey because he was home with me the entire weekend, and my husband would never think about hurting him in any way." I'd hoped it was an adequate explanation as I watched for any reaction. There was none.

We roughed it in our small two-bedroom cabin while Trey mastered the art of turning his left eye towards his nose and holding his right eye steady. He found new ways to torture his teacher and friends by crossing his eye every time he looked at them. Mrs Beasley found little humour in his newly acquired skills, and I figure that she never accepted my response at our last gathering. She sat down and wrote a letter.

Dear Mrs Morelli,

I have enjoyed working with Trey for the last few weeks, but I feel in Trey's best interest, it would be better if he stays home for another year before he starts kindergarten. He daydreams in class, and struggles to keep on a task due to his immaturity. I hope I have another opportunity to work with him in the future.

Sincerely,
Mrs Beasley

Within one week, I withdrew him and brought him home while wondering how to keep him entertained for another year.

Chapter 5

THE WARNING CAME LATE IN THE NIGHT AS Marco screamed with pain. It was a crippling thing, the sensation that a huge hole had been punched through his chest, excising his most vital organ and leaving ragged, unhealed gashes around the edges that continued to throb despite the passage of time. Rationally, I knew his lungs must still be intact, yet he gasped for air. He curled inward, hugging his ribs to hold himself together. Each breath he took felt like a knife stabbing him in the back. "Oh my God, I can't take a breath." He struggled to inhale as the night grew long. Sheer agony met each short breath.

"Get dressed! I'm taking you to the hospital!" I glanced at the clock. It was 4:00 a.m. I woke Adriana and left my mother's phone number if she needed help while I was away.

We drove through the darkness as Marco tried not to breathe. The medical centre seemed hundreds of miles away but was only a twenty-minute drive from our house. We ran into the emergency room, where they were waiting for Marco to arrive. After a thorough examination and some x-rays, the doctor explained that he had pleurisy and medication would help drain the fluid collected in his chest cavity. As we waited, Marco's chest x-ray revealed pneumonia and, he would stay in the hospital.

After Marco settled into his hospital room, I drove home alone and wondered how to handle the kids in his absence. The house was alive as I walked through the door to see my mother's tired face. "The kids were up early this morning and haven't stopped since then. Adriana stepped out to run to the store but should be back soon." She closed her eyes and sighed as I explained that Marco was in the hospital.

The nursing staff was friendly, and we were fortunate the hospital was relatively new.

Marco sat in his private room as the doctor explained that antibiotics would knock out the Pneumonia and chest tubes would drain the fluid. He shouldn't be there for more than a couple of days.

Marco was prepped and taken to the surgery room, where the doctor performed a minor procedure. Four tubes fell from under the sides of his rib cage as he returned to his room. He was in agony as I went in search of his doctor for a more potent painkiller. "I'll prescribe Vicodin. That will make him more comfortable."

Two days passed. As I met the doctor in the hall, he greeted me. "Oh, I'm glad I didn't miss you," he said with a downward smile. "The chest tubes have not worked the way we expected. The liquid is thicker than we thought, so the tubes have been removed. The only possible method to relieve the pressure is to remove the viscous fluid surgically. Tomorrow, Marco will go into surgery. He will need to stay in the hospital until he heals." I took a deep breath. *Oh, God.*

The following day, I arrived at an empty hospital bed as Marco went through the worst possible experience. While sedated, the doctor sliced Marco's back, lifted his shoulder blade and mopped the fluid from his cavity. One hundred and fifty sutures held the open wound together as Marco screamed for more Vicodin and soon found himself in the ICU.

I shuddered as the elevator doors flew open and stood in front of the unit's door. There I was met by the charge nurse. "It's severe. He lost a lot of blood and contracted a very nasty infection. You can see him for a few minutes. The prognosis is poor." I walked in. Marco lay with a tube from his mouth, helping him breathe, but he was unaware of my presence. I left feeling helpless as I returned to the little monsters running wild through the house. Adriana and my mom sat, tired, shaking their heads as I entered the front room.

The house had nothing more than plastic sheets of Visqueen. Marco removed the roof before his hospitalization, and open areas revealed the sky. Many of the house's walls were half up without drywall. The floors throughout the living room had carpet tacks, so I grabbed a broom and tried to make it as livable as possible.

Pans of dirt, sawdust, and nails filled the trash cans outside. I vacuumed cement floors. I tried to hold it together. *How can I do this alone? We were crazy to do this with four small children.* I cried myself to sleep, hopeless and worried.

Marco's stay in the ICU lasted three weeks. Once again, I found myself entering the elevator and waiting for the door to open. I pushed the button on the wall. The charge nurse appeared and ushered me towards Marco. He took a shallow breath and stared at the nurse holding the pan of warm water and a sponge. His mouth twisted the tiniest bit. When he finally looked up, his eyes were different, more demanding. He spoke slowly and precisely, his cold eyes on the nurse's face, watching as she absorbed what he was going to say. "Keep your hands off of me! You are not going to bathe me. My wife will!"

"Marco, stop it!" I stepped into his room as he looked over at me. "You'll be home tomorrow, so let her bathe you." I was tired and burned out. I hadn't slept for weeks.

The following day, I was back at the hospital and collected Marco's belongings. Among them were doctor's orders and two prescriptions, one for antibiotics and Vicodin. The doctor's orders silenced me. It would take six months of bed rest to recover.

As Marco gained more strength, he started taking control of the smaller jobs he had started before his surgery. He stayed on the phone dictating orders to his employees and eventually ventured out to visit the job sites. While the kids stayed at home with Adriana, it was me who drove him from one place to another while he bitched about my driving skills.

"Take a right here, slow down, speed up, stop!" I didn't answer. I couldn't think of a way to protest, but I instantly knew I wanted to. I was not too fond of this treatment. The voice in my head repeated, "This is not fun", repeatedly. Day in and day out, I stayed quiet as I listened to his every order and constant harassment.

"Get me more Vicodin! I'm running low and don't have any more refills." He looked at his empty prescription bottle with cold and desperate eyes. "My damn doctor! Why didn't he refill this?"

"Marco, it's been nearly four months since your surgery. Are you sure you are still in that much pain and need more Vicodin?"

"Yes, God damn it. I need more pills. Call my doctor!" he demanded.

I hesitantly picked up the phone and made the call. The nurse on the other end heard the urgency in my voice as she went in search of Marco's physician.

"Doctor Jones? I'm Leigh Morelli, Marco's wife. Marco has asked me to call you to refill his prescription for Vicodin. I don't think he needs anymore. He's showing signs of addiction and requires more throughout the day. He's edgy and extremely moody." Dr Jones listened, then agreed, and refilled two more pills while I notified Marco that this was the end of the road.

"God damn it! I need the pills! I'm in pain. Call him back!"

"No, I'm done." I walked out of the room.

Chapter 6

TALL PINE TREES YIELDED TO THE WARM BREEZES that blew in the high mountains surrounding the small community where we lived. Lacana was where the wicked Santa Ana winds blew at the end of the long hot summer. The sun had been devilish all season long, rising above pleasant temperatures to furnace-like heat and drying out the brush in the foothills where we called home.

One afternoon as I stood at the kitchen sink, I looked up and gasped as I saw a raging wildfire off in the distance, a short way away. I yelled to Russell and Trey. "Go to your rooms, grab everything important to you and put it by the front door in case we have to leave in a hurry!" The hot winds fueled the fire as it grew larger and closer by the minute. Russell flew past five-year-old Trey and scrambled into his room, looking for his most prized possessions. Trey stood motionless as Russell stacked his toys and games by the front door.

Trey finally looked up at me, confused, with his big brown teary eyes. "What if I don't have anything I care about?"

"Are you kidding? Of course, you do." I panicked as I noticed the fire racing closer. He ran into his room, where I found him crying into his pillow.

"I don't have anything, Mommy. I don't." He cried harder.

"Okay. It's alright." I tried to comfort him but honestly didn't understand after seeing his toys scattered across the floor.

****

The Nintendo's most popular game, Mario Bros, became a distraction for Trey as his playing time increased while Russell was at school. Trey started the game and didn't want to put it down. He was obsessing over the competition, dreaming of it, and at times it frightened him, which seemed to please him oddly. Restricting his time with the video game didn't work; the more I limited his play, the more Trey wanted. He talked about it all of the time and tried to bargain with me. He'd clean his room, pick up his toys, water my plants, anything to get more time. I wondered if this was the first sign of addiction? I pushed the thought from my mind and concentrated on the fact that I would have to face this problem sooner rather than later. *He has difficulty staying on task*; Mrs Beasley's words rang through my mind. They made me laugh as I watched him engaged, oblivious to his surroundings as he played. He found isolation a way to stay focused, and he continuously worked on new ways to win the rounds.

"He should've stayed in school like you wanted him to." I looked at Marco, who was deep in thought about work, and wondered if I had made the right decision to keep him home or if Marco was even listening.

"Take the stupid game away and find something else for him to do." I couldn't argue with that as I listened to Marco's advice. I found Trey clinging to the only thing that meant something to him. He cried as I put it into his closet on the highest shelf and then decided this was an excellent opportunity to get out of the house.

After picking Russell up from school, we went off to get some dessert. The kids behaved most of the week and deserved a treat. "Sit still, and I will buy you an ice cream cone." I threw the comment to the backseat, where they sat quietly. Baskin Robbins was the best ice cream in town and had a vast selection.

"How cool!" Russell screamed in delight. "The kids at school told me about the different ice cream they have there. There's a bunch of cool names like Booger, Cereal Milk and one called Vanilla! The one called Vanilla glows in the dark!!" He was bouncing off the seat with so much enthusiasm.

Mounds of different chocolates, rocky road, chocolate chips, chocolate peanut butter were at the top of our list. The boys' heads swam as they stood with their hands spread across the glass, trying to make a choice. I held Madison in my arms as she pointed and begged for a small taste.

"Mom, what ice cream should I get?" Trey turned to face me.

"Maybe get the one that glows in the dark?" He smiled and flashed that crossed eye at me. *Silly boy! Your eyes will get stuck if you don't stop doing that!*

The no-seat-belt rule in California allowed the boys to roam freely in the back of our station wagon on our way home. Madison sat contentedly in her forward-facing car seat as I yelled to the boys in the back seat. "Stop wrestling, or I'm going to pull this car over and give you the spoon!" I carried a long-handled wooden spoon in my purse that served as a warning.

None of them heeded my warning as I watched Russell sitting on top of Trey, Cameron kicking Russell. I sent another message but with much more strength. "Russell, get off of Trey." No reaction from the now professional wrestlers as I pulled the car over to the curb. With one hand, I grabbed the first flailing leg. Three smacks with the spoon against the thigh sent Russell crying.

Reaching again, I grabbed Trey's leg and delivered another three blows as Cameron crouched behind the front seat. Smack, smack, smack. I felt vindicated and hoped I had impressed them with my actions. I put the spoon back into my purse and drowned out any crying heard by raising the radio's volume. They recovered and sat quietly for the rest of the trip as Madison sat oblivious to it all.

The next trip, I came prepared, and once they started up, I calmed them down with something educational. I fumbled my hand along the footboard, looking for a book about the birds and the bees. I gently tossed it into the backseat where Trey was sitting. "What are babies made of?" He started as he turned the pages, which contained childlike illustrations.

Cameron yelled, "Playdough!" I could barely hide my smile as I glanced at the boys in the rearview mirror.

Trey's eyes deepened as he read on. "Boys have a penis, and girls have China." I was on the verge of cracking up as he read, "Sex between sharks can get rough." His face looked slightly red and puzzled. "Eww," he yelled and then shuddered with disgust. "The woman's vagina is like a pocket." Huh? "The man puts his penis in the pocket." "What?"

"Gross, I would never do that!" Russell shouted, followed by a giggle. We made it home without any wrestling as the boys sat quietly in the back seat with only their thoughts. I couldn't wait to get my hands on the phone and tell Marco that our discussion last night worked out just as we planned.

*****

It seemed the wealthy and snippety neighbourhood had mostly white privileged-class women. As my children gained independence, they forced their boundaries further from the house as the days went by. Their skateboards zinged down the local side street as I heard my doorbell ring. I jumped from my velveteen upholstered couch.

"Good day, Mrs Morelli. First, I'd like you to know this is not a social call." Our neighbour to our right was at our front door. She stood proud but what I saw was not pretty. Her arrogance made me sick, and her pathetic voice caused me to cringe.

"When has there ever been one?" I questioned her with disgust.

"Your dog is killing my chickens! I found one dead underneath my brand new BMW! You need to keep your filthy-dirty dog on a chain!" Her voice didn't waver. I was a bit annoyed at her allegation. *Why wasn't her chicken kept in confined quarters?*

"How do you know it was Olive? There are many other dogs in the neighbourhood, and she has been in the house all day." I knew I had to protect my dog at all costs from such an all great know everything. As I spoke, I glanced over as Olive nonchalantly came around the corner with feathers sticking to the edges of her mouth. I quickly shoved the door closed in front of me with my pink-slippered foot.

41

Our kids never fit into the neighbourhood, which was filled with nannies and maids as the years flew by. They were ordinary, rugged kids that had life by the tail for the most part. They played in the yard, dug holes in the dirt, and climbed trees to their hearts' content. They played together, stayed together, and needed no one else.

As I answered the ringing telephone, it surprised me that little Eleanor wanted a play date with Trey. She lived next door in her noble house surrounded by manicured lawns and had servants who saw her every need. Trey was excited to go.

"Behave yourself and watch your manners." He was dressed to kill in his clean white tee shirt, ironed blue jeans and black high-top tennis shoes. His fresh, clean hair swayed as he walked securely to their front door. The big wrought iron doors swung open to a robust and white-aproned nanny who smiled sternly at him, almost saying, "BEHAVE WHILE YOU ARE HERE".

He entered after I whispered, "I love you. Please call me when you are ready to come home." With that, he went to the backyard, where his playmate awaited. An hour passed as I cleaned the kitchen and kept an eye on the telephone. Another hour passed.

Finally, the phone rang. I expected to hear Trey on the other end, but no, it was Eleanor's mother. "Mrs Morelli… Your son has traumatized my little Eleanor while they played in the backyard. You'll need to Come to get him now!"

I screamed inside but held it together while I remembered my last run-in with her. I wondered why I would even entertain the idea of letting Trey go over to that horrible woman's house in the first place. In some respect, I felt sorry for Eleanor. She was the victim not because of Trey but due to her environment.

I couldn't help but throw some digs in before I hung up the phone. "What did Trey do to deserve such horrible treatment?" I sarcastically asked.

"He dug in the dirt while teaching Eleanor how to use the science kit I bought for her. It was going fine until he decided to pick up the slimiest earthworm he could find and stick it into his drooling little mouth. He chewed it wildly. My little Eleanor is still crying from shock!" W*ow, little Eleanor is a bit sheltered for being a seven-year-old!*

I walked over to Trey, who was leaning up against one of the most beautiful Oak trees I'd ever seen while he waited for me in front of their house by himself. I wrapped my arm over his shoulder and said, "Let's go home."

Chapter 7

THERE WERE TWO REASONS WHY I KNEW I WAS dreaming. The first was that I was looking at my Grandfather George. Grandpa had been dead for fifteen years now, and second, the colours were so bright that this could not be reality.

Ole George hadn't changed much; his wrinkled face looked just as I had remembered it. The dry skin on his spotted, massive hands was rough, withered, and held large creases that hugged gently to the bone underneath. He had no hair except for small patches of white, which embraced the very back of his high hairline. It was common to see him wearing a hat to cover that very bald head. When he spoke, his chest heaved, and the sound was raspy, which came with many years of smoking cigars. But here he was in my dream, and I enjoyed looking at the Grandfather that I always loved so much.

I was about to ask him a question; I had so many. Where are you now? What have you been up to for the last fifteen years? Have you seen my other Grandfather where you are? And my Grandmother Moser, was she there too? But he opened his mouth when I did, so I stopped to let him go first. He paused, too, and then we both smiled.

"Leigh?"

It wasn't Grandpa who called my name, and we both turned to see who came to our small reunion. I didn't have to look to know who it was; this was a voice I would know anywhere. It was my Grandmother's voice, my father's mother, Josephine. The woman that my mother hated so much.

Everyone who knew Josephine assumed that something terrible must have happened to her when she was a child. Josephine was abused beyond recognition as she grew into her teenage years. As a young boy, my dad remembered terrible, hideous sexual abuse and torture by his Grandfather to his mother. What he didn't know was when this behaviour began or why.

They said she needed treatment for dissociative identity disorder when she had a dramatic moment when she started smashing windows and split into "Josephine" from "Edna" at a feed store. She had created two very distinct personalities: the gentle, flower-loving "Edna" who spent hours and hours knitting beautiful blankets. Edna's kind nature enjoyed small trinkets set on her window sills as gifts given to her by the people she loved. Then there was "Josephine", who swore, drank heavily and smoked. She was a big woman, standing five foot eight. Josephine was wicked and a terrible mother. It was then that she had started seeing a psychoanalyst in Idaho, her birthplace, when she was in her early twenties.

Once married to poor George, she lived in isolation and left for months at a time when my father was a little boy. When she would return, she wouldn't acknowledge that she ever left. Maybe she didn't remember? My Grandpa had tried so hard to cope while working in the coal mines and raising two small children in her absence.

While my dad was a young kindergartener, Monday's were her wash day, and she loved to dress him in white. "If you get one spot on these clothes at school, I will beat the ever-living hell out of you!" She would warn him each week with a wicked smile on her face, and a crooked forefinger pointed right to his nose. My father's older sister tried to accept the blame for the stains when he came home from school. Who could expect a small child to stay perfectly clean for an entire day?

"I did it, Mom. Punish me. Please don't hurt Pharis!" She pleaded and then grabbed from behind. She struggled to be free, but her mother's eyes were wild, empty eyes focused only on her. She knew a beating was soon. She didn't care. She didn't want anything to happen to her beloved brother, Pharis.

"Get back, you stupid pig!" Josephine's face was stone-cold as she headed in the direction of my trembling father, who hid sheepishly, a little boy who couldn't defend himself. He tumbled down to the ground by the old tree stump; with his arms thrown out instinctively to catch his fall, he fell into the jagged shards of glass. He felt the searing, stinging pain that ran from his wrist to the crease inside his elbow. She roared and laughed as she left. "That's what you get, you whiny piece of garbage!"

My dad loved her for some reason. I always heard that children protect their abusers but couldn't understand why. When I turned nine, Edna/Josephine came to live with us. It wasn't easy to understand as a child. She was mean, jealous and despised my mom one moment and then the next, the sweet Grandmother that I cherished. We were scared of her, didn't trust her and had wished that she didn't live with us until she died of a stroke one day.

The thought jarred me awake. I woke with a start. It was only a dream, and I realized I needed to get up and pack as we were leaving for Mexico today, but the vision left me with a gnawing feeling that we shouldn't go.

*****

The tires of the new motorhome turned as we barreled down the freeway heading to the gulf coast. Fourth of July was only a few days away, so we soon needed to hit the road. It was two months after Russell turned nine. We packed for a two-week vacation with our family of six and our beloved dog, Olive. Olive was a valentine gift Marco had given to me three months before Russell was born. She was a beautiful terrier with solid, black eyes that looked like olives but was rather possessive. Olive made it her business to bark at me each time I changed Russell's diaper in her earlier days. Her nature was kind, and she worshipped the kids.

We were proud of the new Bounder motorhome and the small Suzuki car trailing behind. Marco and I had purchased them just two weeks before, and we were excited to learn about the things they had to offer.

We pulled into the Outdoor Resorts located just north of Ensenada. It was safe, gated, and catered to Americans. We parked our new motor home on the sand facing the gorgeous Pacific coast as we anxiously unpacked our chairs and beach toys. The kids were ecstatic to get into the warm water that rolled into waves as Marco, and I waited with great anticipation for the spectacular fireworks display later that evening.

After a full day in the sun, the kids tired out early that day—a quick nap before the grand event they welcomed. We locked the motorhome door securing Olive inside, and headed to the beach for the 9:00 p.m. firework show. Marco placed our lawn chairs on the edge of the blanket as I passed out the popcorn. We were excited to watch the fireworks burst above, searing their brilliant light and bright colours into the night. The show was explosive, and with each release, a colourful bouquet followed. As we headed back to the motor home, we were in awe.

Olive was nowhere after we noticed the motorhome door ajar. Could someone break in and take our family pet? Would anyone be that vindictive? We frantically ran into the park, calling her name in the darkness. No one had seen her, but the coyote's screaming in the nearby hills said something different. We were panicked as we searched most of the night, then decided to get some sleep and take up our search in the morning. Everyone was heartbroken as we heard Russell calling for her later that night.

Early morning, we loaded into the Suzuki, Marco and me in front, the four kids in the back. We covered a lot of ground that day as Marco searched every possible place Olive could be. We spent the next two weeks repeating our search until it was time to leave Mexico. With heavy hearts, we all sought a way to cope. After crossing the border and reaching home, I never gave up hope that I would find her sitting at our front door once she found her way back to us.

*****

Christmas came and went in a hurry as we looked forward to the new year. I couldn't help but remember something from so long ago.

My Dad packed up the family and took us to the world-famous Rose Parade. The parade was held on New Year's Day on the longest road on Colorado Boulevard in Pasadena. Thousands of people lined the streets to see the massive parades of floats made of flowers and other beautiful materials. As a child, I was in awe of these fantastic floats with millions of bright blues, reds, and yellow synchronized flowers. The floats combined the flowers to create figures, which towered high into the sky as they debuted one by one. Marching bands with over three hundred members took the souls of the listening audience with them. Their patriotic sounds soared through the air as my Dad filled with pride. The Marines passed as he saluted his country and service in World War II.

The first year we sat in the bleachers for the best possible viewing. Several years later, my Dad planned months to reserve a parking spot. A decked-out work truck on the boulevard held 2' x 6' wood planks resting on top of his lumber racks. It served as our bleachers for the morning of viewing. My mother's jug of Bloody Mary's prepared the night before was poured into glasses before the parade started. Chunks of celery, olives, and jalapenos floated on top, close to where the salt-rimmed the glass.

Each year the show took on new meaning, and as the years passed, Marco and I introduced it to our kids.

Jane Boyle, the mother of Madison's best friend, glanced at me. "What are you doing on New Year's Eve?" Her eyes were glowing with excitement. I looked up at her, shrugged my shoulders and uttered sadly, "I don't think we have plans."

"Well, you do now. We are going to Colorado Boulevard. Why don't you come with us?" Eight of us poured into Jane's Bronco a week later and headed toward Pasadena for dinner near the parade route. After finishing a small meal, she walked out and reached into the car's trunk. She made eye contact and handed Marco and me a can of silly string and a squirt gun. "You have to be ready." She made herself clear. We piled back into the car, and as we cruised the boulevard, we saw people from all walks of life

As we drove down the strip and approached a stoplight, we saw a small group prepping their ammo of silly string and shaving cream. "Use your squirt gun!" Jane screamed in delight as a lather-laced tortilla hurled towards us. I grabbed the loaded squirt gun in my lap and nailed the group on the street. "Roll up your window!" Jane's eyes were shining. A launched water balloon flew and crashed onto the front window. The light changed, and we drove on until the next stop.

Hundreds of people were going crazy defending themselves with herds of others attacking. The kids never had so much fun. The car was a mess by the time we got away from the parade route. Jane laughed when she saw the backseat smeared with shaving cream and tortillas. That was our first experience on Colorado Boulevard before the parade. We realized then that the fun was not on the day of the show but the night before.

*****

Our family's custom was to throw the most outrageous parties. "We are going to do something crazy for Trey's eighth birthday," I warned Marco as my eyes gleamed with excitement. We'd entertained with clowns, tea parties, sleepovers, and magicians for the past few years, and I looked for something new.

"What do you want to do for your birthday, honey?" I looked at Trey.

"I love the mountains and all the creatures there, Mom." His dark eyes grew large.

We stuffed the envelopes with invitations that read, "Join us for an afternoon of hiking. Bring your best shoes and sunscreen." We weren't planning a simple hiking trip. I gathered several items at the nearby grocery store included sandwich bread, meat, chocolate cake mixes, dark- chocolate frosting, black pipe cleaners, a giant chocolate cupcake, and two bug eyes. Stirring the cake mix jarred a memory from my past.

My mother and I spent most of the day preparing to bake together in the kitchen. She reached into the cupboard and placed a box of cake mix in front of me. At ten years old, I was excited about my first cooking lesson. I threw it into her mixer as she watched, correcting my newly acquired baking skills. I dipped my utensil into the batter and, with a lick, I thought, "Ahh, it tastes good." As my tongue cleaned the spoon, I noticed the dough was watery and decorated with white specks. I looked at it closer. I realized the white bits were white wiggly bugs, the larvae of moths. I asked my mother what they were. She broke into laughter. I choked and gasped, trying to clear my mouth. Her laugh I will never forget for as long as I live.

After baking Trey's cake, I grabbed the chocolate cupcake and placed it right in the centre. "This must sit perfectly," I whispered as I stooped to see the cake at eye level. Bending the pipe cleaners, I attached them to the cupcake's outer edges, forming perfect spider legs. The bug's eyes finished it off and made it seem remarkably creepy. It looked just as I knew it would be a chocolate-covered tarantula.

Ten boys arrived promptly at one o'clock as we packed our lunches of bologna and cheese sandwiches stuffed into freezer bags. I was glad I had taken the time to draw red-and-black cockroaches on the outside of each plastic bag. We headed towards an old, burned-out road that led high into the mountains. The forest was green as we climbed the steep paths that led to one side of the summit with a view of the valley below. The dry October breeze picked up as we watched the skydivers jump from the granite peaks above and drift towards the quiet earth below. Marco pulled up next to us in his truck with music drifting out of the windows to offer the group a wormy orange punch in mason jars along with the lunches. We hiked most of the afternoon, and before our return, Trey disappeared behind a bush.

The lizards didn't move at first as their greenish-yellow colour helped them blend into the mountain surroundings. Trey held his hand still for the first scaly-dry creature as he eyed the second. With his hand stretched out, he grabbed the fast-moving critter in his tiny palm, depositing the six-inch lizard into his pocket while moving slowly towards the next. The second slick, shiny beast tried to escape as his backbone slithered and his tail blinked. Within moments, it decided to run underneath a rock, but it, too, couldn't escape Trey's grasp.

Trey presented two lizards, Chomper and Slacker, who cosied up in Trey's small pocket on our way home. Trey loved the lizards, and he'd never forget this perfect autumn day. The leaves had begun to fall, and the rain was in the forecast. On his way up the trail, he stepped on every crunchy brown leaf, savouring it.

Trey's birthday was a massive success as he took a large sharp knife and cut it into the homemade cake. All the boys' eyes were on the vast tarantula, and Trey was filled with nature as the party ended. As their parents started to arrive, the boys left one by one, tired yet thrilled with their new pet geckos they took home as party favours.

Chapter 8

TREY SEEMED TO BE A HAPPY FOURTH GRADER and was provided with a secure childhood until, I believe, he met a new music group, Nirvana. Nirvana was known for its heavy instrumental punk, grunge-style music, and Trey adored it. It excited him when their lead singer, Kurt, jumped onto the stage in worn-out pyjamas, when he lined his eyes with black eyeliner and deepened his lips with red lipstick, and, especially, when he swore. I was horrified when I first saw this dirty-looking performer on television for the first time. *Was Trey old enough to engage with this kind of entertainment?* Not too much time passed when the news came that Nirvana's lead singer, Kurt Cobain, had died of unknown causes. On April 5, 1994, the speculation was a drug overdose, and Trey's heart broke too.

"I'm glad Kurt Cobain died. Nirvana was an evil influence on Trey." I met with Trey's fourth-grade teacher, whose eyes disapproved of my comment. "He's been mesmerized by the group for months, and it seems that I just can't get through to him that Kurt Cobain's lifestyle was not something to behold," I said with worried eyes and was looking for agreement from his teacher.

"I don't know why? My husband and I like them." I was shocked that she, too, had been exposed to the group and liked them. *Was she speaking of Nirvana to her young and impressionable audience?* She embarrassed me and made me rethink my statement.

The child who enjoyed vacations in the family motor home became a different kid after Kurt's death revealed suicide. Daily, he complained of headaches and depression. With a lot of worries, I arranged visits to doctors and took him to multiple therapists who gave me the same answer, "He will grow out of it." I deemed this a preliminary diagnosis, so I searched for other solutions.

Attention Deficit Disorder was the newfound name for kids, a teacher's explanation placed on children like Trey. After much consideration and knowing that Marco, Russell, and Trey were all kind of hyper, I decided to put Trey on Ritalin upon a physician's recommendation. The highly praised drug made him quiet and withdrawn, sitting away from the other kids at school and isolating himself at home. Along with the apparent depression, he was not eating and began losing weight.

"What are you doing in your room?" My eyes carried with them worry about Trey's well-being.

"Oh, I don't know. I guess I like being alone." His voice conveyed sadness.

I was dumbfounded and didn't know where to turn. To add to my concerns, our community was becoming more diversified, with many other ethnics moving into the area. I found myself worrying about gang activity and the influence it would have on my family. Then I thought about Trey's depression and refusal to participate in school, so I decided it was time to move to the country.

*****

The location was secure at two hours south, with sprawling ranches, and where the kids could get lost at an old oak tree. Here a brown-eyed boy could dispel his gloom by playing in the hills and strumming his guitar. Rancho was the perfect town and one of the best places to live globally. At the centre of it all: Rancho was two hours north of San Diego, two hours south of Los Angeles, and Las Vegas a mere stone's throw away. With beaches, mountains, and deserts at its fingertips, Rancho's three most attractive lures were its distance from Lacana, a short commute to work for Marco and its neighbourhood, which was clean and had lots of space.

Our ranch-style home in Lacana sold within thirty days, so we ended up in a rental on a world-famous Jack Nicklaus golf course in Bear's Head, an exclusive gated neighbourhood in Rancho. I knew it was short term, so I continued, endlessly, to search for a more permanent home.

Our temporary location was sealed with a six-month lease and was splendid. Sitting on the golf course in a cul-de-sac, it spanned 3,000 square feet on a single level. Beige carpets and marble floors decorated the space, which suited my furniture perfectly. A beautifully designed kitchen with granite countertops and a huge breakfast nook sat on one end of the floor plan. On the other end, it presented four spacious bedrooms.

I quickly gathered boxes for the smaller items and then placed a moving van on hold. I knew Marco was up to his neck with work, so I began packing while the kids were in school. Before our lease began, our moving boxes occupied the rental's dining room, making our move easy. I unpacked and unloaded them from our car into the sizeable sprawling rental for days at a time. It was uncomplicated.

Marco brought the heavy things from the moving van in for me to decide where to place them. There were empty, half-filled, and packed boxes everywhere. As I unpacked a moving box in the dining room, I heard a faint rattling sound. I glanced inside the box only to see a baby rattlesnake striking in my direction. I jumped back and screamed for Marco. "Marco, there's a snake in the box underneath the bubble wrap!" Marco's eyes grew wide, and he rushed in with a pair of barbecue tongs to try to dispose of the snake.

"Grab the kids," he yelled, sweat dripping from his forehead. As I held the kids back, Marco bent down and grabbed the snake's neck between the tongs, its body wiggling wildly. He made his way out the back door, across the golf course to the ravine with his arms extended out away from his body. He threw the baby snake as far as he could with a grunt. I smiled as I reminisced about my summers in Idaho.

The gate-guarded community wasn't a good fit for four loudmouth elementary school kids who wanted their independence as they approached the middle school. The population was mainly composed of wealthy, older golfers who didn't have the patience for kids. Personal guards employed by the homeowners watched the entrance and wrote offences for any wrongdoings within the grounds. My four kids earned many tickets as they became familiar with the golf course and spent many afternoons in the dried-out washes collecting lost golf balls golfers had hit off the course. Inspecting and cleaning each ball, they set up a stand under an old oak tree near the putting green to sell them back to the appreciative golfers. They made a hefty profit for their afternoon adventures, showing early signs of young entrepreneurs.

Those were offences, broken bylaws against the strict Bear's Head rules. Doug, one of the guards, disapproved of the kids being on the golf course and received many complaints about them. Across from our home lived the golf club president who complained the most.

Private pools for community use were on every other street. The golf course president's home looked as if it had its own, but it was indeed a community pool for anyone's use that lived on our street.

The kids changed into their swimsuits, and with towels in hand, we walked across the street to the pool. I heard them playing Marco Polo as I lay sunning myself and dreaming of a chilled glass of wine. "Marco Polo," Russell called as he said the words louder. Russell was swimming blindly while using only his ears to find the other three kids. He edged to the side, climbed out, jumped, landing in the middle of the pool with a splash that cleared most of the water. The kids were on fire as they climbed out and tried to match Russell's cannonball.

"That's enough!" screamed the golf club's president as he picked up the telephone. His voice was growling and snapping as he lodged a formal complaint. Marco was not too far from home when he received my telephone call.

"The kids got another citation for making too much noise in the pool. I guess having fun is against the rules here!" I didn't try to hide my annoyance as I spoke with disgust. I saw Marco coming around the corner as he drove past our neighbour's house. His eyes glared and were on fire.

"A woodpecker is on that asshole's house—grab the lawn chairs. Let's watch him peck the crap out of that idiot's house." The kids each grabbed their chairs as we lined up along the edge of the street, eager to watch the show. As the woodpecker pecked, we heard a loud punch coming from inside the house.

"The guy's trying to scare the woodpecker," I whispered to our neighbour's audience. The afternoon had turned out to be great, as we sat and listened to peck, bang, peck, bang. The siding on the house began to chip, which made the woodpecker work faster. Our neighbour's perfect golfing arm burned. He was a nervous wreck as he came outside, tried to scare the bird away, and saw us lined up watching the afternoon's entertainment. A "For sale" sign went up before dawn. Doug smiled as he drove by and stopped writing as many tickets.

*****

Except for the world-class golf course, the privately-owned tennis club was empty, and the courts were barren. The net drooped as it hung and frayed at the sides. The club owners knew that something had to happen to spur new memberships. Plans to hold a substantial grand opening for their renovated tennis club came together.

Resurfaced tennis courts and new nets looked fresh. New overhead lights shone down on the newly painted green courts. Expensive equipment in the weight room was ordered and put into place. The pool was drained and refilled with sparkling clean water. The banquet room was re-wallpapered, new carpet laid and long tables and tall chairs arranged in the centre. A well-stocked antique bar stood in the corner. Fresh flowers planted along the walkway, and the new sod finished the look.

The Bear's Head resident's attendance came with hopes of inciting interest. They came in hordes. Sushi on tabletops in the activities room; California rolls and salmon slabs lay on rice beds. Soy sauce and wasabi filled the small white bowls sprawling out near the sushi for everyone's enjoyment. Attendees freely poured wine, beer, and sake. Activities were happening everywhere. The kids were given handfuls of tokens for the arcade in hopes they stayed out of trouble.

Marco and I strolled around while waitresses chased us down, keeping our glasses filled with fine wine and craft beer. Live music played smooth jazz as residents took to the dance floor. Marco, singing, grabbed me and twirled me around until my head spun and I felt dizzy.

Filled with food and drink, we decided it was time to go home and then realized we hadn't seen Trey most of the day. We set out to find him. Russell headed in one direction; we headed in the other. Looking in one of the activity rooms, there he sat. We saw him with a plate of sushi and three girls his age sitting beside him at the blackjack table. *Of course, even a ten-year-old Trey was a ladies' man.* He offered his tokens to the girls to get them to stay. Laughing with his arm around one of the girls, he said, "Hit me," as the dealer threw down a jack onto the ace and everyone cheered.

The kids were having such a good time and didn't want to leave, so we remained a little longer, letting them get their fill, but then we noticed the staff cleaning up, and most of the residents had left. We decided it was time to go. The girls seemed disappointed but smiled as they left with their parents, who were angry that they had stayed so long.

Chapter 9

SEVENTH GRADE WAS RIGHT AROUND THE corner as Trey continued to consider himself an outcast and began rejecting sports. Feeling like the kids needed to stay busy and out of trouble, I enrolled them in after-school activities: soccer in the summer, football and cheerleading in the winter. While Russell, Cameron, and Madison thoroughly enjoyed the sports and the friendships they were making, Trey continually found ways of getting out of participating.

After a thirty-minute drive to practice, Trey purposely forgot his football equipment, so I told him to face his coach. "Hey Coach, guess what? I forgot my equipment and accidentally left it at home. I guess I'll have to sit this one out," Trey coolly remarked, his eyes glowing as if he had gotten away with something. Coach Anderson, his burly coach, didn't think so and looked at Trey with suspicious eyes. The crowded area had Pop Warner football players on the field.

"Do you see that hill over there? You will run up and down it until the practice is over. Don't stop until you see everyone off the field." Trey glanced up quickly with a hint of panic in his eyes and did exactly that. My heart cried as I fought the urge to speak to his coach. Trey slowly ran up and down the hill for the entire time, occasionally disappearing to the other side. Finally, practice ended, and Trey, hot and sweaty, came over to me.

I thought he was going to complain, but instead, he smiled. "Mom, want to hear the good news or the bad?" I hesitated and then watched him speak intently. "Coach Anderson made me run up and down that hill over there." I felt sorry for him as I saw the sweat dripping from his forehead and figured that had to be the bad news.

"I'm sorry you had to do that, but you should have remembered your pads." I knew I needed to side with his coach.

"Want to hear the good news now?" He was impatient to tell. I responded with a nod. "While I was running that hill, I got a girl's telephone number." He smiled then proudly displayed it in his hand.

*****

Trey felt special and loved how his female classmates twisted his hair in their hands as he sat in the bleachers at school. They pulled a rubber band from their hip pocket and wound it around the bundle. He sat back with eyes glued shut while they applied eyeliner and mascara. He watched their reactions as they stood back and approved of the way he looked. "I love how his eyes look like chocolate," Gina commented on how gorgeous his deep brown eyes were and loved his long shoulder-length hair, his pride, and his joy.

"I love his silky, long brown hair." Jessie reached for her brush. Unwrapping the rubber band, she brushed it again and then tied it tightly into a scrunchy she'd remembered to bring from home. After hearing that, it reminded me of my mother.

"Tresimo, come do my hair," my mother softly said as Trey climbed onto the couch in the living room and slid up behind her. His hands slowly fluffed and arranged her every strand of red-coloured hair repeatedly. At age four, his hairstyling techniques made him famous as he smoothed the overly dyed curls that fell onto her forehead.

"Hey, Mom, how about a glass of wine?" I didn't try to hide my thirst for a crisp, cold glass of Chardonnay as I turned to face her.

"Oh, yes, I would love one." She dreamed with anticipation as Trey began smoothing her hair with his fingers. He grabbed a small comb from the table and started ratting, teasing, and styling it. She closed her dark eyes and dreamed of being glamorous, as her hair was tousled and brushed. He grabbed an imaginary can of hairspray to finish the job and then jumped down to inspect and admire his work. Russell couldn't wait to seize the opportunity to get in on the action as he jumped up onto the couch and into Trey's spot behind her.

"Russell is in my place and took my brush," Trey whined and glared at Russell to move. I closed my eyes and exited the kitchen before he had a chance to corner me and force me to get involved.

Becoming the envy of the other boys, they talked behind his back as he skipped off with the girls. "Did you see how stupid Trey looks with his hair in that stupid rubber band? Why do all the girls like it when he puts his hair up like that?" Ronnie seethed with envy.

"Yea, he looks so dumb." Tim was jealous. "But I wish the girls liked me as much as they like him," he added as his buck teeth rubbed against his lower lip.

Trey had the world by the tail as he spent most of his time with his girls, not thinking about school or his grades.

My telephone rang two hours after I dropped the kids off at school. Mr Manny, the middle school's principal, was on the phone. "Mrs Morelli? Please pick Trey up in my office. He's suspended." His words were menacing.

"What? Are you kidding me?" He stuttered to reply as I placed the clean dishes aside on the counter.

"He's wearing women's makeup, and that's against the school's rules and policies." *Oh my God, is this an offence that deserves a suspension?* I grabbed my purse and flew out the door. Outside, the rain came down like water slopped from a bucket. I had to drive more slowly than I wanted to; I could hardly see a car length in front of the van. But I finally made it through the muddy lanes to the school. Before I killed the engine, the school's bell sounded. Mr Manny held the door open while I rushed in ten minutes later. There sat Trey in Mr Manny's office with a full face of makeup. He looked stupid and very feminine. I was shocked by this total buffoonery.

"I was not aware he was wearing makeup to school. He didn't leave the house this morning with it on." I apologized to Mr Manny as I studied his reaction and appearance. His silver-flecked hair had a military look about it, cut short and precisely trimmed around his ears and neck. The skin on his chin was smooth, and his voice was weak with a bit of a tremble. He was shorter than I and seemed nervous and not in control as I expected from someone with such authority. I wondered how he got his job as I noticed his eyes leak signs of intimidation. I apologized once again and left the school grounds with Trey.

Marco was taking his boots off as I told him what had happened. He called Trey into the room. By now, the eye makeup was gone, but small black traces remained, and his eyes appeared bloodshot.

"What are you? Some queer?" Marco kiddingly asked while he eyed his son.

"No, I just like being around the girls." Trey shrugged his shoulders unapologetically.

Marco shook his head in disgust and tried to understand how his son could be interested in wearing makeup. He looked up at me.

"Is he trying to get attention or something? You can still see the thick mascara caked between his eyelashes and the stained lipstick on his lips. What a clown! Don't let him near your makeup while he is home from school."

*****

"Trey, please don't break any rules at school today!" I pulled into the campus parking lot after Trey's long three-day suspension. "I'm going to be busy and don't need any more calls from Mr Manny."

"Okay, I won't." The wind howled as the other students arrived through the gates, hustling and bustling down the corridors as Trey and Cameron hurried into school before the bell rang at Johnson Middle School.

As Trey's eyes fell onto the campus, he realized he wasn't interested in attending school today. He pondered the idea of missing first and second periods because, in his mind, he had already missed three days, so what would it matter if he skipped a couple more of his classes.

Rumour has it his 1st-period teacher was out sick, making the decision easier. He gathered a few of his buddies to meet him at an old, abandoned house a few blocks away. Homes built too close to the wash years before were left empty due to rising floodwaters.

Getting a running start, he hopped the fence, felt free, and headed down the street to the boarded-up old home. It wasn't his first time there as he slipped inside through one of the windows he'd left open the last time. He sat in the corner of a dirty room and smoked cigarettes stashed in the trash-filled cupboards. Taking the butt from his lips, he looked over at Garrett and offered it to him. Garrett smiled, grabbed it, and after a long drag, he coughed uncontrollably. Trey coolly laughed.

"That won't last long! Before you know it, you'll be a pro at smoking. Just take smaller hits and don't inhale so deep." His professionalism showed as he continued to laugh at Garrett's innocence and watched Garrett take another puff, trying to master the art of smoking.

"I want to form a band. You in?" Trey's eyes gleamed as he watched Garrett pass the cigarette back.

"Sure. I'm pretty good at the guitar. All we need is a drummer." Garrett was interested. "I'll get in touch with Mikey. I think he plays the drums." Trey looked at his watch then realized he had missed most of his morning classes, and lunch was almost over. He knew it was time to get back.

Once there, Trey canvassed the school grounds and deemed them clear from security. He rushed toward the fence and jumped up, reaching the top. His converse shoes gripped the metal, but just as he was about to swing his leg over, he lost his balance and fell forward, free-falling, to the pavement and landed directly onto his Adam's apple.

Unable to breathe, Trey remained still while his friends ran to Mr Manny.

"Mr Manny! Mr Manny! Trey broke his neck! Hurry! He can't breathe!"

The principal ran a short distance to his car in the parking lot without thinking twice and followed the kids to the fence. When he reached Trey, he lifted him into the back seat of his car and drove him to the emergency room. Trey's breath was shallow, and he was unable to swallow. A panic-stricken Mr Manny notified the nurse as he burst through the hospital's automatic door in the emergency room. She called for a gurney.

I was informed and told what happened shortly after that, but Trey was calm and comfortable with a doctor by that time. I consulted with the doctor by telephone about pain relief. With no other options, morphine dulled Trey's pain.

I entered Trey's room and asked how he was feeling. Groggily, he replied, "Really good!" I noticed his voice was raspy, yet it had a familiar ring to it. It reminded me of the lead singer of Nirvana. "This morphine is great, and I love it!" He struggled to get the words out. He continued to tell me how much he liked the pain medication as he slowly fell asleep. His first real experience with hard drugs was now; a day that he never forgot.

Everyone knew about Trey's accident as he returned to school a week later with his neck wrapped in bandages to protect his bruised Adam's apple from further damage. The girls rushed to him as he made his way through the crowds of kids gathered during the break. Trey eyed the clock, happy to see his art class teacher was about to open the doors for the students to come in.

"Class, class, quiet down." His pretty eighth-period teacher was beaming in front of the blackboard. "Today's assignment is the following: You have five days to create something that shows movement. If you can visualize a tennis or golf player, that should make the assignment easier." The class used different techniques while exploring papier-Mache. As she announced the new assignment, Trey's face fell into a natural look of disbelief. Twenty per cent of the grade was for the artwork that went into it. The other eighty per cent was for creativity.

His imagination quickly went to work, conjuring up precisely what he wanted to do.

Taking strips of newspaper dipped in water and flour, he wrapped them around the wire that he had formed into the shape of a toilet. He grabbed more cable and bent it, shaping it into a sitting male figure. He placed the paper-wrapped item on the lavatory made of wire and glued them together. Working quickly, he applied layer after layer of papier-Mache, waiting for each layer to dry completely. His mind raced as he completed his project and finished it with a palette of colour. The figure's face strained with purples and blues dabbed across its forehead. Blue jeans, a white T-shirt, and black tennis shoes completed the figurine as Trey finished his project. He felt proud he'd completed the task on time when he presented it to his teacher.

"What is this?" Her impatience showed as she looked around at his classmates' smiles.

"You don't see it? The man is having a bowel movement." His eyes shone with pride as his classmates broke into laughter.

She took the sculpture from him, placed it on her desk and looked straight into his eyes. "You think it's funny? Do you think this class is a joke? Stay after school today and meet me in my classroom," she sternly instructed.

Mr Manny didn't want to make another call but needed to warn me that Trey would be late after school. After hearing about the teacher's choice to initiate another suspension, I reluctantly headed to the school. Trey stood out in front of the gate with his project in his hand and stepped into the car. I saw the look of defeat on his face.

"Let me see your project," I said. Trey handed it to me. I examined it and handed it back. "This project is creative and well done. Your teacher was wrong not to have seen the humour and imagination that went into this. I want to keep it."

Trey's mood perked up as he listened to my words, and once we got home, he placed his project on the lid of the toilet tank.

Chapter 10

CROUCHING DOWN OUTSIDE THEIR BEDROOM window, Trey looked over at Cameron. "There you go." He handed Cameron the lit joint after he inhaled and held the smoke in his lungs for a few seconds. His expression softened into dreaminess as the cannabis worked its magic. "You want to go explore the hills?" Trey knew Cameron wanted to. There were plenty of hidden spots in the mountains surrounding Bear's Head. "Do ya?" He felt the excitement build as he waited for Cameron to reply. Cameron took the joint, hit it, and then handed it back, his head swimming pleasantly.

The rolling hills were beautiful as the sun shone down on them. The boys hiked up a thin trail created by many hikers before them. The cave was only a mile from our house but hidden by bushes and fallen rocks as the slopes descended below. The path stopped abruptly at the mouth of a cave as ivy-covered the rough dark opening. Trey looked over at Cameron, smiled and was proud they found a perfect hangout. Cameron and Trey spent plenty of time preparing the cave and gathering firewood from outside. They heaped wood, sticks, and brush into a pile as they worked together to get the fire started. Three hours later, one, two, three clicks of a lighter and the fire sprang alive. Their tiresome job was complete. They sat back to enjoy a smoke together and savour their hard work. They were pleased by the warmth of the fire and thrilled they found this home, away from home, where they could spend plenty more days together.

Cameron suddenly couldn't breathe as he realized some of the brush they used was poison oak. The boy felt like someone was choking him while his heart raced and pounded. He curled into a fetal position, hoping someone would save him. It seemed like so much fun in the beginning as Trey sat, reflected, and then couldn't believe his eyes. His brain was numb, slow to respond, and he couldn't comprehend what was happening. Trey felt concern filling his mind as he looked at the smouldering fire and then at his brother. "Don't worry, Brother, you'll be home soon!" His brother's breath laboured as Trey slowly grabbed him around the waist and struggled to drag him down the path. "I've got to get him home," he mumbled to himself. Cameron's clammy hands clung to his brother's neck as he gasped for another breath.

He struggled with the words that were finally easier to say as he saw our house in the distance. "I've got to get you home." They approached our property as I was looking out my kitchen window. I could not believe what I saw. It seemed like a nightmare as I watched Trey dragging a pale Cameron down the path and instinctively knew something was wrong.

I grabbed my purse, and after Trey told me about the poison-oak stoked fire, I rushed Cameron to the emergency room. It seemed like an eternity to me as I heard Cameron grunting and groaning, trying to breathe. I saw how frightened he was as he gazed at me with swollen eyes. Every blood vessel in the whites of his eyes had burst as uncontrollable tears ran down his face.

The emergency room was crowded with many sick people, as a door flew open and the triage nurse waved us in. After a quick assessment, the syringe filled with epinephrine slammed into Cameron's thigh, and his breathing quickly started to normalize. "Wait fifteen minutes, and then you can go." The nurse pointed to the exit.

Finally, we headed home, and when we got there, I asked Trey how it had happened. "What made you guys think you could burn poison oak?"

"I don't know. We didn't know it was poison oak until Cameron stopped breathing." Trey found himself searching for a decent answer and knew there wasn't one. His memory was a blur, and the details were tucked away in his fogged brain.

"Didn't you remember Cameron is allergic to it?" I grilled him and forced him to answer.

"We decided to build a fire, and poison oak was the only bush around." Trey's memory faded into the smoke-filled past.

"No one in their right mind builds a fire with poison oak!" I shook my head, mumbled to myself and under my breath said, "You dumb idiots". I smiled when I thought of the movie "Dumb and Dumber" and wondered if my sons fit the roles best.

Trey smiled as he went into the bedroom where his brother waited. They laughed together, remembering the strength of the pot they bought earlier in the day.

Doug warned me about the kids causing trouble with the golfers, so I suggested they play in the cul-de-sac, away from the golf course. I picked up the telephone, made an appointment with a local real estate agent to show me property in the hills above Bear's Head. The area was known as The Plateau, a rancher's paradise. I stood at my kitchen sink and looked out over the golf course as I waited for the appointment time. I watched Russell run by, then Trey, with Cameron following them. Doug, the security guard, was a close fourth. I needed to settle down and buy a house to get these kids out into the country, away from Doug and Bear's Head.

*****

Rancho boasted many qualities that called to families looking for peace, cleanliness, and safety. The Plateau perched itself above the big city lights, the track homes, and away from the familiar streets in Rancho. The house, situated on six acres of land, sat on a flat, two-acre knoll high above the rest of the surrounding area. The home's points of pride were the incredible views of rolling green valleys to the west and city lights of the nearby city to the east. Its Mediterranean style caused the previous owners to spend extravagantly to finish it, but the bank forced them to leave after reckless decisions. I found our dream home, moved and settled in.

The house was missing stained-glass windows above the front doors, had unfinished Spanish floor tiles throughout the house, and all the appliances were gone. Landscaping was sparse, but several small trees were planted and left behind by the last occupants. It was just a house on a hill as the coyotes roamed the area. We heard their crying and yelling at night; one coyote called the others to join him after killing. We saw drawbacks but had visions of making it our paradise. Marco gave up the two-hour drive to Lacana and succumbed to moving his business south. I needed help with the kids anyway.

Outside the property lines grew an old oak tree about a one-half acre away. The tree had the most beautiful skin, every brown from deep chestnut to rich mahogany. It changed too, as the day matured, as the sun came to strength, illuminating the details that made it such art. The kids made it theirs, spending every waking moment there while Marco and I put everything we had into the house. "We're so lucky we sold the house in Lacana at the top of the market." I felt pride as I looked over to Marco while he cleaned the windows.

"Yep, me too, but remember all those late nights?" He was proud too of our accomplishments.

"Yes. How could I ever forget?" I smiled as I drifted into the past.

It'd been a long day with the kids. Marco and I were committed to working on the two-bedroom shack. Marco's tired eyes showed the ten-hour days he worked at his newly-formed construction company before he came home each night, but somehow, we continued our evening ritual.

The new design of our home was what Marco and I planned, with a large open family room and a stairway leading to the upper floor to our massive master bedroom suite. We left the original kitchen intact as we worked around it so I could continue to cook for our family. We worked hard and steady, dreaming of our perfect home, as the paint was mixed and applied smoothly. Marco and I listened to our favourite groups as we sipped our rum and coke and settled in for the night's after-hours. The nights hurried by.

"We accomplished a lot tonight, more than I expected. Tomorrow I'll start drywalling so we can begin moving into our new bedroom upstairs." Marco's eyes sparkled as he thought about our new honeymoon suite.

We slowly made our way to bed as dreams of finishing the house filled our heads. As I began to slip off to La-La-Land, I heard a sound coming from the existing kitchen cupboard.

"Marco, did you hear that?" My imagination quickly went to work. What could that beast be? Was it some giant, hairy half-man creature or something? A bad one? Marco sat up in bed, listening carefully. "There's something in the kitchen!" I mumbled in a frightened whisper, fingers to my lips. Moving in closer to Marco, egging him to get up by pushing and tugging slightly at his arms, I watched him shut his eyes and shake his head as I again heard a knocking sound coming from the cabinet. Marco didn't seem to flinch as he pulled his black army boots on.

I watched him leave the bedroom wearing only his "whitey tight" underwear and heavy black work boots. I followed him down the narrow hallway and into the outdated kitchen. We heard knocking sounds again as Marco reached for his hammer. The sight of him made me smile and proud that he was here to protect me. He looked over at me with straight-line lips then reached for the cabinet.

"You're not going to open the cupboard door, are you?" By this point, I was scared to death and worried while I bit my lip. He then grabbed a nail from the counter and hammered the door shut, leaving the sizeable black rat to fend for itself. He looked over at me and smiled as he made his way back to bed.

The boys honed their carpenter skills as they nailed thick pieces of wood to the tree's trunk. The planks of wood acted as stairs leading up to the plywood landing, and from there, they climbed higher into the towering branches of the grand tree. Inscribed into the trunk were the names of friends who came to the tree fort and wanted their names engraved into history. The boys tied ropes to the branches and swung from them as they spent countless afternoons there. Madison joined her brothers and their friends at the tree. She made multiple trips back and forth from the tree to the house bringing the boys sandwiches and drinks. The tree was their sanctuary and a place of independence away from adults.

Chapter 11

TREY SLIPPED BACK INTO DEPRESSION WHEN HE abruptly decided to let Chomper and Slacker go. The world and all of his senses had turned into nothingness for him. Everything was gone. He paused, trying to hold back the familiar feelings roaring inside him, but he couldn't. A lone tear traced down his cheek, then the wall of tears opened, spilling down his face. He packed his life-long friends up into his pocket, walked to the edge of the property, reached in and grabbed Slacker.

He looked into Slackers eyes as he had so many times before and quietly cried. "I wish I would have treated you better. You have been more than a best friend to me. I could always talk to you, and you just listened. You have always made me laugh, and I never appreciated you the way I should have. You deserve so much more. Now go find a family who can love you like I never could." Trey wiped away his tears as he gently placed the lizard on the ground then watched him run off into the bushes.

Next, Trey grabbed Chomper's petite body and held him to his cheek. He whispered, "Go free, Chomper." His words broke his heart apart as his face soaked up his tears, and he quietly cried uncontrollably. After setting Chomper down onto the dirt, Chomper looked back at Trey, not understanding what he'd done wrong or why Trey wanted him to go. "I don't love you anymore!" Trey shouted. His voice was now gruff, yet his eyes conveyed the truth. The lizard remained there for a few minutes, then ran off, sad and alone. Trey was alone now. He was utterly alone, without anything to comfort him.

The two lizards, which had withstood two big moves and lived as Trey's closest friends, were now free as he walked away with tears streaming down his face. He never looked back as he slowly left the two lizards to fend for themselves in the hills of The Plateau.

*****

Heat penetrated the floor-to-ceiling windows in the living room. As the sun started to descend behind the hills, Marco and I reluctantly watched pigeons build their nests under the eaves of our Spanish clay-tiled roof. The male, boasting bright blues on his chest, carried twigs to the waiting female. They worked in harmony as he fetched the twigs so she could build the nest. The male dropped bird poop onto everything beneath him with every returning flight. It splattered onto the concrete and dripped down the white stucco walls. I observed Marco put up a tall ladder and climb two steps at a time to the top. He placed chicken wire around the nest's opening and nailed it shut. His steady hand held his favourite hammer; the other grasped the ladder as I stood below, stabilizing it. "Leigh, don't let go! Keep both hands on the ladder!" Marco dramatically moaned. I remember many times I'd have gladly let it go.

We were decorating our ten-foot-tall Christmas tree as Marco climbed onto the ladder. I handed him silver and gold balls to hang on the highest boughs. He shook and stuttered as he yelled, "Hold on tighter. You are going to let it slide sideways!" Marco was always concerned about the stability of ladders that leaned against walls.

"No, I'm not. I have a firm grasp on it." I stared up into his eyes while remembering how weak my rotator cuff was.

"Leigh, hold onto it while I climb onto the ledge." The shelf was halfway up the twenty-four-foot wall. "You hold onto the balls while I climb, then hand them to me." He demanded as he made his way onto the shelf. I climbed up a couple of rungs and handed him one of the balls he struggled to hold but then dropped. It crashed to the floor. "God damn it, you almost made me fall. You have to climb higher to reach me!" He glared at me and screeched. By then, I wasn't going to hang onto the ladder or hand him any more balls. I climbed down, moved the ladder away from the wall, and walked away, leaving him alone on the ledge. "What are you doing? Where are you going?" I walked out of the house, leaving him stranded. I stood in the shadow of the house, contemplating if I could leave him there and for how long. What if he fell? He could break his neck. I hesitantly went back into the house, replaced the ladder without saying a word, and watched him descend. The second he was safe, I walked away and left.

"They crap all over the place." Marco dodged a near hit. "They belong at the ocean. What the hell are they doing here at the Plateau?" He complained. Two days later, we called an exterminator.

Surveillance came quickly to Trey as he listened from the top of the winding staircase near Cameron's room. He watched our failed attempts to stop the birds and knew that he could finish the job with his keen eye.

He pled to Marco, "Dad, please let me shoot the pigeons with my BB gun."

I snarled. "No! You could hit and break the stained-glass window above the entry doors, and I'm not willing to take that chance." Marco trustingly looked at Trey and gave him approval while muttering under his breath that Trey wouldn't be able to hit them anyway.

The BB gun was cocked and, in his hand, as he hid behind a tree. He waited patiently as Marco, and I finally lost interest. At the precise moment, he jumped from behind the tall palm while holding his BB gun at his hip after he spied a bird sitting on the eave. He aimed and then shot. It was the loudest eardrum rattling noise he had ever heard. He hit the pigeon on his first try. As the bird dropped from the sky, Trey ran to see the pigeon was still alive. I saw Trey passing in front of the window from the corner of my eye, cradling the bird in his blood-drenched tee shirt. He tried to hide the tears running down his flushed face as I looked over at Marco. "See what you've done!" He looked at me puzzled for a moment, then noticed how upset Trey was.

Marco walked out the front door, grabbed the bloodied pigeon from a sobbing Trey, and headed to the garage. He grabbed his hammer and laid the injured pigeon on the ground. One hit with his mallet, and the pigeon was dead.

He swiftly rushed back into the house. "God damn it, Leigh, see what happens? You made me kill the bird!" *Me?* I looked at him in amazement.

*****

The Plateau's temperatures rose into the hundreds during the summer, making it a breeding ground for rattlesnakes. Rock formations and other shady areas protected the reptiles as the weather sizzled throughout the summer months.

At first, the sound was like something sizzling on a grill as the rattlesnake shook its tail. The rattling sound filled the previously humid, silent air. It eyed our family dog, Tommy, as it slithered up the outside stucco wall near our bedroom. Trey heard Tommy, who rarely barked, so he knew it must mean danger. He came running around the corner with an axe in his tiny hand. His eyes fell to the rattlesnake; all else vanished from his mind. With one solid swing, he lopped off the rattlesnake's head. He watched its head drop to the ground as its body wiggled and the rattle continued to vibrate.

The long-standing family rule pounded in his head, *you have to eat what you kill*, so he decided to skin the snake and cook it. Even with its rough exterior, the snake's skin was smooth and silky to the touch. Trey ran his hands down the snake's back, expecting it to be uneven but found it flat over its entire length. He removed the fourteen rattles from the five-foot-long creature lying on the solid birch butcher block in the centre of our kitchen. His blade slid under the skin along the snake's belly. He smiled as thirty long minutes passed before the snake was undressed and lying on the counter. Trey carefully folded the scaly skin and took it down the backyard stairs draping it on the white picket fence to dry. "Dad will be proud of me." He smiled as he walked back to the kitchen.

He grabbed Madison by her freckled arm and persuaded her to join him in the kitchen. "C'mon, I want you to see this," he coaxed.

"What is it?" She remembered the times he had fooled her before.

With the frying pan out and ready, he filled it with butter and began frying. The chunks of snake splattered and filled the air with smells Madison had never encountered before. "What is it?" He ignored her questions as he finally sliced it into bite-size pieces.

"Here, have a bite." He persuaded her. "Have a bite; you will love it, Maddy." His eyes twinkled. He prepared a big bite on the fork as she opened her mouth, and he plopped it down onto her tongue.

"It tastes like chicken." Her eyes sparkled with pleasure.

He laughed and threw a chunk of the snake into his mouth. "You're eating rattlesnake!" He screamed with pleasure. He pointed over to the skin drying on the fence. She gasped, gagged, and choked, trying to remove anything that was in her mouth.

*****

Close friends who lived close by held the annual neighbour-hood Bring-Your-Own-Booze-Party. We grabbed our unique rolling cooler from the cabinet and packed it with exotic and expensive wines and beer. I gently placed the Chateau Margaux bottle into the container, surrounded by foam to protect it during its ride. *Yummy.* I eyed the label. The second bottle, a Russian River Chardonnay, snuggled next to the first vessel. "We should bring the Chateau Laffite for our hosts." I watched Marco as he pulled it from the wine cellar. Two more craft beers, we were packed and ready to go.

The weather was pleasant as the October Santa Ana winds blew softly through the air.

We could feel autumn in the air as the winds picked up slightly. My mind relaxed as I felt happiness bubble up from within as I flashed back to my younger years and memories of the warm breezes that blew through the windows of our grand home.

"Stay home and behave," Marco instructed the kids with a stern and demanding tone. I reminded myself to lock the alcohol cabinet and hide the key on our way out as I placed the key on the hidden shelf below. "We'll be back in a couple of hours."

Marco, in his exclusive Tommy Bahama shirt and me, in my pink-patterned sundress and white protective hat, kissed the kids goodbye. We drove out the driveway in our Mercedes, entering the small two-lane road that connected the ranches and dotted The Plateau landscape. The drive was less than two miles down the winding road to the much-anticipated party.

Behind the white picket fence sat an impressive Victorian-style home boasting an intricate grand entrance. The pathway led to a wrap-around front porch adorned with turned wood. Gorgeous rose gardens surrounded the house, highlighting the rolling landscapes, deciduous trees, olive groves, and vineyards. We entered through the ornate front doors, impressed by the antiques that filled the foyer. The atrium connected a yellow sitting room to the right. Double doors gave access to another parlour before opening to the picturesque backyard.

Linda and Paul threw one of the best afternoon parties, exclusive to only the elites of The Plateau. Marco knew the group because of his reputation for building luxury custom homes in the area. The party was in full swing as their guests arrived while soft music played in the background. "You can put your belongings in the back, under the trellis." Paul welcomed Marco with a smile. Their backyard, nestled in the vineyards, was where the grapevines wound thickly up supported posts and across the wooden trellis.

"Oh, that must be where we should put the cooler." Marco pointed to the patio. "Where is our cooler? Is it still in the car?" He glanced at me after realizing he hadn't seen it in the Mercedes. "You didn't bring it?" He said harshly.

"I thought you did." I stared at him blankly as I knew this wasn't a good start for the afternoon. We went back and forth as we both denied responsibility and slowly realized that no matter who forgot it, we needed to retrieve it. A quick trip back to our house was no big deal as we prepared to leave. "We'll be back in a minute," I whispered as we passed Linda at the front door.

I saw a white Ford Ranger approaching us on the winding hill as we headed home. Marco's truck grew closer, and I saw Trey with Cameron riding beside him. I immediately began to worry. Cursing under my breath and wondering where they found the keys to the truck, I hoped Marco didn't notice as we slowed down to enter our driveway. As we did, Trey pulled a U-turn to follow us. I waited as Marco jumped out of our car, angrily running to Trey and Cameron.

"You stupid idiots!" Marco yelled. "What the fuck are you doing?" He raged as Trey stood there dumbfounded. Trey looked directly into Marco's eyes and shrugged his shoulders nonchalantly. "We were just taking a joy ride and weren't leaving The Plateau. I'm the one who asked Cameron to go." He was leaning against the truck with his legs crossed. It seemed Trey always took responsibility for others when they got into trouble.

"You what?" Marco screamed as he noticed our Igloo cooler sitting in the back of the truck. "You what?" He couldn't believe his ears as he continued to fume.

"Marco, it's getting late. Come on, let's go back to the party." I grabbed his arm.

"You little assholes better stay home!" He yelled as he swiped the keys from the truck's ignition.

"We'll be back, and I'll deal with you later!" We grabbed our cooler and returned to the party.

Marco was uncomfortable as we made our way through the crowded room at Linda and Paul's house. "Those stupid sons of bitches. I should beat the crap out of them for stealing my truck," he muttered under his breath. I poured a full glass of Russian River Chardonnay for both of us, which quickly made the day's events fade into a blur.

The party kicked into high gear as we dined on live lobster and crab while the gossip began to fly. "Did you hear about Kim and Greg?" Linda leaned over and whispered to me. Her eyes were on fire with delight. "Greg got caught cheating in his office with his secretary." She threw her head back, closed her eyes and visualized what she was about to expose. "Kim walked in on him while he was giving it to his secretary on his desk." She laughed hysterically.

"Oh, my God, I can't even imagine, but I've always known Greg was a cheater," I said as I remembered how he looked at me. I saw Linda look over at Greg, who sat in the corner by himself. Greg was known for his well-kept beard. As I glanced around the room, I saw Kim outside smoking. "Are they going to split up?" I looked at Linda with a puzzled look on my face.

"No, I don't think so. Kim always forgives him." Linda smirked. "I heard Jim has cancer." I wondered if the rumour was true.

"Yes, he does and is starting treatment next week. It doesn't look good. He is sick." She watched Greg. "It's like everyone up here is either divorcing, cheating or dying. What is happening to everybody?" Linda shook her head.

Plastic napkins protected our clothing from the dripping buttery lobster claws. *Aww, it tastes so good with the wine.* Paul sat down beside me. His face showed his age. "Our kids are grown now, and I have a nearly new Yamaha 50 sitting in my garage. I need more space for my toys. Are you guys interested in buying it?" He took a puff from his Cuban cigar. I could see that he had quite a habit by looking at his yellow, decaying teeth.

"Russell wants a new bike for Christmas. His old one is barely running. Let me talk to Marco." I sat next to Paul, avoiding the smoke as it slowly left his lips. I couldn't wait to get the thumbs up to purchase the bike from Marco. We bought it before we went home. The next day Marco moved it into our storage unit at the foot of the hill until Christmas morning.

Chapter 12

THE TALENT SHOW AT THE SCHOOL WAS IN THREE weeks, and Trey had to act quickly. He knew how he liked things. Garrett was called and asked if he could sign up for the gig. Competing against the other acts meant a lot to Trey. He knew they'd have to practice, and it would take time before they got things the way he wanted them. "Let's commit to practising at my house three times a week. I'll set up the garage as our studio. My dad bought a set of drums and gave them to me. I have my guitar and a speaker." Trey's mind raced. "Do you have any other equipment?"

"I have my bass guitar. I know my dad will bring me over so we can practice." Garrett was already checking his notebook for Mikey's phone number. "I'll call Mikey and set it up for tomorrow."

"Let's play one of Nirvana's songs. We can choose which one when we meet." Trey's excitement showed on his face. "I have a pretty good voice, so I'll sing lead, and you can sing back-up." Garrett was disappointed with Trey's lone decision.

The boys practised for hours at a time, and as I listened, I struggled to pick up the tune. The noise coming from the garage was hard to bear as the boys competed for the lead position.

Days passed quickly, and the big event was finally here. The boys worked hard to set up the middle school's lunch area stage. They were third to perform after testing for sound and made sure the amp was working correctly. I stood back and watched Trey as he tuned his guitar.

The soft Santa Ana winds blew as the boys took the stage. Trey wore his white T-shirt; a button-down, blue-and-white flannel shirt; blue jeans; and black-and-white converse tennis shoes. His clean hair blew softly around his face as his lips hugged the microphone, and the raspy sounds began. The music started thumping hard and made his bones vibrate as he felt the song's words of anger, fear, and frustration. His mind drifted into a mosh pit as his fingers went numb from strumming the strings. The girls in the front row couldn't keep their eyes off him as he sang. When they heard the music, it was like liquid adrenaline being injected right into their bloodstreams- not strong as to freak them out, but just enough to make them tingle and start to move their bodies. As I watched the girls admire Trey, I suddenly saw him through their eyes. He was nothing short of being beautiful.

The song slowly ended as Trey drifted back to earth, looked up, his hair covering his face and received the first-place award. He proudly displayed the gold trophy in his room on the night-stand after a long and stressful day. Garrett and Mikey could visit the prize whenever they wanted to.

*****

As Christmas morning arrived, the kids excitedly hurried to the tree to open gifts. "We have to wait until your grandparents get here," I reminded the impatient kids from the kitchen, which exploded with delicious smells of baked bread and egg souffle. As I peered out the front window into the darkness, I saw two tiny headlights coming into the driveway. My parents pulled through our wrought-iron gate and parked. As they approached the house with armloads of gifts, we could hear the familiar sound of Christmas bells my dad rang each year. My parents made their way to the front door, where the kids waited to greet them.

Once we opened the gifts, Russell followed Marco and me to the garage, where his big gift waited. His eyes grew large when he saw the red-and-black Yamaha 50 mini-bike. Russell couldn't wait to take the bike out for a spin on the property.

"Can I take it for a ride?" Trey innocently asked.

"No, but you can have my old bike if you want it. It doesn't run that great, but it still works." Trey graciously accepted it as he carried his new BB gun out to the garage to inspect his gift from Russell.

"A good mechanic has to be prepared." Trey reminded himself as he tinkered in the garage, looking for miscellaneous parts. His hair fell into his eyes as he grabbed a couple of bolts and some baling wire. He seemed bewildered by his newfound hobby. Trey stood looking at the unrecognizable bike, trying to figure out how to make it run better and look presentable.

With a well-thought-out plan, he went to work on it. He screwed missing bolts in, took baling wire, and secured the bumpers. He strapped the steering wheel in place and finally stood back to admire the work he had completed. Everyone laughed. The entire bike was held together with baling wire when Trey finished. He was proud of the job he'd worked so hard on. The bike needed a quick cleaning off with a hose, and it was ready to hit the road. It ran fine as he headed over the pathway to the oak tree and back.

He got his bike ready to take to his friend's house a mile down the hill. Trey noticed Madison as she walked outside. "Want to go?" Trey stood coolly with his right hand on his bike, his other on his hip. Without much hesitation, she agreed. I looked out the window to see Madison sitting on the handlebars while Trey gassed the motorcycle down the long scary road. I shook my head. *Madison is crazy and too trusting. I hope they both make it back safely.* I sat down and felt a headache coming on.

The bike started zigzagging across the street and almost flipped after hitting a rock in the road. "Don't stand up!" Madison screamed as Trey performed tricks on the bike. "Stop doing that!" The heavy motorcycle wobbled underneath her, threatening to knock her sideways. Her stomach was contorting strangely, and she thought her voice might crack. She was frantic and knew that letting go of the grip would be a significant mistake. She tried to tell herself that the fear was pointless. Her stomach wasn't buying it. Trey whistled cheerfully, an unfamiliar tune, swinging his arms and moving freely. His smile gleamed as he stood up, and his hands left the handlebars. Her knuckles buckled as she squeezed the handgrips with everything she had, fearing for her life.

His laughter filled the air. They made it safely to their destination as Madison shook off her fear. The second her feet hit the ground, she turned around with disgust and headed for home on foot, too scared to go into their friend's house. "I will never ride with you again!' She screamed. Trey, on his bike, followed her closely until they made it back to the house.

"I can't believe you got on the bike with your crazy brother." I noticed Madison as she walked into the house.

"I'll never do that again. That jerk almost killed me!" Her eyes bled fright. Trey casually parked his bike and went to his room.

*****

Trey reached for a binder beneath his bed, and with a pen, he continued to finish one of the graphic sketchings he'd started two days earlier. He pencilled lacerations onto a stick figure's neck as he indulged in long hours of thought. The sketching was morbid as his mind raced. The violence burned into his brain as he thought about his artwork. The sickness crawled inside him as the red ink dripped onto the tablet's page. His eyes watched as his uncontrolled fingers continued to draw—one man hanging, another one dead. Upon completion, he autographed his drawings as if he wanted everyone to know he drew them. The pictures were visual and made me worry about him. *What would make him do this? Is he sick? Why would he spend so much time in a dark world like this?*

After dropping him off at school, I reached under his bed for more and pulled out a memoir Kurt Cobain had written. He, too, drew raunchy cartoons. Many of Trey's looked much like Kurt's. Somehow it made me more comfortable knowing that Kurt's mind was sick.

One of his drawings dropped from his binder at school, and when asked what it meant, he laughed. That prompted a call to me from his ninth-grade teacher. "Mrs Morelli? I found a drawing by Trey on the ground near his desk. The picture concerns me, so I decided to contact you today. Trey has been distant the past few weeks and seems to be daydreaming more. I'm worried." I listened to her concerns then promised to speak to him.

I'd been worried too, so his teacher's call left me empty. Conversations and discussions with Trey about his artwork left me with a shrug and a smile. Trey didn't seem angry or dangerous. He was just a normal kid with his ups and downs, or so I thought, who idolized Kurt Cobain.

Trey's raspy screams came from his room, the shower, and the old oak tree as he practised Kurt's howl day and night. He lost himself to grunge bands like the Pixies, Soundgarden, and Alice in Chains and liked the classic artists, The Beatles and Led Zeppelin. At age fourteen, he sat at the table with one of Marco's friends, Rich, and begged him to loan his collection of Roy Orbison's CDs to him.

"I need it because I'm thinking about adding some different music to the songs my band plays." Trey glanced at Rich with pleading eyes.

Rich listened, his dimples smiled, and finally agreed. "Okay, but I need them back by the end of the month. Please take care of them. The collection is valuable." Trey placed the CDs under his arm and left with much gratitude.

Trey rode shotgun in his friend's car, which led a procession of headlights on the street, taillights snaking their way up the road and over the brow of the hill to the bonfire. On an empty, graded pad, miles from occupied homes, they had plenty of privacy for the long evening ahead. He reached into his backpack and grabbed his CD player and Orbison CDs. He pressed play, and the music began. The sweet refrain of the acoustic guitar spoke a musical language to Trey's soul. The strumming sound had a hypnotic, soothing quality that he craved. To lose himself to the melody of the guitar and Roy Orbison's voice was his idea of a great night. Trey blasted the sound for most of the evening, enjoying every moment of it. He then replaced it with Nirvana, and after a few hours and a case of beer, the CDs eventually ended up in the dirt as Trey's friends danced on top of them. The morning came as Trey picked up the CDs from the ground, wiped them off on his dirty jeans and returned them to their cases.

Three weeks later, he responsibly returned the collection to its owner as promised, so scratched they were beyond repair. He was proud as he watched Rich reach in and grab one to inspect. "What the fuck have you done to my collection?" He glared into Trey's downward look.

"I returned the CDs on time. They may not be in the best condition, but at least I kept my promise." Trey's eyes seemed mellow as he cracked a smile. Rich looked at him, admired his honesty, then laughed, too, and within a week replaced the collection. He made a copy for Trey promising not to dance on them again.

Chapter 13

INSPIRATION HIT LIKE LIGHTNING STRUCK WHEN Trey decided to expand his band, so he put the word out that there was an opening for a drummer. The catch was that the drummer had to be a girl. Auditions began in our garage on Saturdays, all-day Saturday.

Marco yelled at me, but he wasn't audible over the music. "When the fuck are they going to wrap it up? I can't concentrate. I have a deadline to meet on this bid but can't do it with all that racket!" Unfortunately, Marco's office shared a wall with the garage, and it didn't provide much of a sound barrier.

I walked into the garage to alert Trey and saw a half dozen girls there to audition. They formed a line that extended well past the garage door. The girl sitting on the stool behind the drum set looked up at me and smiled. I returned her smile as I took in her attire and noticed her distinct appearance. Her hair was long, black, and cornrowed under a Theodore hat. Thick eyeliner surrounded her dark eyes. Her thigh-high black shorts revealed incomplete tattoos. Black combat boots covered her feet as she nervously began her drum solo. She initiated and then stopped to ask if she could start again. A simple nod from Trey gave her the go-ahead. She commenced with a dull sound, which ended with drums pounding to an unheard beat. She nervously stopped then handed the drumsticks to the next girl in line.

The next girl climbed in behind the drum set and nodded at Trey as if she'd met him before. Her face was clean and free of makeup, except her full lips, lined with red pencil filled with blood-red lipstick. Her short hair was shocking pink. Her tongue, pierced, caused her to introduce herself with a lisp. "Hi. My name is Leetha." She made her debut, then left the drum set for the next girl in line.

Trey casually sat on the old sofa donated to assist in the interview process, with his arm wrapped snugly over a girl's shoulders. She struggled to pull her black lace minidress down, which hiked up while conversing with Trey.

"You know, you are good." His mouth slyly found her ear as he stuck his tongue into it. "I'd like to get to know you better." He whispered as his tongue went in for another stab. She appeared to like how it felt as it dashed in and out. She was smart enough to know she'd have a better chance at being in the band if she did what he wanted.

"I would love to get to know you, too." She looked into his dark eyes sincerely. Trey's bedroom, conveniently located nearby, allowed him to carry her in and lift her onto his queen-size bed. Auditions abruptly ended for the day after Trey disappeared for an extended length of time and wasn't available to conduct more interviews. Hours passed as Trey's bedroom door remained closed. Suddenly his door opened, and Trey ran butt naked across the kitchen floor with two cold beers hidden in his bare hands.

"Oh my God, Trey! Put those beers back! Where are your clothes?"

He proudly smiled. "Am I as big as all the girls say I am?" He turned, set the beers down, and ran back to his room to a giggling girl.

Girls rolled on and off the casting couch week after week, always ending the same way. "I will call you and let you know if we have a place for you." The band members acted serious about the interviews, taking notes and writing details down in their notebooks while asking the right questions.

"Do you have time to spend with the band while practising different drum solos?" They'd smile with a twinkle in their eyes.

After questioning the girls that day, two of the prettiest were invited to return that night.

Lounging in the garage, Trey coolly sat with a cigarette to his lips, blowing smoke rings while he waited for the girls to return. He was shirtless and wore his favourite ripped blue jeans when the girls finally showed up. His thick hair fell into his face as he waved them over. "Come here, Sexy." One or both girls, it didn't matter. He was more than capable of taking on both.

After being dragged into the garage by Trey, Cameron got in on the action. He wasn't necessarily attracted to grungey girls but loved the opportunity to make his brother proud. "Go over and meet my brother." Trey nudged one of the girls. "You will love his blue eyes." He winked at Cameron as he made a humping gesture behind the girl's back, suggesting that Cameron might get laid.

*****

While he listened to grunge music, Trey's pot-smoking was totally out of control, and there was absolutely nothing I could do about it. He didn't mind being alone; he almost enjoyed it. As he gained more independence and began experimenting with harder drugs, Trey chose to become a part of a very different group.

It was early Saturday morning when I realized Trey hadn't made it home the night before. I had a pretty good idea of where he was as I yelled out to the tree. What I saw was his newfound friends emerge from under the branches and bushes. They appeared to be wearing black trench coats and army combat boots, and from afar, I saw their eyes decorated with thick black eyeliner. Trey suddenly appeared. I took in his messy appearance. Leaves, dirt and various other gunk from the old oak tree area adorn his unruly mess of dark chocolate hair. He looked tired and worn. Dirt streaked his tattered clothes. With his t-shirt ripped and jeans caked with dried mud, this was just another moment when filth was covering him. And he was perfectly okay with it.

He grinned at me as I felt puzzled and disgusted. I asked, "What were those kids doing out there?" He smiled from ear to ear.

"Oh, C'mon, Ma, they just spent the night. Don't be so judgmental." His breath reeked of cigarettes.

"Well, I don't like them out there and you out all night." I noticed his eyes were bloodshot and hazy.

"C'mon, they're not bad kids. We're only sleeping out there." He wasn't very convincing.

I waited for Trey to go to his room to get some sleep. I slipped out the door and followed the beaten path down towards the tree. The trail was rockier than I imagined, with tons of weeds. I worried about my newly bought Uggs as I eyed the burrs that invaded the rocky road. I finally came to the path's end, and it was there I saw dozens of empty beer cans thrown into a manufactured hole in the ground. Alongside a makeshift fire pit, open packs of cigarettes littered the tree's base. I thought about the fire hazard so prominent on The Plateau as I shook my head. Trey's guests had carved into every branch of the tree with swear words and names.

A cool breeze picked up as I noticed the chilled air. I suddenly heard a sound behind me. It made me shudder. I turned towards it and saw a rabbit dash under some brush. I was relieved to see it wasn't Trey, as I knew I would not be a welcomed visitor if he were to see me there.

Chapter 14

VACANT LOTS WERE PREVALENT AND REGULARLY loaned out to the Fourth of July party organisers. The event was a gala attraction that most Plateau residents looked forward to. I spread the blanket on the ground in front of the stage to en- sure I'd get a good seat for the talent-show performances. In the shade of the massive oak tree, the boys talked to another kid I'd never met before.

"Who's that kid you're talking to over there?" Cameron walked towards me as I pointed to the stranger, who was tall and lean, his face tanned and wind-whipped.

"Oh, that's Chris. He lives up here with his parents." Cam- eron said as he grabbed a foot-long sandwich and went back to join his brothers.

Chris was born into an upper-middle-class family who lived on the Plateau. Both of his parents were ambitious attorneys and worked in high profile offices. The love that Chris had been born with, his parent's busy schedules crushed. They bought him the most stimulating toys and hired a high-priced nanny to keep him occupied and entertained while they worked around the clock. Once kindergarten began, there were pre-school and after-school programs that Chris attended. He hated every minute of it and was very much a loner at school. Each day blended into the next. He hid behind a smile and reinvented himself, learning to keep his feelings inside. The hurt lodged in his heart like a slow-acting poison, and before long, he became a "problem child", destined for a life behind bars. He hated his parents, the system, the government and the whole damn world. It burst forth in his speech, actions, and attitude, and he eventually turned to drugs.

It wasn't long after I met him and noticed some odd behaviour. He avoided eye contact with me, wasn't necessarily friendly and acted nervously. It was then that I discovered he was supplying marijuana to the boys. I instantly ended their friendship and made it clear that Chris would not be welcome in my home. Perhaps I was naive to think Chris would care.

Chris immaturely reacted when he found that I knew of his drug dealings and disapproved of him. Each time Chris saw one of us, he shot his middle finger into the air. He and my boys became mortal enemies, making things very uncomfortable.

*****

I needed to make a trip to our local feed store to buy a dog kennel, so Trey decided to tag along. It felt nice to share some one-on-one time with him. As we drove and shared some pleasant conversation, I noticed he had the familiar scent of beer on his breath. I thought twice about it, knowing that it was pretty early in the day for that type of behaviour but decided it best not to comment as I approached a red light. As I began to slow down, a beautiful, new Mercedes Benz stopped at the light on my right. I inched up and noticed the driver glancing over at me while I admired his car. Trey quickly saw red. His vision blurred as a flame lit in the pit of his stomach. His brain went into overdrive. "Are you fucking looking at my mother? Asshole! Mind your own business, or I'll beat the shit out of you!" His eyes were red, a vein visible in his neck as he screamed out his rolled-down window.

"Trey, stop it! You're making a scene. You are drunk and embarrassing me!" My eyebrows pulled together. The driver took one look at Trey and drove off as soon as the light turned green.

"I don't care! Nobody is going to look at my mother that way!" He sat back, barely recognisable, seething inside.

We pulled into the feed store as I begged Trey to wait in the car. I was so ashamed of his behaviour and was trying to avoid any other disruptions. "Wait in the car. I'll make it quick." My statement was direct and to the point.

Once inside, I found myself hurrying until I heard voices coming from the back of the general store. Beyond the rows of dog food and horse supplies, I saw Trey joking with the manager.

"Come on, give me a job!" The manager just smiled. "Come on." Trey was getting a little more aggressive, his voice more demanding, and I was worried. *Maybe I'll go to the car until he comes out. But I can't leave him here alone. God knows what he might do.* I walked over to Trey and asked him to help me with the dog kennel I had grabbed off one of the shelves. He laughed and told the manager he'd be back to pick up the employment application.

As we pulled out of the store's driveway, I noticed Chris, straight ahead, in his mother's white BMW, stopped at a red light. I shuttered as my car crept up beside him and instinctively knew I needed nothing more to complete my day. Trey casually spotted Chris's open window, and then, with a mixture of spit and snot, he launched a "loogie" onto Chris's face. It dripped down his cheek, onto his lips, and into his mouth.

I screamed, "Stop it, Trey!"

Trey yelled while glaring at Chris. "Fuck him! He deserves everything he gets!"

Stunned by Trey's actions, I barked, "Watch your language," and pressed the gas pedal down as hard as I could in hopes Chris wasn't following us. Trey kept looking back, hoping that he was. We raced into the driveway behind the wrought-iron gate. That only fueled the fire between the boys and Chris.

"You should've seen it. That loogie stretched down Chris's cheek to his mouth, and he was so mad. I just sat, pointed my finger and laughed at him." Trey boasted. The excitement showed on Russell's face as he listened.

"I'd do it all over again if I had the chance." Trey dreamed of the satisfying feeling he cherished.

*****

While meandering across the high school parking lot during a Friday night football game, Chris spotted Russell's parked cherry-red Bronco. Chris slowly approached the jeep with a car key hidden in the palm of his cold hand. It sliced into the shiny red car leaving gouges and chipped paint on the key. He stood back, smiling proudly at his handiwork. Of course, he would probably be the only one to admire it. He then slowly walked away with feelings of satisfaction and pleasure that he finally got even with the Morelli family. After spotting the boys near the bleachers and yelling to get their attention, he smirked while he imagined the look on their faces once they got back to the Bronco. Little did he know there were cameras in the parking lot. A review of the film caused Chris to face the judge who put him on probation and forced him to pay for the repair to Russell's jeep. Russell never forgave Chris and the hate for him intensified.

Planning carefully, they asked their friend Mason to help them set the trap. Mason also had a vendetta against Chris after being ripped off during a drug transaction.

Mason answered his ringing telephone. "Hey, Mason. Remember that asshole, Chris, who keyed my jeep last month? My brothers and I are going to teach him a lesson. You in?" Russell was ready with his strong hands clenched.

"Hell, yeah. That son of a bitch sold me some bunk weed last week. I'm with you guys." Mason remembered he threw the pot away after trying it.

Mason called Chris to deliver a baggie of pot on a nearby street corner on the Plateau with plans set. Russell and Trey eagerly waited for Chris to arrive. Time moved slowly as Chris's car pulled around the corner. It was a black sedan, dusty and dirty. Once parked, Russell and Trey walked boldly towards Chris's vehicle. Nervously, Chris fumbled to roll up his window, but before he could, Russell swung, his right fist connecting with Chris's jaw, left to his nose. Chris's nose squirted blood as he revved his engine and tried to speed away. "Get the fuck out of here, punk!" Trey's pulse raced. Taillights faded as Chris's car went around the curve. A few weeks later, with Chris's parent's house sold, no one knew what happened to them after that.

Chapter 15

DRY ROLLING HILLS COVER THE DESERT IN southern California. The wind whipped up the wispy sand, and the sun's never-ending rays beat down on us mercilessly as we took the easy four-hour drive to the Colorado River during the summer. The river was a welcome sight as we approached the winding blue water meandering its way south.

"It must be 120 degrees." I pressed my hand on the window. The sweat dripped from my brow as we rolled our luggage into the hotel and gladly welcomed our air-conditioned rooms after we registered. The rooms adjoined each other. The kids were in one place, Marco and I in the other. The hotel would be home for our long weekend vacation.

The morning sun peeked its head over the horizon after Marco and I spent an entire night gambling. Trying to shake the tiredness and the lingering headache, we packed our bathing suits and towels and made our way to the secluded beach on the river's edge. We planned to spend the day on the water or under a canopy with a full cooler of cold beer. Across the river, Marco carefully backed the trailer down the long ramp as he launched twin Sea-Doos. Each of them already had riders on them.

Once afloat, they bounced through the waves with ease. Cameron's teeth involuntarily bit down after each bump; his legs squeezed tight, his life jacket was on. Next to him, Trey was pressing the engine for more speed, his face alight with excitement. Unlike his brother, he wore only board shorts and shades. *Pretty cool for a fifteen-year-old.* The Sea-Doos were fast and squirrely and were a challenging ride.

"Hey, Ma, C'mon!" I looked up to Trey's extended hand as he led me over to the ride. He steadied the Sea-Doo as he jumped on. I swung my leg over and reached around Trey's waist as the Sea-Doo began to tip until it dumped me into the cold Colorado River water. Again, we tried, and yet we failed.

Marco yelled from the shore. "Your mom's balance is like an egg!"

Suddenly, I was on, and we were off and running. With the increase of speed, the hull bounced higher and higher, slapping the waves harder and harder with each fall. I closed my eyes and said a late prayer. On the following impact, the Sea-Doo didn't just flip. It cartwheeled across the early summer waves. Soaked and stuck in the middle of the cold river, I saw Marco approaching me on the second Sea-Doo as he sensed that something might go wrong.

He yelled questions that had no answers, "God damn it, Trey. Look at your mother. What are you going to do? How are you going to get her back onto the Sea-Doo?" Trey shrugged, then smiled as he watched me float back to camp and helped me out of the water once I reached the shore. I was in shambles, sopping wet. My hair was covering my face. I looked like I had been in battle. Marco was not too far away as I climbed onto the beach and sat in the sun in my beach chair. Slowly, I wrapped my hair into my hat and slid sunglasses over my eyes. It was then that I realized that hives covered my skin.

"Oh my God, Marco, look at my heat rash!" Marco looked, his mouth dropped. He gawked at me for a moment, then recovered himself and then suggested that we end our beach trip and head back to the casino's hotel.

It was five o'clock and happy hour as we cleaned up and got dressed. I downed a tablespoon of Benadryl in hopes that my rash would fade.

"We are going down to the bar for a drink and some dinner. We ordered and paid for sausage pizza which should be here soon. Be good and stay in the room and out of trouble. Here's a tip when the food arrives." Marco's voice was gruff as he handed five dollars to Russell. He took my hand, and we left without a worry in the world.

The clock's hands barely moved before the kids were hanging off the balcony of their room two stories up. Russell ran to the elevator, jumped in before its doors closed and was out on the walkway under the balcony within minutes. He took a quarter and some super glue from his pocket, placed the quarter in a spot where no one could miss seeing it, then glued it to the sidewalk. He then rode the elevator back to the second floor. There, on the balcony, the boys eagerly watched girls bend down to pick up the quarter after seeing it from a distance. Before the girls had a chance to realize it was a coin glued in place, the boys had already offered them an invitation to come to the room.

The dated hotel room on the second floor suddenly felt crowded with the music pumping, and five girls piled into the small hotel space. The girls dressed scantily, wearing bathing-suit tops and short-shorts. Trey sat in the corner with two on his lap, Cameron was standing on the balcony talking to another girl, and Russell had the rest to himself. Madison was busy chatting on the phone with one of her friends about their day on the river while pulling beers from the cooler and offering them to their guests. The kids found themselves in heaven as they wished this trip would never end.

An abrupt knock on the door ended that moment as the security police decided to investigate the scene. Coolers full of beer cans were moved into the other room, and Marco's and my door fastened. It seemed this was not their first rodeo as they worked quickly and in unison. Cameron slowly opened the door to two bulky men wearing blue suits and badges. They looked around. "Where are your parents?" The heavy-set cop's voice was stern and highly demanding.

"They are having dinner and doing some gambling," Cameron commented politely. "Are you kids drinking?" The smell of beer was invading the air-conditioned room.

"No. We don't have any beer. My parents left their room locked." Madison stepped forward with a perfect answer.

"What are your parent's names?" The cops pulled out their scratchpad, wrote the names down, then reached for their walkie-talkies. "Please page Marco and Leigh Morelli." The kids were worried at this point as the girls filed out of the room slowly. Marco and I were stunned to hear our names over the loud PA system in the casino and knew something was wrong.

"We have detained your children and believe they may have been drinking." The burly cop's voice sounded over the walkie-talkie.

Marco stood firm as we made our way to the second floor. Once there, Marco surveilled the room and deemed it free of alcohol. He then made it clear to the security police that our vacation had ended, and we would leave the Lucky Seven in the dust first thing in the morning.

"I'm glad we don't have anything to do next weekend. It'll be the first Friday night at home." Marco seemed pleased to be on our way home as the dust kicked up, and the long ride home was nearly half over.

"Me, too. I'm tired and can't wait to get home and relax." I yawned as the itching from the heat started to subside.

Chapter 16

IT CLICKED TOGETHER FOR ME. I WAS BORED. THE first Friday night of February felt empty at home as football season ended, and we stopped watching Russell play ball with his high school friends. The boys were fun to watch as we gathered together with their parents and got to know every one of them. While Marco and I sat in front of the television, I realized how disinterested I was. I thought of things I could be doing and decided to organize a bowling league with the parents of the kids on the team. Many of our fellow friends loved the idea of letting loose after a hard work week. I carefully put together eight four-person teams, considering personalities and skills.

Two weeks later, we took up half of the bowling alley as we put on our newly acquired bowling shoes and proudly showed off our personalized balls. Mine was blazing, glitzy pink with my initials on it. I admired the cursive-type lettering I chose and imagined it striking just the centre of the pins. It matched my personality perfectly. Marco opted for a masculine colour, coal-black, and didn't need to identify it with a name.

The night started with wine and pitchers of beer as we shared our workweeks and photos of our kids. Most of us were middle class and heavy drinkers. A few secretly smoked marijuana. We drank socially within our group of housewives and were known to uncork wine in the early afternoon without thinking otherwise. We talked of wife swapping within a few groups and adultery in others. With our vices, we judged each other only behind each other's backs.

The bowling alley attracted many different groups; families with young kids out for the afternoon, big leagues filled with serious bowlers, and losers who stood outside smoking and drinking. Known drug dealers found a perfect place to push their narcotics. Trey became familiar with all of them and dressed appropriately in the dirty pea-green mohair sweater he'd seen at the Salvation Army. It matched Kurt Cobain's attire perfectly; he loved it and made him reminisce about his Great Grandfather Bob.

Trey heard whisperings that his great aunts and uncles were planning on selling off all of Grandpa Bob's belongings after his death, and Trey wanted to be the first one there. Great Grandpa Bob was Trey's favourite. He loved his stories, prayers at Thanksgiving, and especially his polyester shirts when he played shuffleboard with his neighbours at the senior centre.

As Trey arrived, he noticed a woven mat at the door, fashioned from rustic strings, enriched with the mud of thousands of boots- a testimony to his great-grandfather had dwelled in the house. Trey smiled as if he could hear the laughter of his great grandfather as he returned with new memories of the old village. Its edges were frayed and curled, but it was still here. His great aunts and uncles had the floor polished, the curtains made anew, and the walls painted, yet still, it remained, giving treasured

mind-photographs, the best kind of life-nostalgia. Now was his
chance to seize on the moment.

Trey waited patiently until the garage sale sign illuminated,
making everyone know it was time to shop.

As Trey thumbed through the rows and rows of shirts, some
used, other's unused, he felt a familiar feeling across his body. It was
like his great grandfather was there beside him. He looked and saw
the perfect shirt, a yellow and green pullover with two buttons just
down the centre. It was used, which made it more appealing to Trey.

He glanced up at his great aunt, who didn't recognize him,
asked how much the shirt would cost and paid the fifty cents. It
was like he won the lottery as he drove off with a friend peeling
off his shirt and replacing it with the yellow one. He crossed
his arms and wished he could have afforded a few others as he
thought about Bob and Bob's life.

He hung outside with his unwelcomed friends but found
time to come in and greet our bowlers with smiles and hand-
shakes. Trey was genuinely friendly and always polite.

At times I felt embarrassed as I watched the faces of my
friends. They couldn't hide their judging eyes and whispers crit-
icizing these socially unacceptable kids. It angered me that they
judged MY son even though they knew their children were far
from innocent. I'd seen our league's kids smoking pot behind
the school and heard stories about their many sexual partners.
Our bowling league members felt fortunate that their kids chose
to hide their true selves and didn't look like Trey or hang out
with Trey's friends.

*****

Once a year, Marco and I left for a weekend to attend our
bowling league end-of-the-year party held in Laughlin, Nevada,

110

the capital of drinking and gambling. A mere five-hour drive from home, it was convenient to party.

As the yellow, chartered school bus pulled into our driveway, the waiting group piled in with their bowling balls and gloves. The moment it pulled away, shot glasses for Patron tequila were retrieved from our packed bags. Salt and lime accompanied the tequila and was passed around the bus, making sure not to miss any of us. We were professionals, and halfway to Laughlin, our professionalism turned into sloppy drunkenness. The television flashed nudity from a porno someone brought. Marijuana smoke filled the small bus as the driver slowly rolled down her window and rolled her eyes like she was driving a bus full of high school kids.

The elevator's lines at the hotel continued to form as we staggered in and struggled with our luggage. "Leigh, see that empty elevator over there. Jump on." Marco nudged my arm, ran over, and held the heavy steel door open. We piled in as the elevator went up two floors and dove back down to the reception area. "This elevator is a service elevator!" Marco held the elevator doors open to our waiting bowling league. Everyone laughed and waited for the next available elevator to arrive. The night ended late while we gambled and drank—no kids, no sense of responsibility, no problems, no worries. Our room's telephone rang early the following day.

"Michael had a great time with your kids last night." Timothy, his dad, was just going to bed.

"He was with the kids last night?" I was tired and barely awake.

"James called and said the kids had a great party last night." Rick, James's dad, suddenly put the telephone down after realizing that I didn't know about the party.

As I poured my coffee and was more aware of what happened, I suddenly uttered the words I didn't have the strength to say, "The kids had a party last night! I'm going to call Madison!" I dialled the telephone. The phone rang eight times before she picked up. "What's happening there?" Madison held the phone away from her ears but heard the words.

She sounded distant and afraid of getting her brothers in trouble. "Nothing. Everyone is still asleep. What time will you be home?" She tried to avoid the looming question.

"Was there a party there last night?" I already knew the answer.

"Just a few of the boys' friends came over." She scrambled to protect them.

*****

Mastering the art of throwing a great party was a class that my kids should have taught the other students in school. The word spread to the entire high school early that week about a party at the Morelli house on Friday, when we were leaving for Laughlin. Mostly made up of jocks and seniors, Russell spread the word to the senior class. Cameron, a sophomore and involved in sports, spread the word too. Trey targeted the rest who had not heard. Every social group in school came. The boys lugged cases of beer into the backyard once they were delivered. Madison, in eighth grade, stood in the corner with a few girlfriends the boys approved of earlier in the day.

Before they knew it, hundreds of kids rushed the house. Girls dressed skimpily in tight designer jeans and push-up brassieres came early. Their tanned little bodies were the epitome of California. The jocks came to guard against theft and fights while Trey mastered the beer bong.

Christine, the prettiest girl in high school, rolled out from behind the bushes. Cameron followed closely behind her. His chin-length blonde hair was messy but thick and lustrous. His perfect lips are perfect for kissing. His strong hands, slightly rough from working after school, held hers as he stared deep into her eyes. She couldn't help but blush as she watched his smile. His body was warm and toned. His skin, newly kissed by the sun, covered his strong muscles; his eyes, sky blue. Cameron, a sophomore in high school, had high grades with mathematical skills above average. He won state awards, year after year, without desiring to be noticed or congratulated by his family or peers.

Trey stood watching his brother with his arms crossed and a smile on his face. He approved of his brother's actions and was proud of the many times they sat together and discussed the perfect sexual act. He felt his schooling served his brother well.

The party raged into the wee hours of the morning when Madison found herself and a friend knee-deep in empty beer bottles, cans and red solo cups from the party. She slowly navigated as she tried to clean up the mess while her brothers slept it off.

I burst into the house after the bus pulled away, and the bowlers were gone, expecting to see a big mess and bodies strewn throughout the house. I knew a party was here over the weekend as I searched for overlooked bottles and caps, but fortunately, I didn't see any damage. I was surprised and pleased to see the house was in pretty good shape. I was not happy but could reflect on my teenage years.

My parents had gone to Las Vegas for the weekend, so I invited some friends to come over Friday night. I found myself surrounded by over one hundred kids later that evening.

Pulling beer from the stocked refrigerator in the bar, I filled plastic cups with alcohol, one after the other, while the music blared through open windows. The party was large, and as I went outside to the pool area, I saw Nancy practising her jumping jacks in the nude while skinny dippers enjoyed the heated pool. The doorbell rang as I looked over at the clock that ticked to one o'clock in the morning. When I opened the door, there stood the cops. I flashed a welcoming smile then invited them in. They canvassed the party area where drunken teenagers slept, stumbled, and tried to stay awake. After a beer, the cops left and promised to return after work. They returned at four in the morning when I entertained the chief and deputy of the nearby police department until noon that day. I was exhausted and drunk when they finally left. I became good friends with them after dating each of them several times.

Chapter 17

THE SUMMER SHOWED PROMISE AS WE PREPARED for yet another river trip. Susan and Dean were close friends and members of our bowling league who had invited us to spend a long weekend with them at their river house, which fronted the Colorado River at Parker Dam.

We entered the trailer park and passed the rented storage units, palm trees, and an entrance decorated with native rock, which had come from the desert across the main highway. It read "Twin Palms" as we drove through the mighty arches. The home's perfect location was two rows back from the river's edge and within walking distance to the park's restaurant and bar.

Directly in front of the home were the community pool and a large boat dock where Susan and Dean kept their boat for the summer. The furnished house had old Salvation Army couches heavily worn on the arms, suggesting more than one owner might have been there. The front porch faced west, so the early morning sun didn't have time to reach the sleeping area until late afternoon. That was where we placed the sleeping bags and slept for the next two nights.

Susan greeted us with a hug and the perfect Vodka Tonic she had waiting for us. It tasted good after our long ride through the desert. "We're expecting nasty weather tonight." Dean greeted us with a smile, his beer belly hanging over his board shorts. He liked the drama. "We should get the golf carts ready for our moonlight cruise. The beer is already on ice."

I loved the excitement the summer's thunderstorms created as we watched them roll in from the trailer's patio. The storms were dignified while we watched wild donkeys rush down the hills trying to escape the downpours and flash flooding. Each bang pushed them further across the main road and into the trailer park, where they stood confused. The lightning was jagged as it cracked and lit up the sky. We sat in amazement of nature's beauty on that hot summer night, not wanting it to end.

"Whoa, did you see that one?" Madison jumped as the sky roared. The booming thunder called the rain to leak from the sky. All at once, it started raining in sheets, and we had nowhere to hide except on the porch of the old river house.

Gas-powered golf carts were parked in front, ready and waiting for the thunderstorm to pass. Coolers packed full of beer were placed in the rear; two equipped vehicles sat six passengers each, two in the front and four in the back. Our goal was to find the highest vantage point to view the incredible painted desert at night. The storm passed as we loaded into the golf carts, one following the other. The washed-out riverbed was narrow; I looked back and saw two small headlights following behind us as our tires kicked up the road's mud.

Crisscrossing the washed-out roads, back and forth, we reached the higher ground as we drove. An occasional wild donkey appeared and disappeared just as fast and left me wondering if the mule was a hallucination. The music was blaring as the golf carts continued to climb. Finally, perched on a cliff, we sat side by side as we viewed the desert and all of its beauty as the night slipped away. At 3:00 a.m., we finally got into our waiting sleeping bags for the rest of the night.

The morning sun bore down on the small trailer park before we had a chance to wake. "The temperature is going to be one hundred and ten degrees today," Dean's neighbour announced.

"We'd better get on the water early." Dean struggled to gulp his bloody Mary, hoping to lose the hangover he had from our night in the desert. We eagerly boarded the pontoon boat, loaded with plenty of sunscreen and beer. The day started at the south end of the Parker Strip, where the Blue Water Casino sat. The Blue Water Hotel and Casino was not anything like Las Vegas. The hotel on the water was rundown and meant for people who didn't have a trailer or the desire to camp. Susan and I ran in with fistfuls of money, hoping to have time to win the big pot.

Marco waved me over as he ordered breakfast complete with scrambled eggs and bacon. "Do you want a Bloody Mary?" He sipped his drink as he eyed the chunk of celery peeking over the top.

"Yes, a Bloody Mary sounds good. Make it spicy." I returned to a nearby slot machine.

After my last coin brought back no return, we decided the time had come to go.

Dozens of sandbars dotted the area and had already started rocking as people found their spots. Some people weaved between the shallows, waist-high in water, holding their beers above their heads. That was the place to be as we drifted alongside them in our boat, listening to Sublime playing loudly on someone's parked ride. The day became lost as we raced up and down the long snaky river hitting each floating bar along the river's front.

Trey had brought along Lisa, a new girl he'd been seeing. As she bounced in Trey's lap, her wind-whipped blonde hair tumbled forward over her face, bleached whiter by the sun and looking pale against her summer tan. "First stop is Foxes." Dean navigated the boat alongside the floating dock. We all headed to a seat at the bar as we ordered drinks and watched the boats race. The next stop was Sundance as we glided past, looking for some action. Dean knew the bars well and explained that Sundance didn't get going until nighttime. Then, we noticed the Roadrunner, its crowded dock with people, and the bar was standing room only.

Russell jumped off the boat, eyeing the bar's speciality, The Roadraper. "I'll take six Roadrapers," he ordered, knowing Arizona's drinking age was eighteen. Our under-aged group could grab sodas from the cooler on the boat. The Roadrunner souvenir mug held thirty-two ounces. The concoction was a mixture of Rum, Ever Clear, Schnapps, OJ, pineapple juice, cranberry juice, and grenadine.

Two Roadrapers in, I looked around the crowded bar, wondering what had happened to Trey and Lisa. "Where are Trey and Lisa?" I slurred my words from across the bar. I looked over and saw Russell flying high on a swing in the grass-covered lot next door.

"They went to the bathroom." Cameron pointed in that direction.

Climbing off my barstool, I motioned to Marco that I was going to the restroom to look for them. I talked to someone coming out of the men's room. He told me they weren't in there, so I decided to go into the women's bathroom. I heard Lisa giggling from behind a stall door. "Hold still," Trey whispered while holding her up against the wall behind the toilet. I peered under the door only to see Trey's feet planted firmly on the floor. "Trey?" I only heard silence. "Trey?" I asked again. Nothing. I walked away. *Of all places, the women's bathroom!*

I went back to the bar and told Marco what I'd found. Right on cue, Trey bounced out of the bathroom, smiling from ear to ear while holding onto Lisa's hand. Her face was shining, and the grin on her face did not go unnoticed as they approached. I then noticed Trey's long brown hair styled into two ponytails. He looked silly as we stumbled back onto the boat. Russell was upset and embarrassed by Trey and his newfound hairstyle. He looked over at Trey. "Take those stupid-looking ponytails out. You look ridiculous trying to look like Kurt Cobain!" Trey looked away, avoiding confrontation.

The pontoon boat barreled down the river as we headed back to the river house. It was a fun ride as we bounced against the wind and waves. The air conditioning felt good after a day in the sun, and it cooled our sunburned skin. Dean announced that he was loading up for another desert ride, but all I could think of was sleep.

After we awoke and thanked our gracious hosts, we headed home. The journey from the river was long and hot as the sun beat down into the car. I noticed the kids were asleep and anticipated a long week ahead with temperatures expected to hit the 100s.

*****

August is always hot in California, I thought, as I checked the degrees on our outside thermometer. According to the local news, it read one hundred and five degrees, and it wasn't going to cool down anytime soon. Madison was anxious to have a sleepover and invited her friend Connie to spend the night. The two girls wanted to camp in the backyard, pitch a tent, and stay up half the night. Our large picture window in the family room overlooked our pool and the park-like grassy backyard, which afforded me a viewing stage of the designated area. Marco's tent went up quickly, and they decorated the inside with soft sheets and fresh pillows. After dinner, everyone retreated to the garage, and the kids gathered around the large television while Marco and I retired to our bedroom before going to bed.

Some of Trey's friends joined in as he made plans to head out for the evening. "C'mon, Madison." Trey looked over at her but saw that she was worried about getting into trouble for leaving without asking. I had a watchful eye over Madison as she entered her teens and trustingly allowed her to venture out as long as she was with one of her brothers and had permission. Trey reassured her. "I will take the blame if you get caught. Mom doesn't normally check up on you anyway." They loaded up and sneaked out.

A few miles back into the Plateau, they came upon an empty and partially built home overlooking the green fairways of Bear's Head. In the distance were the shining lights of three surrounding cities. The views extended to the mountain range the kids knew from Lacana. They could see the ocean in one direction, Big Bear in the other. The house had been carved out on the lot by a custom home builder, who dreamed of selling once completed. The shack appeared to others as discomforting, but it was the kids' only place of escaping from the rest of the world, the only place where they could go when they wanted to be alone. The home was called the Lookout, and the only way to it was on foot because of the wide crevasses and ruts caused by a washed-out clay driveway.

Rarely awake at midnight, I found myself wide-awake and scanning the backyard for any signs of life. There was none, so I decided to check on the girls in the tent. After peering inside, I realized they were nowhere. Fuming, I jumped on the telephone and paged Madison to get her ass home! No answer. I waited—another call. No response. I left another message. That one was more direct. "You have ten minutes to get home!" Madison's eyes grew large, and she shot a panicked look over to Connie, who was buttering up to one of Trey's friends.

"Oh, shit! Am I in trouble!" Her fear rose, and her face showed it. "We need to get home right away," she worried as she spoke to Trey.

Trey took a long, calm drag off his cigarette as if nothing was wrong.

"Don't worry. I've got this. Let's finish our beer, and then we'll go." His face was relaxed. He wasn't worried in the least.

Ten minutes later, Madison headed for home. It was forty-five painful minutes since I first paged Madison, all the while envisioning her lying dead in the street somewhere. Every second that went by, I became angrier. Finally, I saw a dim headlight in the distance and watched it as it pulled into the driveway.

Trey got out of the car first and walked up to me with a mouthful of excuses. "We weren't doing anything. I'll take the blame. Don't be mad at Madison." I looked straight through him, and my only thought was on Madison.

I screamed at Madison. "Get your ass inside. You're in trouble!" Her friend was by her side, and her eyes were downcast as she started to walk past me. My arm wound up to deliver a blow to the back of Madison's head. Her hair flew as the back of my hand connected. She rushed past me and into the house without a backward glance.

I felt satisfied with my swing as I smiled at Marco. "I got her pretty good." I could hear the girls laughing in the tent and wondered what could be so funny. *Maybe I didn't get her that good?* I lay in bed and doubted myself while the lantern in the tent stayed aglow. I finally, peacefully, slipped into a deep sleep after experiencing so much tension. Daylight broke as I watched Trey come out of the tent.

"What the hell were you doing in the tent?" I was surprised that he was there.

"I kept Madison and Connie company all night." He didn't blink his eyes which were an off shade of red and tired. I smelled marijuana on his breath as he stood near me and sensed that it wasn't the only drug he had used during the night. His eyes were cloudy, pale, and hid a wealth of well-justified mistrust. "I was sorry for getting her into trouble and felt bad that I didn't keep my promise. I decided to stay up with the girls until they went to sleep." I stared at him as he headed in the direction of his bedroom.

Chapter 18

SAN FRANCISCO AND THE BEAUTIFUL WINERIES that surrounded it was what I needed. We had planned to attend the "Grapes to Glass" celebration for six months, and now the time was here. I picked up my favourite summer dress and placed it in the suitcase. I was ready as I put other items on top of that. The sun shone brightly as Marco and I checked on the kids before leaving. Madison was busy practising her cheerleading routine, Cameron was studying for final exams, and Russell was getting ready for a date. I went in search of Trey.

Unnaturally still and white, with his large dark, lifeless eyes intent on his guitar, Trey was perfectly motionless in the centre of his bedroom. He appeared as if he'd crawled inside some invisible shell and was unreachable. Trey moved his eyes slowly towards me as if they were heavy and an effort to control. He looked overwhelmed with sadness. It was severe depression.

"What's wrong?" I walked toward him.

"Nothing. I want to be alone." He slowly looked away and acted as if he were unattached.

"Your dad and I are getting ready to leave for the weekend, and I wanted to be sure you are okay." I watched him closely.

"I'm fine. Just go have a good time." He glanced out the window. I bent down and kissed him on his forehead, noticing the thick nicotine smell in his hair. I worried as I left his room. I felt uncomfortable leaving Trey at home but knew his siblings would watch over him while we were gone. I calmed myself as Marco poured me a glass of wine and convinced me that he would be fine.

Trey had been distant for the past week and was acting defiant. He chose to surround himself with a group of kids with bad reputations, and I sensed he was getting involved with something he would regret. He became highly defensive of his friends, and I couldn't help but notice how he rushed to the phone when it rang to protect their calls from me. Kim was one of the girls Trey was seeing. She wasn't beautiful but was typically grungey, just like Trey liked them. Her jet-black hair was short and often left unbrushed. Her face was pale, and her eyes were downcast. She acted as if the only thing she wanted to see was Trey. I wondered what Trey saw in her.

*****

We made our flight with seconds to spare, and the torture began. The aeroplane sat on the tarmac while the flight attendants strolled, casually, up and down the aisle, shoving the bags in the overhead compartments to make sure everything fit properly. The pilots leaned out of the cockpit, chatting with them as they passed. *I flashed for a moment on my brother-in-law, a pilot for Southwest Airlines. I remembered how he regularly drank before each flight until he finally lost his position.* At last, the plane rolled slowly from the gate, building speed with a gradual steadiness that terrified me. I finally received some relief when we achieved liftoff.

Marco and I were off to beautiful Northern California. We checked into the quaint bed and breakfast after a short ride to the beautiful community of Healdsburg. The Inn was a two-story stone cottage. A large chimney poked out of one side of the roof and a small smokestack out the other. A creaking wooden sign advertised the Inn with a picture of a horse and fox frolicking in the vineyards. The accommodations consisted of several small, beautifully decorated rooms, each with a massive king-sized bed in the centre. The majestic breakfast room was where the buffet and cocktails in the afternoon were served for the three families staying there. Two large picture windows let in natural light. A spacious cellar stored and preserved wine. A neat pile of firewood was stacked against the house by the owners. We were excited about our plans for the weekend, which included canoeing down the Russian River, picnicking at wineries, and wine pairing at Fred MacMurray's.

On Saturday night, Kim showed up at the house to take Trey to a small, intimate party. As they drove, Trey remained quiet, which caused concern for Kim. She loved him, a love that he didn't return and didn't like to see him so down. They pulled up to a house where the party was. As Trey walked through the front door, he began looking for anyone who had cocaine. His desire to stay high was insatiable, and he grew angry when he wasn't.

"Doesn't anyone have any fucking cocaine?" His eyes bugged out of his head as he screamed and looked around the room. 'Kim, what the fuck are we doing here?" He stormed out of the party to the front yard, where she followed him.

"Trey, please wait. I'll find you some." She panicked and didn't want him to be mad. "Leave me the fuck alone. Go away!" She quietly went back into the house. Trey made his way into the street, where he found shelter by the curb. He sat calmly, alone and depressed. An hour passed. He curled up, holding his knees and rocking to the beat that played over and over in his mind. His clothes looked like rags. His greasy hair hung in a mess over his face.

The white-and-black cruiser spotted a teenager in the street that appeared homeless. The cruiser stopped. The boy was sitting on a concrete curb that was damp from the early morning dew. The cops took a look at his face. He was despondent.

"Hey, you there." They shone their flashlights into his face. He didn't look up. "Hey, look up." He just sat and stared. One of the police officers looked at the other and deemed it necessary to take him in. "Get him into the car." They cuffed him and pushed him into the back seat, where he rode until they pulled into the station. He spent the night on the cold bench inside the cage.

It was Kim on the phone when I answered. "Mrs Morelli? Trey wasn't doing any drugs or anything. He was sitting on the driveway when the cops pulled up and arrested him." *I didn't believe a word she said.*

"What do you mean, Kim?" I was disappointed that, once again, Marco's and my weekend getaway was interrupted.

"I swear—he wasn't doing anything. They just cuffed him and threw him into the cop car!" She sounded upset.

"Okay. I'll pick Trey up from the police station when we get home this afternoon." I hung up the phone, tired and disappointed. I rushed to our car after the plane landed. "Drop me off at the house so I can get my car, and I'll head over to the police station to get Trey." I panicked as I watched Marco speed through the streets. We finally reached home, and I headed for the jail, where I sat and waited. There I stayed for four hours as my blood pressure went to boiling temperatures. All of a sudden, Trey was standing there. He had his shirt slung over his shoulder and was wearing a smile.

"What are you smiling about?" My lips tightened into a fierce line. Four long hours added to my apparent anger. He stared into my eyes, and I stared back.

"I mean it," I whispered.

"Oh, nothing. I'm glad you are here." He grabbed my arm without hesitation as I yanked it back. Touching me was not something he should have considered.

"God damn you, Trey! Why were you arrested?" I couldn't even look at him in the eye; I was so upset.

"I wasn't arrested! They brought me to jail for my own good. I needed protection from myself!" He laughed and threw his head back. He looked over at me slowly, his eyes bright with excitement. "It was fun!"

"What are you talking about?" I opened the car door and climbed in. My eyes were straight ahead as I noticed people watching us argue. He got into the passenger side.

"They thought I was homeless!" This time he laughed harder.

"You think that's funny? I just rushed home from vacation and have been waiting four long hours for your release! How can you think it's amusing to be homeless?"

"I wasn't arrested." He looked away, disappointed that I didn't see the humour in it.

*****

The new school sat in the hills west of Rancho, a twenty-minute drive from home.

Behind the school were massive mountains that protected it from the early ocean breezes and the typical morning overcast. Winds picked up in the afternoon, kicking up the area's dust, typical for the under-built area. The school was medium-sized and housed students in ninth through twelfth grades. Halls crowded with mostly white teens whose parents had found a safe town for their families to grow up in and where the chaos was minimal. Trey had little desire to be accepted by the groups that occupied the school and found peace outside its doors. He had no interest in his classes and often made them a joke.

His strict English-class teacher assigned homework for creative writing to her students, who had to have it completed within two weeks. She made it clear that there were specific guidelines to be followed. Trey's imagination exploded.

How I became the person, I am . . .

On October 15, 1983, I was born without a doctor's help. After twenty minutes of child labour in an elevator, my mother and father delivered me. I now know why my life would be different from the norm and that these would be talented people in my life.

I am the second oldest with three siblings (two brothers, one sister). When I was between three and nine, my mom called me "the peacemaker." My mother thought for all those years that I was the only child that could make or want peace. I would go on for days without ever noticing that I even had siblings. I could hear them fight, but it didn't affect me. I would live in my little world, thinking of things that probably didn't matter, but to me, they did. Then, after those ages, she found out that I was nothing close to being a peacemaker. I am sure she regrets calling me peaceful because I have shown her that peace is not what I am.

I get my personality from a mix of things. My artistic talent is from my mom's side, my humour is from my dad's, and I'm pretty sure that I got a big part of my attitude from my Great-grandmother, Josephine, the skitso nut. I don't idolize her or anyone around me. Maybe it's because I have so little in common with everyone. I have never made crucial decisions wisely. It's a bad habit that must go. On another note, I am grateful for my proper raising and all my parents' support.

Living in the Present Moment . . .
 Right now, at this moment, I am okay. I'm a little angry and maybe a little sick, but I'm okay. If anything, I have a massive problem with certain people and their personalities. No matter how much I hate someone, I can't express myself orally unless I'm pissed off. Then, that usually results in a physical fight
 If I had a bumper sticker, it would read, "If you ever need anything, please don't hesitate to ask someone else first," because I don't have time, I'm too busy thinking . . .
 The only thing that makes me happy now is being left alone. I don't want to hear about how I need to fix my problems. If you're going to hear about what makes me unhappy, it's "psychiatrists." I know more about them than you care to remember. They are the worst, if anything. They try to understand what is on your mind when they don't know their own. Shrinks are many stupid, idiotic people who think they need to make money off other people's emotions.

Future Fantasy . . .
 My ultimate fantasy would be to be a rich rock star who would be living in a dumpster so no paparazzi would invade my modest lifestyle. My dumpster would be a two-story cardboard hut with aluminium car stabilizers and wind-resistant trash-bag

tarps, which would keep all the rain out and keep me dry. I would have a metal can built into the trash below me, and that trash can would give me all my food and keep me warm at night. I would also have a stash of rocks to throw at opposing dumpster divers. My lifestyle would be good enough for me and anyone else into the business of free merchandising. My food would be free because my dumpster would be two stores down from Jack in the Box, so I could eat out of their trash if I were hungry.

The only thing I would spend my money on would be my instrument equipment. I would use the rest of the funds for firewood chips. Oh, yeah, my bumper sticker would be on my dumpster.

My Real Future. . .

My real future would be a little like my fantasy future. I will probably still be a rock star, but I can't predict the future. I will be an underground rocker if I'm not a rock star. I can assure you that it will be one of the two. I don't think I will live in a dumpster with all those special features, but I may have to find an appropriate trash bin if things go wrong. I don't know what type of people I will associate with, but they will likely be people I can see being my friend. All the other people will still be around, but I wouldn't bond with them. The truth is I can't predict the future because many things change in ten years.

Death with Dignity . . .

During my funeral, I don't need a eulogy. I mean, what is the point of having people talk about your significance if you can't hear it? But I do want to be cremated along with some of my prized possessions. Some of them are my guitar, amp, and pics. These are the prizes that I don't want to leave behind on my incredible journey to Nirvana. No one should be sad because they will be dead soon too.

I want my ashes buried somewhere away from the typical cemetery, with a headstone that people can visit. I don't want to be buried six feet under; I want five feet under for all those lazy diggers.

His teacher found little humour in all he wrote, and he failed his creative-writing assignment. As I waited in my car for the kids to leave school, I watched the students as the bell rang, signalling the end of the day. The students carried backpacks filled with books and homework and had smiles on their faces as they casually chatted with their friends. They acted as if they had the world by the tail as they joked, laughed, and celebrated that school was ending for the day. The football field was full of practising jocks, who dreamed of big careers in the NFL, and cheerleaders performing their stunts as they thought about Friday night's game. They planned for college and dreamed of being married with children someday.

As my eyes canvassed the school grounds, I saw Trey leaning against the fence by himself. He was completely and utterly on his own in his mind, body, soul, and most of all, entirely alone in the world. He didn't carry a backpack like the others or dream of Friday's night football game; he only conveyed sadness as I watched him through teary eyes. He was lost without plans for the future and only saw satire and the emptiness surrounding him.

Chapter 19

THE GYM CLASS RAN DOWN THE HIGH SCHOOL driveway out to the busy street. The twenty-five students stayed in a single file as if they were in boot camp, keeping few gaps between them. Trey's instructor kept a close eye on his students as they jogged past newly built tract homes.

As Trey ran, the rhythm of his footsteps started to numb his mind as he broke formation and headed into one of the neighbour's front yards. The orchard was small, filled with peach trees and beautiful flower gardens. There he found and picked the firmest, juiciest peach. He looked up and locked eyes with his teacher, who had followed him there. He then, with bold disobedience, bit into the peach and let the juice run down his chin. Fuck you, he said under his breath. His teacher's eyes glared with fire as he snapped at the whisper of the words and demanded Trey meet him after class. Trey earned himself a suspension and a short vacation from school, which allowed his teacher a three-day break from him. As he lay in bed smoking pot on his first day off, I wondered who this was benefiting, indeed not Trey.

A week later, he slowly inhaled and took a puff from his cigarette. Smoking on campus was forbidden but not unusual for Trey as he sneaked a cigarette from his shirt pocket, satisfying his heavy addiction. He knew the consequences were significant as the smoke-filled his lungs. He looked around as he fumbled for another smoke when he caught the eye of one of the security police who regularly patrolled the campus. Trey received a ticket for a court appearance.

As unhappy as I was, I escorted him to Department E. Standing in front of the judge, Trey awaited his punishment. "I order you to pay the court $300.00." The judge pounded his gavel. I stood up and pleaded to the court.

"My son doesn't have any money, and it'd be me who'd be penalized. Please reconsider your ruling." I pled as I made eye contact with the robed and overweight judge. After much thought, his dark eyes surrounded with black-framed glasses looked up at me, and he carefully changed his order, which sent Trey to smoking-cessation class. I was pleased with the judge's reversed decision and hoped Trey could successfully stop smoking.

Trey's designated meeting place and the date was assigned. The class was one and a half hours from home, every Saturday at 7:00 a.m. for the next six weeks. As I drove Trey there and back, I swore while watching him sleep. *You little asshole. When are you going to grow up?* There was no conversation, only silence as I drove down the freeway and wished I had paid the money.

Soon his grades began to collapse, and I started grieving for the bright future I'd hoped he'd have. He purposely earned an expulsion from school by bringing an ornamental eight-inch butterfly knife he'd received as a gift from a buddy when it fell from his torn pocket. I sat with the school board, arguing that sending him to Brookside Continuation School would not be in Trey's best interests, but I finally conceded. He would no longer be with his brothers at the good high school but transferred the following week.

*****

We were ready for our annual September trip to the Colorado River, and we all, except Trey, anticipated a great time. He, becoming more reclusive, made it clear he was not interested in going with us on family vacations. I made it clear he had no choice. I was not particularly happy with the company he chose to keep and instinctively knew he was not in a healthy place. I certainly wasn't going to leave him home alone to do whatever he decided.

There were many signs of drug abuse. Trey became withdrawn, his personality sunk into dark thoughts. Money was disappearing from purses, and items of value vanished. He wasn't the same boy anymore. His happiness had been stolen from him, locked uptight, and put out of reach.

We arrived as a family on Friday, earlier than usual, and unpacked our bags and belongings into our friends' mobile home. We'd been here plenty of times before and knew exactly where to put our things. The house was large and accommodated our family with two bunk beds in the back bedroom, each with a queen-sized bed on the bottom and a twin on top. The weather was hot as usual, so we appreciated our awaiting drinks.

We couldn't wait to board the thirty-two-foot Charger jet-powered boat that awaited us at the dock. It would carry us to the northern sandbar near Parker Dam, where we would celebrate happy hour and the setting sun.

The sandbar was quiet when we arrived, which was unusual. It typically had fifty people climbing onto it to get out of the water. I thought about all the people who would be arriving here the next day as I pulled another Bud-Lite from the cooler.

We kicked back, cracked a beer, and turned up the tunes when we saw other speedboats racing on the water. We watched a V-haul going south with four teenagers, all under the age of eighteen, and heard screams of delight as they passed the vacant sandbar. The second boat on a northward path was on a test ride and proceeded to show off its muscle when it struck the southbound boat head-on. Both vessels were in pieces as we jumped into our boat to seek help.

"One of the teenagers is unaccounted for!" Someone yelled as we watched unsuccessful attempts at CPR on the other three who lay lifeless on the pier. Trey dove into the water in search of the missing teen. He came up for air.

"There is so much fuel in the water; I can't see anything!" His eyes were bloodshot as he tried to wipe the gasoline from his face. "It looks like there's something wrapped around the prop." He pointed hysterically and took another dive. The three teenagers were gone with no hope of survival as the police and paramedics arrived and asked us to clear the area.

The following day, the newspaper headlines read: "Two of the teenagers killed in the boating accident near Parker Dam were siblings from Southern California who were testing the boat they drove, anticipating a purchase for their dad. The third teenager was one of their friends. The fourth and missing teen was found in critical condition near the shore by the wreckage. The owner of the other boat fled the scene and faces prison time if found guilty."

Down and out, we went back to the trailer. I looked over at Marco. "I never want to come here again." Tears filled my eyes as I glanced around and noticed everyone had left and gone to the trailer-park bar.

Marco wrapped his arms around me as we slowly walked towards the bar with only the thoughts of the day's event on our minds. Trey was in the bar, sitting alone, doing shot after shot as he screamed at the top of his lungs to the tunes of the jukebox.

"Trey, slow down a little bit." His eyes were on fire as he laughed at me and took another shot.

"Calm down!" I implored as I noticed the river rushing past. For a moment, I wondered if I could stop him. He was entirely out of control and not listening to anyone. He suddenly jumped from his chair and ran out of the bar. Susan glanced at me with scared eyes and chased him down the street, where they ended up in the sand by the river's edge.

Trey felt dead, and his eyes were fixed and vacant. Susan stooped next to him, one hand over his shoulder. She picked up his hand and touched it to her newly wet cheek, closing her eyes just for a minute. In that second, she felt his pain. The time ticked forward as I approached them and noticed that Trey's spirit was gone. He was crying and saying that he wanted to kill himself. "I don't want to be alive. I want to die." I knew at that moment that there was nothing I could do to console him and no precautions I could take. There was no place I could hide. No one could help me. With a nauseous roll of my stomach, I realized that the situation was worse than ever before.

"Are you crazy?" I whispered. "You're suicidal?" That question caught his attention, and my eyes focused on him. He turned away, numb.

Susan looked at me teary-eyed. "We have a serious problem." I looked back at her and admitted I already knew.

The drive home through the desert was different this time as everyone sat solemnly after the weekend's event. No one talked or even wanted to listen to the radio. We just wanted to sit in the quiet within our thoughts. Trey sat in the backseat staring out the window without a sound or expression on his face. He was down and out, showing visible signs of defeat.

*****

Brookside Continuation School was for losers who didn't want to comply. My heart wanted to believe Trey didn't belong there, but my brain knew there were no other choices.

The school's halls decorated the blank areas in black and white. The whole building sent a chill down my spine and reminded me of something from my nightmares. It sat next door to the big Rancho High School and only steps from the local middle school. The wind howled through that area as if it understood the kids who went there. The institution was sterile, without posters supporting and rallying their football team. I guess because there wasn't one. It resembled a prison with high walls surrounding the gathering areas. The teachers were not as friendly as they were on the other campuses; they knew what type of kids they dealt with daily. The educators had rap sheets on the problem kids, instructing them on how to deal with specific situations. The old picnic tables which sat outside displayed graphic images carved into the distressed wood. The janitor's full-time job was keeping the benches clean and picking up food thrown in the area.

None of the kids wanted to be there, none of them wanted to be in any school, but the law forced it, making it mandatory for them to attend. The students snarled as they talked about how society had mistreated them and blamed their parents for the things they'd done wrong. The school was a place for bad kids. Trey would spend the rest of his school year there, and unfortunately, it was his behaviour that had brought him there. There was no going back, and it was too late for me to help him.

*****

"Oh, Leigh, you won't believe what I just saw!" It was Judy, a close friend, on the phone. "Russell, Trey, and Cameron were beating the shit out of a kid on the corner as I drove my kids to school this morning. That kid must have done something wrong for the boys to do something like this. This kind of behaviour is so out of character for them!" Judy knew the boys well, as her daughter and Madison were best friends.

Hitler, or so they called him, was one of those kids who didn't want to conform, and whispers ran rampant around the Brookside campus that Hitler slept with Madison. He had not forgotten how the last Morelli party was, how everyone treated him as an outcast. With his bloodshot eyes and unbrushed jet-black hair, he sneaked around from one place in the house to another. The girls avoided him at all costs during the party. He had no cares as his target was Madison, who was only in eighth grade and preparing to graduate into the nearby high school. She didn't need any false rumours following her.

One day on the Brookside campus, Trey heard the nasty rumours Hitler was circulating, and he didn't take it kindly. He immediately organized his brothers to put a hit job on Hitler scheduled for the following day. As school was about to begin, Russell, Trey, and Cameron hid behind a tree waiting in the shadows for Hitler to exit his car. A fist pack of quarters that Trey held in his palm smashed into the back of Hitler's head, leaving him stumbling. Cameron had no choice but to follow with a solid right-hand punch to bloody his nose. Another giant punch thrown by Russell finished Hitler off. As Hitler regained his balance, he displayed a pale face and a watery black and swollen eye. Trey prodded him. "Hey, fucking Hitler, if you don't want this to happen every day, you will admit you fucking lied about my sister to every one of your asshole friends. I will follow to make sure you do, fucker!" Hitler agreed to do what Trey demanded. Trey smiled throughout the day as he begged him to detail his lie as his peers listened. "Why did you lie, Prick?" This day pleased Trey, as he knew he had and would always protect his little sister. The word spread quickly about Hitler's demise, and the boys made it clear to stay away from Madison; she was off-limits. She became the most protected sister in school, and there weren't many who wanted to mess with the Morelli brothers.

Chapter 20

HE LOOKED JUST LIKE ANY OTHER SKINNY GUY and only attracted girls in a friendly sort-of-way, that is, until the summer between his junior and senior years when Russell shot up five inches. He began gaining weight, and his thin frame started filling out with muscles from working in construction throughout the summer at his dad's side. He grew into his features; his bone structure was subtle and perfect. Russell was striking, and with each year that passed, his inner beauty showed on his face. There was a softness in his blue-green eyes and gentleness in his smile. Suddenly, the girls' heads turned, and he found himself returning smiles when he caught an admiring glance. The popular-girl crowd began jokingly calling him "Russell the Muscle." Madison's friends only dreamed of one day calling him their own.

Russell earned a reputation around the campus as a fighter who quickly saw red, and his strength backed him up. He was strong and coordinated. Russell didn't look for a fight but would defend his friends, some of the biggest jocks in school. As he

clenched his fists, he knew how big and strong he was. An iron punch landed ninety-nine per cent of the time where he intended it. Loyal to friends and family, everyone liked him. Russell was simply a happy person, and he carried that happiness with him, sharing it with whoever was near him. It was natural, a part of who he was. His humour was unique. In his senior year, he, too, earned a suspension after he confiscated the school's PA, locked himself in a bathroom with a friend, and proceeded to accuse that same friend of "spanking his monkey" over the school's speakers during final exams. Through frequent meetings, Mr Adams, the high school principal and my friend, barely held a straight face as he spoke of Russell's disciplinary action. The school's year-end couldn't come too soon for Mr Adams. They watched Russell receive his high school diploma and graduate into the fire department academy, a nearby facility, which allowed Russell to live at home while he completed his training.

*****

Mike was the poor sap who had never heard the Morelli name before meeting Madison. He smoothly asked her out for a date, and when he picked her up, Marco sternly said, "You better act like a gentleman." Mike nodded and headed out the door, not giving it a second thought. That night the movie theatre was crowded as Mike's hand fumbled to find Madison's breast.

"Let's go out to the car." He whispered. "I thought that I'd like you to kiss me."

Madison was stunned as she searched, studied, met, and surveyed his determined eyes. "No, why would I?"

He laughed and then sighed. "Heaven forbid that I would do anything you don't want me to do," he said in a strangely desperate tone as he reached for Madison's face to his. He went further towards her as he leaned in to deliver a wet, slippery kiss. Suddenly his lips became more urgent; his free hand twisted into her hair and held her face securely to his. She pulled away, knowing she wasn't in the least bit interested. She wasn't ready to give in to his promise of a pleasurable night. He became a little more forceful as he tried to reach between her legs. She stood up and looked at him with cold eyes—she knew how to take care of herself. He looked into her face and continued to tell her his car was perfect and where most girls in the neighbourhood gladly gave out blow jobs. She spat at him and demanded Mike take her home.

I eagerly waited that morning while drinking my creamed coffee for her to come downstairs. While taking her to school, I asked her how her date had gone. She cried and told me what Mike had done. I was furious and found it hard to keep the car on the road as I headed for home.

Marco's eyes turned red as I told him what I'd heard. The boys were summoned immediately to Marco's office and left with instructions to "Go get him!" The three boys drove to a local oil-changing business where Mike worked and demanded to see him. After his employer heard the story, he paged Mike and asked him to come to the front office and take it outside. That's when he saw three pissed-off boys. Adrenaline coursed through Mike's system as a fight-or-flight instinct took over. He wanted to run away with his tail between his legs. He had to get away, but he knew he would never outrun them. He looked at them as they surrounded the poor boy. Russell escorted him outside by the arm. "Hey, Bud. You made the mistake of a lifetime last night. Now, you're going to make three phone calls. One to my mom, one to my dad and one to my sister."

Mike pleaded and cried. "I don't have any money. I'm sorry, but I didn't do anything. I don't know what Madison told you, but nothing happened. I swear!"

Russell made it simple. "Well, you are going to get some money and make things right. I don't give a damn what you say. Madison made it very clear how you acted last night. Now you will pay." Trey, Cameron, and Russell surrounded Mike as they crossed the street to the nearby bowling alley. He shook as he retrieved five dollars from the ATM.

Russell had a face of utter nonchalance as he rested against the pillar. Russell didn't slump; his body was too muscular for that. He was smiling as if something good were about to happen. Suitable for Russell was terrible for Mike. Very bad, as he made his first call.

"Mrs Morelli? I'm sorry for how I behaved last night with Madison. I didn't mean to hurt her." He barely spoke the words; he was trembling badly. I sat back and bathed in the warmth of his scared voice. He shook as he turned to Russell, hoping that Russell would show mercy. Russell stood cold and stared at him with disgust. Next, a call to Marco, who wasn't happy.

"What the fuck do you want? You son of a bitch! I should kick the shit out of you. I think I'll let my boys do that instead. You are trash and not worth my time. Don't ever touch my daughter again!" He slammed the telephone down, hitting the top of his desk and carving out a dent in the wood.

Russell stood firm as Mike dialled the last name on the list, hoping the call was left unanswered. His voice cracked as Madison smirked. "I'm sorry, Madison. You deserve better than that last night. I promise I've learned my lesson and will never treat another girl the way I treated you." Madison sat on the phone with a satisfying grin as Russell released Mike's shirt collar and shoved him into the street.

The following morning Madison returned to school to face boys too afraid to look at her. Her last name followed her like the plague. Russell's friends who had already graduated showed no interest; they were too old for her and had their sights set on more mature girls. They certainly didn't want to face Russell either. Most of Trey's friends were creepy, and the few who weren't wouldn't even look at her. Cameron's friends were a little different and closer to Madison's age, but they, too, were afraid.

Madison was classically beautiful; her large, deep-brown eyes held a calmness that made it impossible not to be fascinated by them. They showed her soul. Long black and curled eyelashes surrounded them, eyelashes her friends could only dream of having. Her cheekbones weren't exceptionally high, but her nose was perfect and kissed by tiny freckles from God. There was absolute perfection to her features, which held her audience prisoner. Her hair was long, dark, and curly. It gently flowed over her shoulder blades, caressing her soft skin. She was tall, thin, and naturally endowed. All the beauty in the universe could not compete with a straightforward thing she had: Passion. It made her emotions beautiful, which didn't hide on her innocent face. Her passion sparked her eyes and, in them, you knew she'd fight for her life and those closest to her. She was a warrior for her brothers and would stand up to anyone who crossed them. They knew who she was and were proud that she was their little sister.

*****

As the holidays approached, we began to feel the familiar excitement in the air and planned another visit to the famed Rose

Parade. As we pulled our motorhome into the crowded parking lot, we spotted the parking space on our left that we had reserved for a two-day stay. Trey's skin was pale and broken out, and he had lost a lot of weight in the past few weeks. He had a heavy cigarette habit, smoked nonstop, and showed more signs of drug abuse.

The motorhome was old, rickety and set up for the parade. We placed chairs on the roof, giving us a good vantage point for viewing the event in the morning. The kids ventured into the streets, staying close and trying not to get lost in the hordes of people.

After a dinner of grilled hamburgers and corn, the kids started prepping their stations with tortillas brought from home. The kids formed a line on the boulevard and were ready to start the night's events. Hundreds of people on the road that night were throwing things at cars that were passing by.

We sat on the dirty curb and saw a commuter bus pull up to a nearby bus stop. As the doors flung open, a dark-skinned woman climbed down the stairs and flipped the bird at her audience, a group of parade-goers. She appeared to be homeless. She was thin and missing teeth. Skinny Trey laughingly eyed his target while filling his tortilla. One fling of a tortilla, and the woman started screaming, "Fuck you, bastards! Fuck off!"

Trey shouted back. "Fuck you!" She wiped the cream off her face, trying to get back into the bus. Trey seemed angry and determined as we sighed in relief when the bus carried the madwoman away. Fifteen minutes later, we looked up, and the coach was back with the woman frantically looking for the guilty party.

I grabbed Trey's arm. "Don't, Trey." He pulled away defiantly and disappeared behind a motorhome for a moment. As he came back around, I noticed a different look on his face as he continued at his station.

"Trey is on drugs." My mouth took on a straight line as I looked at Marco and pointed over to Trey.

Marco looked over. "Why would you think that?"

"He seems animated. Watch him." I knew he was high just by the way he looked. His eyes had a strange, sunken look, and they appeared pink. His cheeks glowed under broken veins; his actions were fast and careless. His hands trembled as he closely monitored his surroundings.

The kids had a great time as they assembled a group of like-minded teens, who hovered close by, using the seemingly endless supply of "throwables" we brought. Marco and I sat on our lawn chairs at the curb, watching the kids. We looked over and saw Trey eyeing his next target, a police car's open window. The cruiser was squeaky clean since everyone had the common sense not to throw anything at it. Not Trey, though. Once again, he quickly foamed the shaving cream into the tortilla without losing eye contact with the cop car and then gently, methodically, threw the tortilla up into the air. It landed perfectly into the vehicle and onto the officer's lap.

We heard a sudden blast from a siren, and a police cruiser appeared with red-and-blue lights flashing. "Shit! Trey is going to get arrested!" I noticed the officer getting out of the car. He paced as he approached us with his flashlight in one hand and a billy club on his hip.

Standing up to look over the crowd, I felt Trey pull me backwards and onto his lap as he quickly sat down on my lawn chair, using me as a body shield to hide from the police officer.

Questioning passersby, the cops decided it was pointless to find the perpetrator. With a stern warning to all, he drove off.

I screamed at Trey. "Are you crazy?" I pushed Trey away from me. "Of all cars, why would you throw it at the police?"

He blew smoke in my face. "Fuck them." He walked away. *I secretly wished he had stayed home.*

Morning arrived as we climbed to the motorhome's roof and enjoyed the parade. I poured Bloody Mary's and decorated them with chunks of celery, olives, and jalapeno. Sadly, I knew we would not be returning. Not only because of the growing police presence but also because Trey was out of control. He didn't care about anyone or anything.

Chapter 21

THE PRINCIPAL AT BROOKSIDE CONTINUATION school called to inform me that Trey had quit. He was eighteen, and there wasn't anything I could do. Holed up in his room using drugs and writing music for his new group, he dropped out of life.

For Marco's forty-sixth birthday, I planned to throw a huge party complete with catered food, a full bar, and live music. It took weeks to organize down to the last detail. I announced to the kids. "I don't want any high school parties, so please don't invite any of your friends."

As guests started arriving, I looked around and noticed Trey had not shown up. I worried he might not make it and knew Trey's absence would hurt Marco. I lost myself to my entertaining duties, and halfway through the party, Trey appeared with a girl on each arm. His hair was bleached blonde now, and he sported stark-black two-inch roots. His face was pale, his skin scarred with giant pockmarks. His yellow and decaying teeth were disgusting. He looked horrible.

Brigette, on one arm, was a tall redhead. Her back displayed a massive tattoo of a smiley face peeking through her sloppy see-through blouse. Kathleen was medium height, sporting her barbed wire tattoo crisscrossing across her flat chest. Both girls were grungey, pretty, and friendly but stoned. Trey circulated through the party proudly, showing off his prizes as I watched him chain-smoke. He lit each new cigarette with the old one. His eyes were tired, the colour of moss and dirt shovelled together, with apparent signs of insufficient sleep. I watched him closely in a distrusting fashion noticing his skinny frame, and wondered what had happened to the son I once knew. Russell acted embarrassed by him. Madison, Marco, and I felt sad. Cameron seemed distant as he tried to stay separated from Trey. In his eyes, he knew he had lost his best friend. I then remembered hearing about their last trip to Mexico.

Trey was desperate to make another trip down south. He'd been holed up too long and needed a break when he asked Cameron and another friend to make the trek with him. They left early one Saturday morning. It was easy to cross the border in Tijuana from California for three teenagers who knew which restaurant was best in the Mexican village. They'd been there many times before. As they took their seats at the bar, Trey ordered his drink, "I'll have a shot of tequila!" A young Mexican kid who recognized him came over. Trey pulled a wad of money from his pocket and sent him on his way. Time passed as the boys proceeded to allow the tequila to dull their minds when Cameron suddenly realized Trey hadn't made it back from the bathroom.

It could have been the drug cartel that pointed their guns at Trey. Instead, they never fired but cuffed his arms and legs and bound his mouth. They glanced at him, peering down from their Mexican faces with appreciative smiles. "We'd offer you some tequila, Trey, but you seem somewhat tied up." The main guy laughed. Then they loaded a syringe from a small brown vial and plunged it into Trey's thigh.

Cameron and the other kid searched for Trey, across the street and throughout the town. Hours passed as Cameron panicked. His thoughts vanished behind a wall of worry. Half his brain believed Trey was all right, and the other saw a horrible ending. He saw the funeral, his brother a hollow shell. Cameron was too empty to cry anymore, and he felt the accusing eyes fall on him from all around. It was all his fault for going to Mexico with Trey. His brother was gone, and he wasn't coming back. The search continued as the night drew near in the foreign country with a horrible reputation for drugs and murder.

Suddenly, two men approached Cameron. They claimed to have Trey. The men escorted Cameron and his friend to a nearby hut where Trey was bound and gagged. Cameron pleaded to the strange men to let his brother go. They refused as they searched Cameron for anything valuable. He was scared to death.

The Mexican banditos finally saw something they would take in exchange for Trey. They pointed at Cameron's jacket. "Give me that fucking coat!" His dark eyes glared at Cameron. "And take the other mother fucker's too!!" He pointed at Trey. They unbound Trey, stripped his leather jacket from his back and shoved him towards Cameron. Trey was weak, sleepy, and drugged as Cameron dragged him down the pebble-stone pathway and back across the border. The silent ride home was long, and Cameron swore this would be his last trip to the country just south of California.

As the musicians improvised on the patio in the warm summer air, the music danced out of their instruments in a bluesy, swinging rhythm. Trey's foot began to tap, and his head nodded and swayed. He loved that sax, deep as the soul and so soothing. As the band played, everyone jumped up to dance. The dance floor was full when the group finally decided to take a break. Trey broke free of his dates and approached the members of the group. He then convinced them to let him sit in on one of their songs. As the music resumed, I looked up and saw Trey shirtless, a cigarette hanging from his upper lip, his guitar strapped across his shoulder, playing with the band. He got lost in their rhythm and blues. The girls hung all over him while he played song after song, taking the lead from the band's main singer.

"Do you like the girls, Mom?" Trey broke from the band to ask. "Huh, do you like them?" He elbowed me, and I noticed faint bruises on his inner arm. The night ended with howling from Trey's mouth while white cocaine hugged his nostrils. Trey stayed home with the girls in his bed that night.

*****

I felt tired and stressed from drinking too much the night before, so I went in search of my bottle of Xanax. It treated insomnia and anxiety. I fumbled through the drawer where I was sure I had left it. Finally, I realized it was gone, and I had a good idea of where it was. I peered into Trey's room, he was fast asleep, and the girls were gone. I moved quickly out to his blue Toyota truck, opened the front door, and slid into the front seat on the driver's side. Putting my hands under the front seat, I located a secret box, which I slid out and opened. I was not surprised to see my Xanax and other containers there. One contained marijuana; the others, pills. Small rolled-up pieces of aluminium foil contained dark powdery substances. I found a court order rolled into a ball, ordering him to attend rehab two times a week for six weeks for attempted suicide. I remembered his failed attempt like it was yesterday. I left the court order there but took the rest of the box's contents with me. Making my way into my bathroom, I flushed the drugs down the toilet. The drugs and stolen merchandise spoke for themselves and made me realize what a big problem I had on my hands. I had no obvious solution. Trey had been going down the same path for years, and I'd done everything I possibly could to help him.

*****

A letter dated June 16, 2003, dropped from his jacket's pocket as he left the house in the afternoon to go back to James's. I picked it up and started reading.

> Trey, listen to me. You're not as fucked up as you seem. You're just different—Unique like many people. But what separates you from most other people is that you don't stick and brag on one thing. That's what makes you unique! So, please, Trey, take advantage and motivate yourself. Search your artistic ways and expand your creative and unique ways. Trust me, Trey, you are not fucked up! You are just lost.

> Love always, Jackie.

Trey's dreams of writing and producing music became a reality as he fell deeper into drug addiction. His anger increased with his drug usage, evident in the piece he wrote.

Scribbled on a piece of cardboard I found in his room, he wrote lyrics that barely made sense.

I am So Broke
Get out of bed, pack your bags, you're out on your own
Where should you go now that you are out on your own
Is there anything you could say to make my thoughts change?
Stop your complaining, always are blaming
Get out of my home
Stand up straight; your family is disgraced.
Take a slap, you ungrateful brat
You don't need to dwell any longer; you said you
are sorry. Just take your apologies
You still have other good kids you can save.
Now, you are alone and have nothing to
show. Is it neglect or just constantly sad
How modest is that? You are such a
brat. Soon enough, the sickness will
kill you Cashing your points for your
sympathy

Trey was on a path to destruction, and problems were ahead. He could not get along with the band members because he always looked for perfection. They came and went as Trey wrote music. He practised singing, playing bass and drums, and worked hard to produce a CD. His band was falling apart while he grew impatient with himself and found that writing was more accessible on heroin. Trey was alone and angrier. He recorded and re-recorded song after song but couldn't get it right, so he dove deeper into the drugs that offered him the creativity and escape from reality he desperately needed. An opportunity to move in with some buddies came, and Trey took it against my wishes. He was nineteen and didn't care what I thought.

Chapter 22

BUSINESS HAS BEEN BOOMING SINCE WE SURVIVED the recession. "Guess what, Leigh? I got that framing job in wine country that I've been working so hard on." There was excitement in Marco's voice over the phone. He knew the 4500-square-foot home would take just under two months to frame if all his employees showed up for work on time and worked a solid forty hours a week. He would be on a tight schedule, so everyone needed to be on the same page. He couldn't wait to tell his crew as he drove to the job where they were working.

As he opened the temporary fencing, he listened to Phillip, his superintendent. "Trey is here on the job and is hallucinating. He believes there are Indians in the hills behind us. He's on drugs." Phillip had a history of drug abuse in his younger years and found freedom through classes and AA support. Marco listened while walking to Trey, who sat on a beam smoking a cigarette.

"So, what's up, Trey?" Marco noticed the big black circles that appeared under his bloodshot eyes.

"Don't you see the Indians, Dad? They're in the hills right over there. I swear. Don't you see them?" Trey pointed in the direction where he thought they were.

"Those aren't Indians, Son. Those are rocks." Marco tried to reason with Trey, but Trey wasn't listening. He was filthy. He appeared as if he hadn't eaten in weeks. Trey was unreliable for work and missed days at a time. Marco routinely called and fired him, reasoning that if Trey didn't have any money, he couldn't buy drugs, and eventually, he'd have to come home. But in the end, Marco, feeling guilty, always gave Trey another chance.

"Get him into my truck," Marco told Phillip as they helped Trey into the front seat. As they drove down the dirt road, Marco called me. "I am going to take him to his apartment to sleep it off. Maybe you can check on him later."

*****

He had forgotten who he was, and he was living in an apartment with a group of friends who had one thing in common. Drugs. Not long after Marco's call, I jumped into my car and headed to the apartment, worried about what I might find. I opened the unlocked apartment door and, at first glance, noticed its dark and musty odour. There was no sound, so I assumed no one was home. To the right, dishes and stagnant water overflowed the sink, and the trash grew high in the kitchen corner. The floor was filthy, and signs of cockroaches filled the cupboards. In the breakfast nook sat an old wooden table where carving took place nightly. Names and artwork gouged the once perfect pinewood, and a large buck-knife was on the table. An old, filthy couch splattered with stains and cigarette burns was in the living room. A piece of a broken mirror glued to the armrest was covered in dust and small remnants of cocaine. Small empty ziplocked Baggies and used syringes were scattered everywhere.

Trey's friend, Will, had recently turned eighteen and had received a large sum of money after his father's death. Will had put up the money for the apartment's security deposit and first month's rent, and in return, he had gotten the most oversized bedroom. His room was the first bedroom I entered. Pornographic trash scotch-taped to the walls filled the walls, and as I looked around, I saw pipes, pot, straws, mirrors, and bags of cocaine strewn across his bedroom floor. His room smelled obnoxious, with dozens of half-smoked cigarettes littering several ashtrays. Will had been a cute-looking kid before he inherited his father's money, which gave him an avenue to abuse drugs.

Trey's room was to the left and down the small hallway. Trey didn't desire or need to decorate because he only slept there. His bedroom was just a place to hide his loneliness while using drugs. A simple bed was pushed to the corner of the room, covered with musical instruments and drug paraphernalia. As I entered his room, an eerie feeling came over me. I sensed him there as I walked towards his open closet door. I looked in only to find him fast asleep. Lying near him was his guitar and several used syringes. A dirty strap used as a tourniquet was still wrapped around his arm, as his head hung and his shoulders slumped. His hair was greasy and bleached blonde, and Trey's black stubble covered his once-handsome face. When I finally woke him, his subdued, pale-green eyes were blurred as he gazed at me. They were rigid and cold as he struggled to recognize my face. In them, I saw pain and loss that nothing could cover up. He showed no emotion and didn't try to speak. At that moment, I knew he was far away.

*****

Trey isolated himself from family, but court-ordered rehab classes for attempted suicide forced him to contact Marco and me twice a week. The order did not require us, acting as sponsors, to accompany him to the outpatient rehab, but we chose to anyway. So, twice a week on Tuesday and Thursday nights, we made it a ritual to pick Trey up and drive to the group meeting. If we didn't, he most likely wouldn't have gone.

We walked up the driveway to a brightly lit centre. We noticed rows of chairs set up for the attendees and their sponsors as we entered the building. Trey was familiar with many of the strange faces there and felt comfortable as he walked in casually and carefree. To him, this was a joke. The counsellor called everyone to order as we took our seats. Marco, Trey, and I sat in the sixth row from the front. He started, "Thank you, everyone, for being here tonight." Trey took one look, then quickly excused himself to the restroom.

As I sat and searched the room, I noticed many people in Trey's position. Their faces were cold and uncomfortable. They didn't want to be here, and only a few participated. I suddenly noticed a small number of people who seemed like they were there seeking help. They had been going down the wrong path for years, tried to escape independently, but found they couldn't avoid the abusive behaviour. They were desperate for a life change and a place that offered it to them.

We sat and listened to a counsellor speak about the steps toward freedom from drug and alcohol abuse for two long hours. The program seemed ineffective for those who didn't want to be there. It was about the drug use and nothing of the problem that drove these teens there in the first place. The treatment was

157

useless for them, but it was different for those who wanted to be there.

The counsellor's empathy extended to the group at the centre seemed like a bridge.

It just took time for those who wanted the change to trust the counsellors' professional advice. The professionals extended hands and stayed, while those who sought help showed them their scars, mess, and fear. The adults who ran the program allowed the users to come in close to them, hide from their past, and permit them to return for help without shame. The addicts were shown patience by the counsellors. They swore they never wanted to be this way. They tried to be strong, though they hadn't been. They promised they'd be reliable, as they made their pleas for help.

We learned that true healing takes time; there are no magic wands for deep pain. I only wished Trey could have been one of those people who had come for help because he knew he needed it. Marco and I sat, worried. We heard a sigh of relief when someone signalled the class had ended. Trey was nowhere.

After Marco did a quick search of the empty men's room, we headed to the car. I found Trey sleeping in the back seat with a used syringe hidden under the seat. After six weeks of dreaded classes, he had somehow completed his rehabilitation class and walked out with a certified copy for the courts. I know Marco, and I learned more in those six weeks than Trey or any of the other court-ordered attendees there.

*****

I quickly began gathering information about how to help Trey and started contacting counsellors for advice. They all said the same thing. "Tough love. Stop seeing him. Do not employ him. He must hit rock bottom before he wants to be clean." I knew they didn't understand. Trey didn't want to be clean. He didn't need to see us, nor did he need to work. Trey didn't care about living; Trey wished to die. He dreamed of it. If we walked away, death would follow, and I wasn't ready for that. I knew I had to pour in more love first, show him how much he mattered. He had to want to live and get better, and it would take love to bring him to a place where the professionals could step in and help.

One of the counsellors mentioned a doctor who was prescribing a new medication to help Trey fight addiction. The drug was called Suboxone, a form of methadone, but was far more effective and less addictive, according to the Center's director. We were encouraged. We met the doctor within a week and picked up his prescription that same day.

Two months passed quickly as his doctor shared that he believed Trey was beating addiction after putting Trey on antidepressants and other drugs. However, there were no signs of recovery that I could see.

I started to realize two things. Firstly, I saw Trey only when I was driving him to and from the doctor's office. I found myself pressuring his brothers to bring him to our house more often. Trey nodded off during our one-on-one conversations the few times they did, which caused more frustration. Secondly, as I looked into his tired eyes, I noticed his pupils were pin-sized, and his eyes were no longer brown. His irises had changed colours into a cloudy hazel-green hue somewhere along the way. I learned that when the pupil changes size, the pigments in the iris either compress or spread apart, which causes a change in the perceived eye colour, a condition known as meiosis. The repeated use of opioids, nicotine, and antidepressants caused constriction of the pupil, all of which Trey was using excessively.

Chapter 23

AFTER COMPLETING HIS STINT IN REHAB, TREY decided to move into an apartment with Lisa, a girl he'd been seeing off and on. He felt that he could concentrate on his music and clean up his life with Lisa. There was a beauty about her. She had safe eyes and a purity that made those grungey girls look ridiculous; she seemed honest. We'd met her before and liked her drive and ambition in life. She was easy to talk to and fun to be around. Trey seemed happy, and Lisa appeared to be a good influence.

Lisa and Trey visited the apartment complex as the day drew near to sign the lease agreement. It was not far from home and was in a decent neighbourhood.

Before Lisa had even landed her third knock, the apartment door opened sharply. At first, she imagined a middle-aged woman, but when her eyes landed on the face of her future landlord, she let out an involuntary gasp. It was more wrinkled than she imagined. The age spots gave the skin a coffee-stained look, and her jowls hung an inch below her chin. Lisa opened her mouth to introduce herself when the old bag delivered a substantial interruption. "Why are you here?"

Lisa sheepishly replied. "Hi, we're here to sign the lease agreement."

The woman took a step back, opened the door more expansive, and the lady narrowed her eyes, pulling her thinning mouth into an actual frown. After a second or two, she revealed a walking cane from behind the door frame and allowed Trey and Lisa to enter.

The rental sat on the second floor and was friendly and airy. The kitchen had enough appliances to cater for a small army, and everything glistened. The colour scheme was neutral; the wood floor was polished. Lisa claimed that the balcony was her favourite part of their future home by far. It was a place to let romance into her soul as the world passed by on the city streets below.

While the elderly landlord reviewed the tiny print on the lease agreement with Lisa, Trey started looking around the apartment and stumbled upon a cupboard. He climbed in and closed the door. The landlord looked at Lisa, puzzled and confused, as Lisa signed the lease. The older woman left with the document held in her left hand, the cane in her right.

Lisa, a bit miffed, went in search of Trey, who she found in the cupboard, grinning from ear to ear. "What are you doing in there?" Lisa thought it relatively immature of him, especially at age twenty.

"I dunno? I thought it would make you laugh!"

She wasn't quite sure why she loved him so much but knew that he was constantly making her smile by doing some silly thing.

Trey seemed like he was finally getting it together. He was staying at home more and entertaining friends and family frequently. He was carefree when I saw him, and I felt he was on the right path to happiness living with Lisa, and the new medication seemed to be working.

*****

Our sleepy little puppy slept, curled up next to Marco in our oversized king bed as I thought about how happy I was now that Trey seemed to be more comfortable.

Pinot Grigio Morelli came into our lives at six weeks old after Marco, and I had discussed whether we needed to replace the pet we had recently lost. The day I met her seems like yesterday.

The scales tipped 150 pounds for each parent who was jumping the pen's high walls and trying to escape.

"Are you sure you want a pit bull, Marco?" I quivered at the thought.

"These dogs are well trained," the breeder explained. We could barely hear him over the dogs barking as he ignored them leaping the fence wall. I froze while I watched them nearly succeed in their quest to break out. We looked around the grounds, which were not a place where dogs bred professionally. It was an old rundown home in the middle of nowhere with old, dilapidated trellises covering his side yard. He seemed friendly and unfazed by the dogs barking as he disappeared around the corner for a few minutes. I convinced myself that we didn't need another dog until he returned with two exceptional spotted puppies. One was male, the other female. As he approached me the teeny dogs wiggled and wormed excitedly in his arms.

I reached for the female and felt her dotted, light-brown coat smeared with spotted black flecks. Marks all over her face looked like freckles splattering across her cheeks. I held her against my breast as she licked my face. I felt excitement as I watched the constant wagging and wriggling. This puppy was adorable, and for me, it was love at first sight. I smiled at Marco and knew we had found our dog.

The Catahoula/pit-bull mixed puppy, Pinot, chased at my heel's day and night, nipping at my loose pants. When she would get a firm bite, she would shake her head back and forth. When I bent down to push her away, her jaws clamped tight. But there was no malice in those big doggy eyes; they were the eyes of a baby. So, I would turn the pup onto her back and firmly hold her in place. She would release her grip and scamper away, ready to pounce again a few seconds later. We were in love with this sweet thing.

The obvious pit-bull traits appeared when she, at eight weeks, aggressively wrestled the other puppies in obedience training, which ultimately earned her a timeout. Being held in a position of submission while her fellow puppies filed one by one past her, she quickly learned her lesson. Her days in timeout ended as she learned to be friends with other dogs and a companion to people.

*****

The double date, Trey with Lisa and Madison with Alexander, began at our house. They left after packing the car full of beer and two bottles of Jack Daniels. Alexander was a guy Madison had been dating for the past few months, and the first she showed signs of serious interest. They took Lisa's car to a local hangout at the end of a dead-end road. The area was dark, with oak trees surrounding the old sports park and dimly lit street lights barely covering the unused street. Deserted picnic benches laced the field, and it seemed like a quiet place to drink with no cops to interrupt them. It was a familiar place where they had all been before.

The night began as they searched for a picnic table on which to sit. Once seated, they pulled out a bottle of Jack and a twelve-pack of iced beer. Trey couldn't wait to get started. He grasped the bottle between his fingers, poured the brown fluid into his mouth, and slugged it down. The amber liquid slid down his throat, and it felt good as it warmed his stomach. He couldn't wait to pour another. Madison didn't think so. "Give us all a chance to have a shot!" Trey's demeanour began to change as they drank, and after a half-hour had passed, he turned into a demanding idiot.

"Give me the fucking bottle, Madison." He grabbed the bottle, tilted it back, and filled his mouth as his throat opened and allowed the juice to roll into his stomach.

"You're an asshole, Trey!" Madison remembered how he changed when he drank and couldn't believe he could act so stupid. Trey drank heavily, making sure to drink more brutal and faster than the others. He gulped shot after shot and complained he couldn't catch a buzz.

"C'mon, Trey. Be happy." Lisa tried to console him, but her words went unheard. "Well, I'm driving home." He glanced at Madison with bloodshot eyes and insisted he was sober enough to drive. Madison disagreed and hurried Alexander to get into the driver seat before Trey had a chance to. That infuriated Trey, who refused to get into the car and took off on foot through the hills. The alcohol had numbed him. Fog settled into the nearby field as Lisa chased him through the park and found him standing behind a tree.

"Please, Trey, you've been drinking a lot, and you should let Alexander drive," Lisa pleaded with tearful eyes. He scoffed at her but finally agreed. They found their way back to Madison and Alexander, who were tired of waiting and wanted to head home. Trey reluctantly got into the car.

"Fuck all of you. I'm not riding in this fucking car!" He screamed as the car headed for home. As soon as it stopped at a red light, he jumped up, climbed through the moonroof, and took off running again.

"Fuck him!" Madison was tired of his game. She told Alexander to keep driving. Lisa worried about leaving him and feared the worst as she had seen this before.

"He could get arrested. You know, he's been hanging around some of his old drug buddies lately," she pleaded to Madison. Madison reassured her that he would be okay but worried about this discovery. Once home, Lisa climbed into the driver's seat and sped down the hill, searching for Trey. She found him lying in a gutter. His eyes shut. As she gently woke him, he screamed.

"Fuck them! Take me up to my parents' house! I want to talk to my bitch sister!" They headed back to our house to confront Madison, who had gone to her room with Alexander.

The harsh scent of drink smelled on Trey as he struggled to keep his balance. Lisa watched his legs swaying left and right. He finally faced Madison's locked bedroom door. "Fuck you, you little bitch. Open this fucking door." Trey slurred every word. He continued banging on the door and then finally decided to wait downstairs.

Madison's eyes filled with tears, which forced Alexander to smooth things over and calm Trey down. Trey had a different thought as he ripped his shirt off over his head and began to challenge Alexander. "C'mon, mother-fucker. C'mon. I'll kick your fucking ass!" His face darkened bloodred.

"C'mon, brother, you don't want to fight. Let's talk in the morning." Alexander tried to console him. His usual playful smile had drawn into a hard line across his face.

"Fuck you, Alexander. Keep your fucking hands off, my sister." Trey raged with tears running down his face.

"Trey, go home!" Marco yelled from our bedroom as he awoke to the fighting.

Trey heeded the warning and jumped into the front seat of Lisa's car. He called Lisa to join him as they sped off into the darkness with Trey behind the wheel. Trey awoke the following day to a letter written by Lisa on her empty pillow.

Dear Trey

I'm sorry that I left our house last night. I couldn't handle watching you so wasted entirely. I can only see you like that so much. I want to tell you that I love you and care about you so much. It's hard to see someone you feel so strongly about getting fucked up daily. I am not trying to lecture you, but I can't just sit and watch you do this shit. I want you to be happy and sober even if that takes you and I not being together. Now that you are hanging out with your old drug friends, I worry more. Why would you go back to that scene? Trey, you are so much better than that. I wish I could do something to help you. I feel useless like I follow you around and watch you. I want to thank you, though, because you have always treated me right. I am so happy with you, Trey; I would love for us to be together and see where it leads, but what future do we have together when you are unwilling to change. Let's compromise, and more than anything, you should do it for yourself. I know it's impossible to change

someone who does not want to change, but why wouldn't you want to? Why would you risk dying so young? You are twenty-one years old, isn't it time for you to grow up? You are talented and intelligent. Go for your dreams. You lack a reason to do all this shit. Last night, you told me you like getting drunk because it makes you depressed and enjoys being sad. Why? You seem so much happier when you are sober. I do not know, maybe I'm wrong, but you should learn to deal with depression without drinking or drugs. Start to sober up now while you are still young before it's too late. You say you cannot ever keep a girlfriend due to this. Change then. You have an awesome family who loves you and great friends who love you, and me who loves you. Aren't those reasons enough to change? Eventually, you will lose all that and have nothing. It makes me sick to think of not being with you. I wish things were different. I will marry you tomorrow. I smile when I think of you. I enjoy every second I am with you, and I hate going a day without being with you. God, I feel like a bitch always lecturing you but tough shit. I love you and care about you, so as long as I am in your life, you're going to hear it. If you and I do not end up staying together, I want you to know that I will always be here for you and support you. I cannot imagine you not in my life. I love you so much, Trey, and please start to listen to everyone. I know it's hard, but you better look because I want that wedding on the beach!
Love always, Lisa

Chapter 24

TREY FELT DIRTY IN THE MORNING. HE HADN'T slept well; his head ached. He knew he had to talk to Cameron, maybe about last night, maybe about Lisa? He wasn't sure. The anxiety seemed to ratchet up the intensity of the pounding in his head.

He picked up the phone, "I have something I need to talk to you about." Cameron held the telephone to his ear as he wondered what it was that Trey needed to discuss.

"Okay. I'll meet you at one o'clock." Cameron knew he'd been down this road before.

Trey was waiting for him at a neighbourhood park where a group of guys, five deep, formed a circle. Seth, the most brutal guy around, was in the middle. He stood in the centre of the ring with his shirt off and his fists tight. His temper was explosive. Once the sparks started to fly, there was little time to duck and cover. He shouted and paced, waiting for anyone to take his challenge. Finally, he eyed his opponent and stepped back to give him room to enter the ring.

Like trained boxers, they circled one another. It was fighting time. Tempers were hot until Seth threw his final punch and his opponent was down on the ground. He smirked, turned his back, and walked away, again eyeing his next opponent.

Seth was robust, coordinated, and wore a massive chip on his shoulder. "C'mon, any of you. I'll kick your ass." He challenged anyone stupid enough to fight. The next guy stepped up, and after two punches, he dropped to the ground. "C'mon, pussies! Anyone?" Seth screamed as his eyes caught fire.

Trey watched Seth kick the shit out of everyone who entered the circle. "Fuck that!" Trey stepped into the ring as Cameron tried to grab his arm to stop him. Trey watched Seth and headed to the middle as he clenched his fist, and a vein popped out of his forehead. Trey swung his arm with a coordinating punch, but it fell short. Seth stood back, waited, and then his fists connected to Trey's face and body. Tiny drops of blood ran down Trey's forehead and blurred his vision. He began to feel light-headed, his legs gave away, and he crumbled to the ground.

Cameron dragged his fearless brother from the park, knowing he was sick and filled with rage. He tried to wipe the blood from his brother's face and then shuddered when he noticed fresh tracks on his brother's arm.

"Leave me the fuck alone." Trey scrambled off alone as Cameron stood with tears in his eyes, feeling helpless, defeated, and confused. He still didn't know why Trey wanted to meet him there. He picked up the phone and convinced Lisa to go home to Trey.

*****

Each time that Trey opened his eyes to the morning light and realized he'd lived through another night was a surprise to him. After the shock wore off, his heart would start to race, and his palms would sweat.

It was Friday, the morning of April 9, 2005, when I picked Trey up at the bottom of the hill. There I would meet him at a local Quickie Mart to take him to his doctor's appointment.

The meeting with his doctor that morning was the same as it always was. The doctor explained that the prescribed drugs acted slowly and advised us to be patient. "Mrs Morelli, these prescribed drugs take time to work, but once they do, Trey will begin taking small steps towards recovery. I've seen many people in the same shoes recover in just a matter of months. He's young, and with your support and the prescriptions, I'm sure he will be fine." His words left me empty. He was sure that Trey would find sobriety. I had my doubts. After all, it hadn't been long ago when the doctor had claimed victory that Trey was close to being clean. We left, and after the forty-five-minute silent drive home, I dropped him off at his truck.

As Trey pulled out of the parking lot, an illegally parked truck blocked his view. He inched forward into the street to be sure there were no oncoming cars when a auto struck the driver's side door of his truck. The only sound heard was the crushing of metal. He found himself there, glued to the wheel of his wrecked truck. His muscles ached. His head smashed up against the steering wheel and his vision kept flashing from dark to white light.

Shrieking at his wheel, at himself, and, most importantly, yelling at the idiot driver who had crashed into him, he realized the exterior of his truck was damaged even worse than he thought it might have been. He took no responsibility for the mess. The woman climbed from her car, convinced that it was all Trey's fault. "You weren't watching as you pulled out of the driveway and left me no time to react. All I saw was your truck illegally entering the road!" He knew otherwise. He knew she was speeding, and the illegally parked truck had caused the accident. He grabbed his forehead with his hands, then reached for his phone and placed a call to me. He explained he was involved in a traffic accident. I dropped the telephone and rushed to Trey, who I found standing on the curb. He was shaken up and held by the police, who conducted a field sobriety test. I watched Trey touch his nose and walk a straight line. He successfully passed the test, as I knew he would. He'd been with me most of the morning.

After I noticed a small gash above his right brow and he explained how his head slammed into the steering wheel, I suggested he go to the hospital for a possible concussion, but he refused. Holding his head in his hands, he complained of a terrible headache. I invited him to come home with me, but he insisted on going back to his apartment, even though his headache continued to thump behind his ear. I finally gave in.

Once we got to the apartment, Trey insisted I go home. I put the car in reverse, inched out of the driveway, and drove off through the pretty town of Rancho. I drove up Avenida la Plateau, a steeply sloping street, and all I could think of as I navigated the steering wheel were the mistakes I had made. *I should have listened to the counsellors and played tough love; no, that wouldn't have worked. I should have been softer; no, I couldn't have been. I didn't care enough; no, I did. I was too tough on him; no, maybe not enough.* The questions and answers filled my mind as I searched for solutions. What could I have done differently?

A big party to celebrate my birthday and Cameron's would occur the following afternoon, yet I worried about Trey. I had unexplained anxiety that wouldn't go away. I reached for my Xanax. I only pretended to be okay. We had invited sixty guests, and I was as ready as I could be for the gala event, even though I secretly wished there would be no party.

Chapter 25

TREY DOESN'T WANT TO GO TO THE CASINO tonight...... He isn't looking forward to the loud bells and flashing lights. All he can think about is his splitting headache. His girlfriend, Lisa, has been a little quiet but persists in wanting to go. She needs to go out and blow off some steam. "Come on, Lisa, get dressed, and I will take you." She hurries to get dressed as Trey lights up a cigarette and tries to forget about his pounding headache.

Not long after Lisa disappears into the bathroom, she reappears in her barely-there black shorts, low-cut sequined tube top, and four-inch black heels. She throws herself into Trey's lap, letting her thick long blonde hair fall into his face. Trey laughs. "C'mon lover, let's go!" Her heavily made-up eyes are bright with excitement as they climb into her white Camry, making their way out for the evening.

Trey's headache continues to bomb as they drive ten miles to a buzzing local casino. They meander through the crowded high-limits area, happy and glad to be together. Trey sits down at the bar pulling an old crumpled twenty-dollar bill out of his pocket. He shoves it into the machine before grabbing Lisa's hips, guiding her onto his lap. After their drinks are gone and, a few video poker hands played, they give up and head to a place where a few friends are partying in the hotel room.

Walking down the decorated and quiet hallway, Trey notices how pleased Lisa is as she stops to reapply her lipstick in a mirror. She lines her mouth with blood-red lip liner and then fills in her lips with lipstick a shade slightly deeper. She glances at Trey, winks, and then blows him a kiss. "You'll get yours later." He mutters under his breath. They make it to the stark room filled with friends drinking and smoking pot while Marilyn Manson plays on the portable CD player. Trey's headache is pounding harder as he reaches into the cooler and grabs a barely chilled Bud Lite.

Newly decorated walls with soft pastels smell of nicotine in the nonsmoking room on the sixth floor. The downtown lights from the nearby city glowed in the distance. Blackout curtains hang in each corner, which begs use after a long night of gambling and drinking. The casino knows no time limit as the clock races forward.

Advancing toward two o'clock in the morning, Trey excuses himself to the bathroom away from Lisa and to a place where he finds peace. He methodically takes out his syringe, spoon, and lighter and places them on the marble countertop. He's done this so often he's not concerned about his surroundings, only consumed with his thoughts of what is yet to come. Next comes the tiny balloon with the $15-chunk of heroin wrapped in plastic, purchased from the guy in the room outside. He slowly places a small piece of tar onto the spoon and, using his lighter, he lights the flame. Trey watches as the smoke begins to dance, and once the dope turns into liquid, he sucks it up into the syringe. There's only a faint smell of vinegar as he wraps a thin rubber strap around his arm. His slender fingers press into his skin, prompting the tired vein to appear. His whole body shakes, anticipating the future that looms before him. Inserting the needle filled with heroin into his arm, he waits for the drug to flood into his system. He closes his eyes and drifts into slumber and fantastic dreams.

Lisa fills with worry each passing minute, deciding to search for him. A knock at the bathroom door finds no response. She places her ear to the door, afraid of what she'll hear, then catches weird choking noises coming from inside. Lisa tries to stay calm as her eyes fill with fear. She shoves the door forward and finds Trey convulsing on the bathroom floor. She can't believe her eyes. And now Lisa is seeing something her eyes won't be able to erase. Adrenalin flows through her veins, but she can't seem to move a single muscle, not even to scream. Utterly terrified, Lisa wants to run away. She reaches for him, white with fear, then rushes out of the tiny bathroom where Trey lays with his eyes rolled back and his body shaking. She feels as if someone is strangling her and can't breathe. Her heart is pounding. A choked cry for help pushes itself up her throat, and she feels a tear run down her cheek.

"Hurry, call an ambulance! Trey is fucking overdosing!"

One of the kids' shrugs and says, "Nah, he'll be alright." Though there is fear in his chest, there is none in his heart. Then one by one, by their moral ethics written in slaughtered ink, they condemn her and beg her not to call for help.

"Oh, c'mon, Lisa. You worry too much. He'll be okay; just let him sleep it off." Once again, fear finds her. She pushes back, grabs her phone, and dials 911 as the cowards, who would do anything to save themselves, file out of the room as quickly as possible, hoping not to be stopped and questioned.

The paramedics arrive at an otherwise empty room, where Lisa cradles a lifeless Trey and her phone. She steps aside and dials my number. Desperately trying to get his heart to beat, the paramedics pound his chest. "Come on, come on, start beating. Come on!" One of them continues pressing Trey's chest as he lies dead on the cold bathroom floor. Trey's brain starves of blood and oxygen for over twelve minutes, but a sigh of relief finally comes when he takes his first breath. The sigh is long.

"Oh my God, Leigh, he's breathing . . . he's breathing." Lisa sobs.

"I will meet you at the hospital . . ." Anxiety floods my system. My body wants to run fast for the hills, but instead, I stay right here while I try to digest what has just happened.

Chapter 26

MARCO AND I BURST INTO THE INTENSIVE CARE unit after the three o'clock call that morning and the long drive to the hospital. There we see an unrecognizable body lying on a gurney, with lines attached to his nose, mouth, and arm. A machine is helping his lungs inhale and exhale as he struggles to remove the tubes. The beep on the device is the most reassuring sound I hear, but it doesn't stop the dam of tears from bursting open as they roll down my face in a constant stream. Marco stands by the bed as I grab Trey's hand. *He isn't my son; it can't be my son.* It is all a dream, a nightmare.

After waiting in denial, I searched for the nurses' station and demanded to speak to the doctor. After a short wait, the doctor walks from behind the curtain. His face is like a brick. His movements are sharp and purposeful. He analyzes the chart for a few seconds and then looks up without emotion. Behind the gunmetal spectacles, his eyes are stone-cold grey, matching the washed-out bed sheet that covers the rollaway gurney. "We don't know much yet, but we do know he overdosed on some drug he shot into his arm at the hotel. He seized, which resulted in a massive heart attack. He was without oxygen for over twelve minutes. I've stabilized him by sedating him with medication but don't expect him to survive. I will update you if anything changes."

"Well, isn't it a good sign that he is trying to remove the tubes from his chest and face?"

The doctor looks at me. "That's agitation. His brain simply isn't processing fast enough for him to remain calm. I doubt he is even aware that he is doing it." I sink into the ground. *God, you can have him; it's your turn now.* Hours fly by while he lies on a gurney in the emergency room, shaking, posturing and comatose. The minutes turn to hours. We watch in denial without saying a word.

Twelve hours after his overdose, we leave the hospital and head for home, lost in thought and remembering with a shudder that our guests are going to be arriving within two hours. Once home, both feeling exhausted, I phone our guests, cancel the party, and swear there will never be another one. I struggle to hold back the tears. The doorbell rings while I am standing wrapped in a towel after a long hot shower. As I rush to change and notice the clock striking five o'clock, I meet our neighbours at the door. I forgot to call them! My eyes filled with tears. "Trey had a massive heart attack last night."

*****

We relocate our motorhome to the hospital's parking lot, where I can constantly contact Trey's doctors while they work to keep him alive. First, the tracheostomy is performed on his thin neck to assist him in breathing. His head leans heavily onto the pillow while the awkward tube climbs down his throat. Then, another surgery for the feeding tube is needed. Trey is ushered by the technicians down to the operating room. "It's a simple procedure." The lead doctor's words ring through my mind. One hour passes as the charge nurse at ICU approaches me slowly.

"The feeding tube mistakenly punctured Trey's colon; he needs surgery to repair it." I sobbed. *What? Another surgery? Why doesn't the doctor tell me he will be all right?*

This surgery leaves yet another scar with twenty sutures holding it together, straight up the middle of his stomach, just above his belly button. Trey didn't sign up for this. He thought all along that if he ever overdosed, he would die. He never dreamed this could happen to him.

I find myself worrying about Trey and his siblings. They have spent most of their free time with Marco and me at the motorhome and are utterly heartbroken. None of us, especially not any of them, ever thought this would be Trey's fate, and as the days get lost, I find it hard to stay positive.

And yet, another problem we face is our new puppy, Pinot. Although she's been in safe hands with Madison and Alexander, who have made it routine to take her to her puppy classes, she still needs to be with Marco and me where she belongs. God, she's so tiny, only a baby at eight weeks old.

It seems everyone in the city has decided to visit Trey. As the word gets out, we notice more and more people coming to the hospital. A line starts to form at the heavy metal ICU door. A bunch of random strangers seem to begin spreading rumours. "He's a vegetable." "He's going to die." "He drank himself to death." "He overdosed." "It was drugs." These murmurs echo down the quiet hallway. I need to stop this insanity—it's none of their business, and there's only one way to do it. Tears roll down my face as the nurses in ICU are put on notice. Trey's only visitors will be family. I don't want him put on display.

A call comes from the East Coast. "Sorry to hear about Trey. I'm heading to the West Coast to see you guys. I will be there on Thursday." Joseph is an old buddy of Marco's, a friend Marco hasn't seen in years, and a pal who would report his findings to the entire East Coast. A nosey friend who I didn't need to see.

"I don't want anyone to see Trey, Marco. I want you to call Joseph and tell him not to come." I'm serious but calm while Marco calls him and insists Joseph change his plans. Joseph agrees to our request.

Thursday morning arrives after many sleepless nights, and we awake to the RV's empty refrigerator. Still feeling uncomfortable letting anyone see Trey, we give up the defence and head to the grocery store. While we are gone, Joseph arrives at the hospital. He goes to the ICU and rings in to see Trey. The charge nurse tells him that the family doesn't want any visitors, but Joseph convinces her that he is Trey's long-lost brother from the East Coast. The nurse permits him in. After taking off his shoes, he stands over Trey in his long hemp tunic. His feet feel naked on the cold refrigerated floor, and his bald head shines from the fluorescent light above as he bows and delivers what he believes is a prayer to his demigod. He's brief as he studies Trey's jerking body. Not long after Joseph leaves the hospital, the nurses reported that Trey had a visitor.

"He's not his brother. Damn you, damn him!" I scream. As I lie in bed in our small motorhome that night, all the thoughts in my mind are of Joseph leaning over Trey, watching him struggle to stay alive. The image haunts me well into the small hours of the morning as the stress and betrayal go beyond anything I have felt before and never want to feel again.

*****

As Trey's neurologist reads the results of the EEG, he looks at me through his black-rimmed glasses. "There is no brain activity." He points at a scale that measures Trey's ability to see and recognize visual stimuli, make sounds and control motor movements. The lower the points, the worse the condition. The lowest score is a three, and Trey's scale is a three! *The score cannot be. He is going to come out of this at any minute. It's all a dream, a nightmare. I can't believe this is true because it's all a lie.* I have to see Trey. I motion to Madison, who helps me make my way back to ICU. The charge nurse meets us at the locked door. She is serious and has a careful look on her face. "At this time, I am sorry to say. There's nothing more we can do. Trey has been seizing for a half-hour, and we can't stop him." I fall into Madison and break down.

"I can't take anymore." We sob as I find comfort in her shoulder. We slowly pick up our telephones, and while Madison notifies family, I telephone Father John from our neighbourhood Catholic church, who I summon in for last rites. As I sit, absorbed in a thousand thoughts, I see a priest pull up in an old Ford sedan and walk across the crosswalk. He holds his Bible close to his heart under his clerical shirt. He enters the ICU unit, where our family grimly awaits. Father John begins absolution for Trey's sins, prepares his soul for death, leaning over his shaking body. Then, he starts praying for relief of pain as the five of us huddle around Trey and try to say goodbye. The afternoon is blurred as we try to make sense of what has happened and accept that it's true.

My cell phone rings in the morning. Trey has survived the seizures and has stabilized.

After being in the ICU for four weeks, he needs to move to a subacute unit, to wait until he is ready for acute rehabilitation. Trey is comatose, weighing 106 lbs., down from 147. His muscles are deteriorating; his body is dying while his organs fight to stay alive. He is storming, unaware of his surroundings.

We encounter obstacles as we search for the best possible place for our son while knowing it needs to be close to home. "Sorry. Our unit is full." The administrators disappoint us after each visit. The only available units are the unacceptable hospitals with pungent smells and a small staff.

"I am going to bring him home!" I scream after each tour. Marco doesn't speak. He only wraps his arms around me as we both cry. "We can sell everything we own and hire someone to live with us and take care of Trey." I cry through my irrational thoughts.

Then, the ICU nurse hands me a piece of paper with a hospital's name on it, saying she has heard good things about them. I call the number scribbled down on paper and schedule a tour. It's a subacute unit near the beach, nearly an hour and a half from home, but we go anyway. At first glance, it's clean, and after making the hard decision to move Trey there, we find their waitlist is six months out. "I will submit his information anyway." I hand the admissions clerk Trey's medical records. I feel defeated as we return to the motorhome.

Marco decides to leave the motorhome and go home for dinner and a shower before we return to the hospital in the morning. He heads to the deli for food in his truck as I drive home in our car. It's pouring rain, and the tears are falling just as hard. I blink tears from my eyes as I search for answers. I pray as I drive down the long and lonely freeway. Please, God, show me a sign that Trey will be alright. Please, God. I plead and promise to give anything for an answer. Suddenly, what appears are three beams of light shining down above our home on the hill. *Oh, My God, is this a sign? Is this a sign?* I wonder as I try to blink away my tears. What appears in the clouds makes me beg for more. The clouds begin to shift and spread into a beautiful angel. It's a sign, damn it. It's a sign. I pray the words. I can't wait to phone Marco and tell him about my experience. My voice begins to tremble then breaks. "I saw a sign, and I think I heard the angel sing." Marco cries while standing at the deli counter.

After our long and much-needed showers, we share dinner and gaze at each other, knowing we met with God today. Shockingly, the following day, Trey is moved to the top of the waitlist and will be transferred to the new facility in three days. Marco and I vow to Trey that he will never face a day without us by his side.

Chapter 27

THE AMBULANCE RACES DOWN THE FREEWAY
while lies Trey lies inside. The sirens are loud, and their lights
are blinking red and blue. They remind me of one night while
Marco and I watched Russell during his Friday night football
games.

Trey, at sixteen, needed money to expand his music col-
lection, buy musical equipment, guitars, and a new drum set.
He needed a job, which required a driver's license to get him
there and back, so I arranged for a class at our neighbourhood
driving school. The date for his first lesson of six was set as
Trey anxiously waited. He loved his new course and drove his
sleeping instructor from place to place. Trey hit up the local
hangout outside the bowling alley, waving at all his friends.
Next, he gave a quick honk, trying not to wake his instructor,
while he coolly drove by the high school and then up the hill,
where he proudly sped past our house. A solid week of driving
alone taught him well by goosing the engine everywhere in town.
He passed the driver's test in one swoop and displayed it in his

hand. He proudly showed it to whoever was interested. "Mom, can I borrow the Mercedes Benz for a couple of hours? I'll drive slow." I shook my head in disbelief. "Dad, can I borrow your truck tonight? I have plans with a new girl I met; I promise I'll drive carefully." He secretly nabbed a beer from the refrigerator. Marco couldn't believe he asked and, after a few weeks, finally broke down and bought him an old blue Toyota pickup truck to call his own. "He can upgrade after he grows up a little and has a bit more driving experience." Marco looked at me and rolled his eyes.

For a solid week, Trey drove his truck all over town, running lights, driving on sidewalks, and speeding. "I hope he doesn't kill himself." I cringed after watching Trey fly down Avenida la Plateau without a care in the world. "He's the last person who should have a license," I mumbled to myself.

After a few weeks of reckless behaviour, he successfully found a job. I hoped he would finally grow up a little. After the dinner hour, he washed dirty dishes and snuck a few cocktails while he dried them. He was happy with the few dollars he made and saved money for the items he needed. Then one night, as he cruised down the dark road after work, the police pulled in behind him and flipped on their flashing lights.

It was the last Friday night of the football season as Marco and I sat in the bleachers of the grand high school and watched Russell's game. We prayed Trey was safe. An hour passed, and then over the noisy crowd, we heard sirens that broke the sound of the game. We looked at each other and prayed to God it wasn't Trey. We heard our names over the school's PA system and learned Trey had gotten a DUI within fifteen minutes. Due to his age and the zero-tolerance policy in California, he lost his license for a year. Trey took residence at the Bear's Head fire *station again and washed fire trucks and floors for thirty days. He didn't seem to mind.*

With his truck and license gone, Trey seemed happy. He strapped his old guitar over his shoulder, jumped onto his older blue BMX cruiser, and headed down the two-mile hill. Trey raced down the street, lifting his feet off the pedals. As the bike zigzagged, scaring the drivers of the cars behind him, Trey imagined the looks on their faces. It was his bike, his freedom, and nothing could break his spirit. Nothing fazed him. He didn't care.

The crystal angel, a reminder of what I saw in the sky, hangs from my rearview mirror, and as it swings back and forth, I try to keep up with the ambulance in my car behind them. It seems like years before we arrive at the hospital, precisely one and a half hours away.

*****

Trey's strapped to a gurney, his arms tied down beside him as he arrives at South Beach Hospital's new home. Nurse Linda enters the room without breaking her stride. One moment she is in the hallway, her eyes straight ahead, and the next, she grabs Trey's arm to take a pulse. Her pasty-white face is round, framed by short red hair. Her eyes, bare of any makeup, are small and stern. Wearing a white uniform that cannot hide her ample breasts, she takes a breath and writes in her chart. "You must be Trey's mother." She looks up and makes eye contact. She is just five-foot-four, yet her controlling personality and extensive education put her in charge of the other RNs working on the floor. She points out that Trey has come to them with five staph infections and two bedsores. She motions another nurse to remove the rusty chain Trey wears around his wrist and sets out to assess his condition. Linda has seen it all before and is immune, hardened by repeated exposure and overwork.

The hospital sits on a cliff overlooking the most beautiful shoreline on the California coast. In the distance are Catalina Island and boats playing on the crystal-blue waters. The well-kept hospital runs efficiently. The highly polished floors are bluish grey, and the walls off-white. Above the ceiling are grid-like frames made of polystyrene squares. The light is bright, and I find it harsh. This place certainly isn't run by risk-takers. I should find comfort in that. Beside every door is a hand-sanitiser dispenser, which the nurses use before and after entering the patients' rooms. Their hands are rough and show visible signs of constant overuse.

The cramped Adventist hospital is on the hillside along a two-lane highway that wraps itself along the jagged Pacific coast. A small vacant chapel sits at the entry, reminding new-comers where they can find peace if they need it. The chapel is unlike any other that Marco and I have seen. It lacks windows and relics of other massive churches. The minimal pews are lined up in an orderly fashion with an empty pulpit in front. There are no stained-glass windows. There are only solid walls and wooden floors.

As we walk through the corridors, we notice the hospital is void of a heavy urine smell, and no patients are lying helplessly in its hallways. This place is clean and peaceful. Even though the hospital is far from home, the facility is the best one for Trey.

Today has come and gone as I gather my belongings and know that I must leave my son again. This time I won't walk across the parking lot to the waiting motorhome but will slowly step out the hospital door to my car and drive away, leaving him with strangers who won't hold him in their arms as I have.

They won't care for him the way I have or love him as much as I have. I feel the tired tears roll down my face as they cloud my thoughts. I pull onto the cold highway and drive into the darkness, not wanting to listen to my heart that tugs at me to stay.

I reach home and climb in between the sheets, and I feel a strange sense of peacefulness. Tonight, for the first time in a long time, I know where my son is and where he'll be. No more late-night calls. No more worrying. No more wondering if he's lying dead in the street somewhere. That, in itself, helps me drift off to sleep as I try to ignore the void.

*****

Marco and I return to the hospital early the next day, and Danny, Trey's new nurse, introduces us to the sixth floor. He speaks with a Bostonian accent making Marco feel comfortable and also miss his friends back home. Danny begins to describe the sixth floor. "It consists of sixteen rooms and originally reserved for elderly men who've had strokes, but as it grew, we began accepting others with different ailments."

The unit is divided by one central nursing station. On each side are eight rooms sitting side by side. By the elevator is a small exercise room outfitted with an electric bike and an old treadmill. Straps and belts hang on hooks above the small exercising mat. At the other end of the unit is the lunchroom that also lends itself as an activity centre. Next door to that is a cold room with a large circular table.

As we tour the floor, we meet the many patients. Andrei, whose a native to Romania, is a forty-one-year-old male patient who worked as the charge nurse here before he experienced an aneurysm that interfered with his promising career. The aneurysm left him aware but unable to move or communicate verbally. Andrei is in the room to the right as I stroll down to Trey's new room. "Knowing the doctors and nurses before his accident helped in accommodating Andrei with the only private room on the floor." Danny points out. "His wife Ana is here every day, waiting for him to recover." Ana's face is older than the thirty-eight years she has lived. Her Romanian heritage keeps her strong for Andrei as she sits by his bedside day after day. Her dark eyes are encased with dark circles, emanating the pain she has long survived. She has suffered so much since Andrei's accident.

Two doors down is Julie. Julie is thirty years old, overdosed on cocaine, seized, and then a cardiac arrest at age nineteen. Her parents dropped her off at the hospital, never to return.

Julie was the youngest patient ever admitted to the sixth floor. Her loneliness is felt on the whole level as she slowly withers and dies, by herself and scared.

Across the hall is fifty-five-year-old Paul, who has Huntington's disease. He can't hear or see anything. He has been obese for many years of being bedridden. His father has never given up hope, even after Paul's mother died of heartbreak.

Then, Christian lies there, two years older than Trey. He was hit by a car while riding his skateboard in a parking lot. He lays motionless while being kept alive only by medical intervention.

The list goes on and on, one patient after another whose stories are different, but all have two things in common. They are hopeless, and their futures are dim.

The sign on Trey's door reads, Isolation. "Slip on this paper yellow gown, gloves and mask every time you enter Trey's room." Danny hands me my gown. "You will also need to wear these paper booties. Trey is in Isolation due to his staph infections, and we need to keep his room sterile." Danny is educated and sounds professional. We wear the gowns over our clothes and notice how hot and uncomfortable we are. The plastic gloves, which come in only one size, are hard to slip onto Marco's hands. The mask's elastic band snaps my face while my plastic-gloved hand fumbles to find my ears. Danny tells us that this daily routine will continue until the infection is gone.

Trey's room, number 12, is as sterile as possible, with white walls, grey slate floors, and a thick cotton curtain drawn down the middle of the room between him and his roommate. His bed is closest to the window, overlooking a partial ocean view where homes are on tiny patches of land. His roommate, Jerry, is next to the heavy door that leads to the hallway. Jerry has been in the unit for several years after suffering a stroke in the middle of the night. His prognosis is poor due to his age and numerous staph infections.

Parking is limited, and cars line the narrow streets. As I look out Trey's window, I wonder how people live in such tight quarters, recalling the space we have in Rancho. His bed is small, nothing like he had at home, where he had enough room for another person. The sheets are clean, and the rough hospital blanket covers his frail body. A tear forms as I close my eyes and wish I could turn back time.

The liquid food bag hangs from a hook and measures how many ounces Trey is receiving. Another plastic bag from that same hook drips fluid and medication into the PICC line buried into his arm. His hair is no longer thick but thin and stringy. Danny motions; we deposit our gowns into the bin marked "Infectious Material." The nurses hurry in and out of the room, each time securing new gloves, a new mask and a gown.

Trey's legs kick about, but he is unaware of anything going on around him. He is "storming," as the nurses call it. They explain that he cannot control his reactions as he thrashes around. He has been in this state constantly since he came into ICU.

Room 12 is across the hall from Deb Dunne, the sixth-floor social worker. Here she keeps an eye on Trey as his legs jerk and kicks, and his body shakes. A bandage is used to conceal Trey's chin's abrasion and protects his chin from rubbing against the trach in his neck. His teeth clench as he wrestles with abnormally high body temperatures.

Deb is soft-spoken with a sweet disposition. Lean in stature; her straight red hair compliments her fair skin. She hands me the insurance paperwork that she has filled out for me. "You are fortunate that Trey qualifies for Medi-Cal. It will be paying the cost of his hospitalisation and care while he is here." She watches me briefly look at the paper on top, where I see a list of services Trey has received. The bottom number reads one million dollars! Trey has racked up that massive sum of money within seven weeks since his accident. I struggle to accept it as the seriousness begins to sink in.

Linda rushes down the corridor, and I overhear her conversation with Dr Striker, who leads the nurses in the subacute. "Trey's body temperatures are above normal, and he is highly agitated. Is it possible he is withdrawing from drugs?" Linda gathers her chart as Dr Striker looks up from his paperwork, impressed by Linda's instincts.

"I'll prescribe methadone and order some tests for AIDS." Dr Striker rubs his chin. *Is it possible he is withdrawing from the drugs, cigarettes, and the life he'd been leading for the past five years before all this happened?*

The substitute for heroin makes me uncomfortable. It's a Band-Aid, something he could become addicted to and have to withdraw from again. I wouldn't say I like it but lack another choice. I must follow the doctor's orders, or so I think. As the syringe is filled and added to Trey's PICC line, I see a stillness cross his face. A serenity that I have seen before. He is home again, finally at peace and comfortable.

Chapter 28

THE LETTER I RECEIVE IN THE MAIL SERVES AS notice that the first team meeting to discuss Trey's prognosis and plan of action is the first Friday of the month, June 3rd. Marco and I expect to be there.

Deb leads Marco and me to a big room at the end of the hall. At a large table, Dr Striker sits directly across from our vacant seats. The place is small, with a dirty window facing the salty ocean air. Deb Dunne introduces us. "This is Mr and Mrs Morelli, Trey's parents." We smile and take our seats, not knowing what to expect.

"I'm Dr Striker. I head the department. I've been here for ten years." He smiles softly. Linda, who reads her chart and states Trey's weight and medications, sits on his right.

Mona bursts through the door, realising she is late for the meeting. She is the head of the physical therapy department. Mona appears strong with long blonde curly hair pulled into a low ponytail. She's wearing a baggy worn-out sweatshirt with tight jogging pants below. She's barefaced with no makeup but seems friendly as she apologises.

"I'm sorry I'm late. I never seem to know what time it is. Next week, Trey will begin with stretching and range of motion, but I don't expect much from him. He's lost most of his muscle mass, and it will take years to rebuild it if we ever can."

Sonny, a speech therapist, smiles and reports. "Trey is not appropriate for speech therapy at this time." The same is said to be true about occupational therapy. They all gather around the table, introducing themselves and speaking of their plan for Trey until it's time for Dr Striker to talk again. He starts slowly.

"You both know Trey has a long history of drug abuse." He stares at the chart that sits on the table in front of him. "His accident left him bilaterally paralysed. His right elbow is frozen against his stomach and cannot move; his left leg does not react to touch. His eyes are locked in an iced gaze, which means he is blind." I look around the table and feel the coolness of everyone attending the meeting. "Trey will never recover. We don't expect him ever to walk, talk, or eat again. He won't leave this hospital. He's in good hands here, and you both should get on with your lives. We will do everything we can for him." Dr Striker concludes as he closes his chart. *I think of Julie's parents and wonder if they even attended one of Julie's team meetings.*

I look at the faces surrounding the table and watch them nod approvingly. I drift into the past, remembering I've heard these words before.

It was early afternoon when Russell and Cameron found themselves hopeless as they picked Trey up from the apartment and insisted he joins the rest of the family for a barbecue. Trey had become somewhat of a recluse and was now heavily addicted to drugs. We sat outside enjoying the beautiful sum-

mer breeze and pool when I heard Cameron scream for help. Trey was in the bathroom with a plastic zip tie around his neck in a half-hearted attempt to commit suicide. He slowly slipped it on and pulled the end tighter. He suddenly realised he may have tightened it too much as he gasped for air. Russell pulled out his buck knife to sever the zip tie but was afraid of cutting his thin neck. Cameron released it with his small pocketknife and then let out the scream. Trey gasped for air as everyone gathered around him, shocked that he'd consider such a thing.

I knew I had to do something. Trey pleaded that he needed help. Cameron was crying hysterically. This afternoon was entirely out of control. I had to decide that it was time for him to go for treatment. I quickly made a few calls looking for the best possible facility. "Bring him here. We'll take care of him." The receptionist told me.

As soon as we entered the psychiatric centre and Trey realised I had signed the admission papers, he began throwing chairs against the walls and swearing at me to take him home. "Fuck you; I didn't want to come here. Get me out of here, goddamn it. I swear to God I'll ruin this place!" He screamed as he picked up another chair and threw it against the wall, barely missing me. I told him to be quiet and that he was making a scene. He continued screaming, "Fuck you! I hate you!" He was hysterical.

"Trey, calm down!" I watched the whites turn a pure black in his eyes, and his irises glow a dark, muted, sage green. His lethal stare felt painful and piercing as if his glare were tearing my heart apart with a blinding dull light.

"Fuck you! You've always wanted to put me away somewhere! I hate you!" He spits, screamed, and then with his arm,

he cleared the top of the desk of books, the phone, and other items.

"Stop it!" I grabbed his arm. He reached back as if he were going to strike me.

Finally, an ex-marine nurse came around the corner to take him away. He was big, tall, and black. He calmly asked Trey if he would go with him voluntarily or involuntarily. Trey responded with a smile after realising the nurse meant business. As he led Trey down the stark white hall, I heard Trey ask, "Hey, Brother, are there any hot girls here?"

"Nope, you're in the wrong place if that's what you're looking for." The nurse turned and looked at me as he wondered what Trey was thinking. Trey never looked back.

Trey was introduced to the Psychiatric Center by the centre's nurse. His items were taken and placed in a secure vault. He was led down the dark corridor and shown where he would sleep. There were two rooms, just large spaces divided by a wall, and in each room were beds spaced four feet apart. One room was for the females, the other for males. Trey called me, collect, from a payphone daily, claiming he didn't belong there and that I needed to get him out. He said the first day he had woken up to a crackhead having a bad trip, and the next day he had heard a guy crying himself to sleep.

His pleas went unanswered after I heard he was introduced to confinement after the charge nurse found him in bed with a girl who was there seeking help. He called me frantically, "Mom, get me out of here! They've got me in a padded cell!" I waited a few days, and after he reentered the general public, I visited him. He was proud as he showed me off and introduced me to all the new friends he had made, many new friends. These friends wandered around looking for another smoke. They came in all ages and many styles. They were the tortured and the torturers. They all had one thing in common, though, which had brought them to the same place—mental illness. A court order followed Trey's inpatient psychiatric stint. It required him to visit an outpatient rehabilitation centre twice a week for six weeks.

Anger boiled deep in me as I sat at the table listening to Dr Striker. It churned within, and I knew it was too much for me to handle. The pressure of this raging sea of anger forced me to express the thoughts I had suppressed for weeks. I abruptly took Marco's hand, stood up, and without thinking, yelled out, "Fuck all of you!" I glared into each and everyone's eyes. "I don't care what you say. You don't know anything! Marco and I have been living in our motorhome for weeks to be near our son and will continue to do so until he returns home to us. We'll find a way to be here, and I promise every one of you he will recover!" We turned and slammed the door as we left them all in silence.

I struggle with my light-yellow gown as I try to hold back my tears. "I hate that man; he doesn't know anything. I hate him!" I cry while Marco holds me in his arms, and tears begin to run down his face. We sit with Trey while thoughts run through our heads but never say a word. *What if the doctor is right?* I wouldn't repeat the words I just thought. Shortly afterwards, we head for home in silence, knowing we need a well-thought-out plan.

Chapter 29

SATURDAY MORNING COMES, AND THE WEATHER matches our moods. The sunrise wrapped itself with freezing fog like a grey and damp blanket. The familiar everyday sights of the streets are quiet as we call together a family meeting. Marco pours the coffee as he looks at me. "Everything will be alright." His eyes question his words. Marco and I are strong. We have to be for ourselves and our family. The past few months seem long ago and a mere memory as we struggle to handle the stress.

"We need to talk." My voice cracks and I try to muster up a smile. I look into my three children's faces as I relive the team meeting. It doesn't go over well.

"The doctors don't know anything!" Russell snaps defiantly. His eyes seem on fire. "I will do what I have to." Cameron looks away, hiding his tears.

"We made a promise to Trey that he won't face a day alone," Marco repeats his vow to Trey to the kids.

One by one, the kids begin to volunteer their time to Trey. "I can be with Trey on Mondays after school and take Pinot to her classes on Thursdays. Don't worry about her too, Mom. She is doing great with Alexander and me." Madison volunteers her time. High school is merely a memory since she successfully was accepted at Saint Mary's College.

"I will go on the weekends. I can stay with Ray." Cameron lovingly puts his name on the schedule, then grabs for the phone.

"I'll go on Tuesdays and Fridays," I said as I planned my schedule and know both Marco, I and Cameron well cover the weekends. Marco arranges his schedule to be at the hospital on Wednesdays, and Russell promises he will make time when he is not at the fire department. The plan works out well, and I'm proud to be the mother of these three kids. They are solid in character, and the power of love makes them warriors.

*****

I'm comforted to know Madison will be at the hospital to-day. I'm relieved I don't have to be there and face the nurses after Friday's failed meeting. I will begin making calls to the hospital requesting an update on Trey's progress.

Emily answers the phone. "We don't have time to answer families' questions by telephone. That's the team meetings job." I knew at that point that the entire sixth floor knew about the meeting and thought to myself with a sarcastic undertone. *Really? What if we don't go to the team meetings?* Emily's nursing education comes from her homeland, England, and with it comes a thick accent. Her dark, straight hair moves freely over her chubby cheeks the way it had since childhood. Her black scrub uniform fits tightly around her hips, and the sound of her voice was to make me think she is in charge, which I already know that she isn't.

"Emily, I want to talk to Trey's nurse." She hears the directness in my voice and puts the phone down. She immediately calls the nurse in Room Twelve.

Candy answers the phone and reports the same information I've heard for weeks. "He's doing great. He is very comfortable and is progressing." *How does she know he's progressing? He's in a damn coma!*

I phone the hospital requesting paperwork, hoping to find something positive. All of the information is negative. I research terms that appear to appear in conversation or the medical records. Anoxic injury. Cortical involvement. Cortical blindness. I find hope in knowing that the swelling in his brain will decrease with time. *Or do I even know that there is swelling?* I look for answers the entire day. I speak to a successful psychologist woman who has had many years of school studying the brain.

Her voice is soothing as she speaks. "Leigh, you will need to be strong for Trey. It would be best if you learned to do everything you can to save your son. It isn't easy, but as a loving mother, you will succeed. I once knew a woman who was so committed to saving her son she offered herself sexually to various doctors in exchange for their help. I'm not suggesting you have sex with Trey's doctor, only that you prepare yourself to give anything you have for his recovery. He is a tight-budded rose beginning to bloom. He will slowly emerge, but it will take time and energy from you to help him."

There was something so warm, something that felt right in her words. I let my body sag; my muscles become loose. As she spoke, her voice cradled me as if I were a cherished child. In that embrace, I felt my worries loosen and my optimism rise. She continued, "You will begin to see changes in him, but you'll have to watch closely. His brain will begin repairing itself, and you will see his muscles begin to relax. You must take care of yourself for him and stay healthy. He will need you along the way. Please listen and follow this advice carefully."

The phone goes dead, and it feels like a dream. I awake at my desk as I realize I must have fallen asleep while working on my computer. *Was that conversation honest, or did I dream it?*

I am in a daze and feel lost as the phone rings. Lisa is on the phone. "Leigh, I have to give up the apartment. I don't have any money, and I'm late on the rent. I wanted to save it for Trey and me, but I couldn't afford it. My parents won't help me. I'm sorry. I can't do it anymore."

"Tell the landlord I will pay for the rest of this month, and you will move by the thirtieth," I said with a heavy heart as I hung up the phone and put the date on my calendar.

*****

Information about Stem cells is over the news. They are the "fix-all" for any ailment. They repair many kinds of damage done to the brain, so I search and buy some online. Could this help Trey?

I look forward to introducing Trey to the stem cells that came in the mail on Tuesday morning.

The phone rings. "Mom, I don't have school today, so I'm going to go to the hospital with you." Madison is devoted to Trey's recovery, and I'm thrilled to have her along for the ride.

"Ok, I'm leaving in fifteen minutes. I'd love to have your company and hear about your success in school. Can you be ready by then?" I smile as I speak to her.

"Yes. I'll be there in a few." She grabs her purse.

Driving over Deer Highway between home and the hospital is dangerous because the road is narrow and squeezed between mountain ranges and cliffs on each side. It snakes its way from the inland valley to the beach with two lanes and an occasional passing lane. Commuters frequent it during the week, and cafe-style bikers find it a field trip on the weekends. Impatient drivers flip off navigators of slower cars every day of the week.

I can't wait to get to the hospital today because I feel energized and excited. I feel encouraged. Once at the hospital, we slip past the nurses' station and enter Trey's room. He is fast asleep. His new roommate, Kevin, is motionless. Kevin suffered a heart attack at work one day, two years ago, and is one of the patients who doesn't receive any visitors. His wife gave up on him one day during the team meeting and left Kevin to be cared for by the nurses. It jars the memory of Dr Striker's words as I wonder if the first team meeting is the same for all families.

Madison's eyes fill with tears as she glances at her brother and remembers how close they were while they were growing up. She draws the curtain while I pull out the stem cells, which come in a green concoction ready to be shot into Trey's feeding tube. Madison watches for anyone who might enter the room. Once I filled and inserted the syringe into the stomach tube, I slowly pressed the syringe, which seemed somewhat clogged. I push a little harder but still no return. Then suddenly, the green stuff explodes all over his pyjamas and bedding. Oh, crap! I glance at Madison. "What should I do?" She rushes over, grabs a towel and begins trying to remove the green goop from the sheets only to make a bigger mess.

Sharon enters the room, a heavy-set woman in her twenties with big breasts and a deep jolly laugh. Her long bleached-blonde hair is held back with a white scrunchie. "Oh, my! Did someone have an accident?" Her dream of being a nurse begins as a certified nurse's assistant as she reaches for fresh sheets and proceeds to clean Trey up. She never says a word about the incident after that.

Chapter 30

TIME PASSES QUICKLY, AND SIGNS OF ROAD RAGE become common as I go back and forth to the hospital. As I drive, my thoughts begin to flood my mind. *What if he doesn't come out of or recover from the coma? What if Dr Striker is correct? What are Marco and I going to do if we lose him? What are the kids going to do? Are they going to be all right?* Then, a flash goes through my mind, and I remember seeing Dr Wayne Dyer on television. I remember him there on the screen as if it were yesterday. "What-ifs" are not reality. They don't exist. It would be best to concentrate on the present, the here and now. These words I repeatedly repeat under my breath, the here and now, the here and now. I need to focus on positive energy. I need to stay positive for as long as possible. I can't listen to the Dr Strikers of the world. I can't listen to the negative gossip circulating.

As I drive the angry road, I see people in their cars speeding by to get to work on time. Oh, how I wish I could be one of them. How I dream I could only think about work. I want to yell, "Go to Hell!" to all of them. I hate them because they don't have my life. I make myself calm down. I have to stop thinking. I need to force myself to stay positive and prevent my mind from straying. The tears start to well up in my eyes. Oh, God. My makeup! I'm a mess. How am I going to do this?

While I park my car at the hospital, I look into the mirror on the visor. I look horrible. My makeup smears under my eyes, and the circles are newly formed and dark. The last few months have taken years off my life.

I enter the stark elevator to the sixth floor when Deb Dunne gets on from the fifth. "Good morning." She's perky. "I have some great news for you. After you left on Friday, I met with the hospital's administrator and asked if you could park and leave your motorhome in the hospital's parking lot so you don't have to drive as much. After a few phone calls, they told me yes, maybe short term, but yes." I stand shocked. I want to hug her, but all I can do is cry as I remember the motorhome and how it came into our lives.

I was ready to take a gamble and make a deal as I agreed to take a look at my client's motorhome in exchange for my commission. I was proud that I'd had enough success in real estate to make this arrangement. "What the heck, let's have a look." I walked down old rickety steps made of two-foot railroad ties sitting on dirt and made my way to an old barn that had seen better days. Twenty years of rain and the baking summer sun had taken their toll on the structure. The building that kept the summer sun off the 1994 Airstream motorhome was broken down and weathered. The cedar shingle roof, the same as the house's that sat above it on a hill, was worse than the old windmill next door. It had missing and rotten tiles sticking up at strange positions. Inside sat the old, dilapidated motorhome, once someone's treasure. The tires were old, barely capable of holding the weight above them. The exterior had lost its shine since it had been on the road in its past. Inside, dust-covered, the once brand-new upholstery was now chafed and peeled. Rats that had taken a liking to plastic and needed a warm place to live chewed the wires. Dirty plates lay in the sink, and the old blankets were in threads. Rat droppings were everywhere. As a girl who could see the good in things, I saw a lot of potential despite its shortcomings. "I will take it."

Excitedly, Marco stumbled down the same path I had walked and opened the old barn door. "It needs work, and we'll have to have it towed home." He smiled. It wasn't long before we had that beauty on the road and looking like its old self again.

We lived in this motorhome at the hospital while Trey was in ICU. It's the same one that we moved to the parking lot at South Beach Hospital.

The parking lot sits below the tiered hospital on Coast Highway. It is where alcoholics and drug abusers fumble for cigarettes during their breaks from the court-ordered rehabilitation that the hospital staff offers. Backing the Airstream into the tiny parking lot wasn't easy. The parking area is long and narrow, and a spot is marked off by cones, showing us where our home-away-from-home will be. It will be easier to stay close to Trey and bring Pinot with us on the weekends.

*****

I stumble up the lightly lit path and make my way to the elevator. It must be midnight by now. The hallway to Trey's room is dim, and the nurses are quiet while the patients sleep. I sneak into his room and peer at Trey, overwhelmed by how much I miss him. I climb into the twin-sized bed beside my son, away from the cold air that chills my body. The full moon shines brightly through his large window as a constant stream of tears rolls down my face. I pull the small thin blanket over both of us as I gaze at him and tell him how much I love him. His body is cold, and the only sound is a whooshing noise coming from his trach, in and out. My heart pounds as I hold him close and know that I can't cling to him enough. I whisper to him. "Trey, I pray you can hear me. I promise I will never abandon you. I will always be at your side. I love you so much. Please come back to me. I need you and can't live without you. Please, I beg you. Please come back to me." Through the tears and sadness in my heart, I swear I felt his cold hand struggle to squeeze mine.

Occasionally, a nurse down the hall checks the chilled room and sees me cuddled up as I clutch the one thing I've lost, Trey. I lay motionless with my arms wrapped around his thin silhouette as I wondered how I would do this. How am I going to survive? I listen to the silence and feel my heart swell. I drift into total sadness, remembering holding him as a baby.

My heart aches as I think of the child with so much compassion, the boy the girls always loved, the funny teenager, and the person I adored. I close my eyes, and then memories begin to engulf my mind. They are the memories I so desperately want to forget. The memories I don't have answers. The hollow feeling swallows me, and I cry as the night slowly turns to morning.

*****

The month's end is nearing. Marco and I drive to meet Lisa at the apartment that was once Trey's and hers. She meets us with tears. The studio once alive with laughter is now dead. A cloud sits over the high roof, and a deafening silence exists as if everyone knows what happened to Trey. The once so nicely furnished living room now has only a couch that has gathered dust and has one of Trey's favourite flannels clinging to its arm. The curtains move as a breeze blows through, softly trying to comfort our minds. The bedroom still houses the king-sized bed that Trey loved so much, and where Lisa dreamed it would be the place where she would start their family. His closet is full of dirty clothes. I quietly sit while I fold them and place them into a suitcase brought from home. His favourite toothbrush and floss sit on the ledge in the bathroom. The refrigerator is empty except for a couple of cans of beer.

Sadness fills the place, and the air is cold. Trey hasn't been here for months, and Lisa is a wreck. She cut and dyed her long blonde hair. It's now short and black, which matches her spirit. Her eyes are heartbroken, and she can't forget the night Trey overdosed. I started packing the belongings that he stored on his nightstand. Old packs of crushed cigarettes are inside the drawer, and there are notes scribbled in his handwriting. Two, three, four bottles of Suboxone are there.

"Wasn't Trey taking his medication?" I look over at Lisa.

"No. Trey was giving it away." She grabs her pale cheeks and cries. "You know, I will always love him." Her teary eyes are tired as she watches Marco and I remove Trey's belongings.

Chapter 31

WE BARELY SURVIVED THE LONG THREE MONTHS since we came to South Beach Hospital in the middle of May. His bouts of withdrawal are finally over, and he now lies motionless. Mona doesn't care, as she bursts into his room and asks her accomplice to slide Trey onto the tilt table. She straps him firmly to the table and presses the button, forcing him into a standing position. His head dangles as his hair falls around his face. She jolts him with electric stimulation, trying to get a reaction. Nothing. Again, another jolt. Nothing. Tomorrow she will try again. She smiles and leaves as she rolls the tilt table to the next room.

Candy bounces into Trey's room with a cheerful attitude. She's Trey's nurse this week and begins her report. "Trey is having a good day today. He's listening to me. His weight is one hundred twelve pounds, up a pound from last week, and his vitals are all fine. I will be here if you need anything. Oh, by the way, one of the night nurses told me during their report this morning that someone has been calling Trey nightly." She flings the door shut with her red hair swinging behind her, humming enthusiastically. I can't help but wonder who has been calling.

My heart overflows with love as I think about my kids. I am so proud of them as they keep their promises to Trey. Russell's made time in between the hospital and the fire department to see Trey as often as he can, and he is the one who finds time to say goodnight to him each evening. Cameron spends weekends at the beach and Trey's side. Madison sees him every Monday, driving an hour and a half north up the crowded freeway from college. In between their designated times, one by one, they each find additional time to stay with Trey. I lie in bed trying to sleep, but my family weighs heavily on my mind. So many things have changed since Trey's accident.

*****

There may have only been 250 steps in total, but it felt like 1000 to Cameron as he climbed the stairway from the beach to the main highway in front of South Beach Hospital. He wasn't thinking about the beauty of the California coastline, the blue waves crashing on the sand behind him, or the tide pools filled with an abundance of sea life. He only thought about the many memories he had had with his brother in their younger days and the emptiness he felt inside. He had never experienced this kind of hurt before. Every memory played like a song in his head, repeating itself for what seemed like forever. He was lost, and a big part of him was gone, vanished into thin air. He thought grief was something foul, but he learned that it was just the price he had to pay for loving someone so much. He missed Trey, and there was nothing he could do to bring him back. He thought about his brother with his daring brown eyes, wily heart, torn mind, and kind, tortured soul as he entered the elevator on the hospital's first floor with Lisa and Kelsey.

The phone scares me as it rings. It's Cameron. Gosh, it's 9:00 p.m. His voice skips with excitement. He sounds pumped, excited, and more alive than he'd been in months. "Mom, you won't believe it!" He is in tears as he speaks, "I walked into Trey's room with Lisa and Kelsey about an hour ago. It was quiet as usual. We weren't planning on staying long due to the dark drive home. I was joking at first and started teasing Trey about his bedsheets. 'Hey, Bro, you look like you're pitching a pup tent!' Under the loose covers was his boner!" He was out of breath as he positively howled and could hardly breathe from laughing. Fat tears rolled down his sun-kissed cheeks, and it was several minutes before he continued. *I can't help but wonder if that's cheering in the background as I hang on to his every word.* "Trey, all of sudden, burst out laughing uncontrollably. Tears were rolling down his face so hard, and he couldn't stop!"

"What? What did you say?" OMG! I hear nurses' voices yelling for others to join them.

Even Nurse Linda was there. Cameron passes the phone to an impatient Lisa.

"Oh, my God, Leigh! He's awake!" Her voice screams into the phone. Adrenaline was coursing through her veins. Her hands trembled, and her eyes were wide. She was animated and chatty. It was like she'd stored up the last few months' worths of talk, and it was all spilling out now.

"He's out of the coma! I can't wait to see him and tell him how much I love him!" I scream to Marco, looking at me like I've gone mad. He can't comprehend what has happened. It felt like a bad dream.

Enthusiasm fills me as Marco, and I head to the hospital. Driving through the mountains on Deer Highway seems fresher and more alive. I can't believe this is true. It's a miracle I so desperately needed. We pull into the hospital's driveway and jump into the elevator, racing to the sixth floor. It's midnight by the time we arrive, and Trey is sleeping.

I lie in our bed in the motorhome and can't sleep as I anticipate this nightmare has come to an end. We hustle up the stairs after a short night of sleep and find Trey is still sleeping. *Damn it! Wake up!* We sadly walk down the corridor as I see Linda hurrying towards us.

"Do not get your hopes up," she declares, "This is rare and probably won't happen again." It's her this time who doesn't believe what she is saying. "You will be at the team meeting this morning, right?" She coldly walks away.

I'm amazed as Marco and I sit at the round table, waiting for an explanation of what had happened last night. No one wants to talk about it. I've been to three of these meetings now and know the routine. Doctor Striker begins by reassuring me that my life needs to go on. *Goddamn it! What about last night?* Linda again claims it's a fluke and probably won't happen again.

Mona reviews the past few weeks' sessions and never brings it up. Sonny and David still refuse services to him. On and on, the team meeting continues to disappoint us.

Disgusted and feeling sick inside, Marco and I leave and decide to avoid future team meetings. As we make our way into Trey's room, we are left with mixed feelings as he lies in bed without a look on his face. His eyes look straight ahead. I move closer to his bed. "Trey, can you hear me?" His expression doesn't change. "Trey, I heard about last night. Cameron is so happy!" Then, a slight movement of his lips appears that turns them slightly up. "Are you smiling?" We hadn't seen the grin that cracked his face since before he started using drugs. It continues to grow bigger as I look over at Marco. "See? Everyone is wrong."

Chapter 32

THE MOTORHOME HAS ONLY BEEN AT THE HOSPITAL parking lot for three months, but it's time to move, Deb tells us. Some arrogant neighbour complained enough to the city to require us to leave. I wondered how the motor home being there was hurting him as I studied the sadness on Deb's face.

We are at one of the most active beaches in California, where the cars line the streets and the parking lots are full. The cosy restaurants are full of beachgoers, and the beaches are crowded.

After planning our next move, we first visit the stuffy yacht clubs that we notice have designated parking lots. We receive cold stares as we state our needs. We feel desperate as the county directs us to the County Director of Parks. They permit us to move the motorhome to a parking lot at one of the few motels on the dock, The Inn at the Harbor. It's a short term solution, but we are relieved.

The shaded parking spot is perfect. It overlooks one of the most beautiful harbours in Southern California at Dave's Point.

It's filled with gorgeous yachts, some over fifty feet in length and fishing boats that can't wait to race to win the biggest catch of the year. Rented slips line the harbour, and the ocean air is alive with joggers and cyclists. Tourists come from everywhere to see the beauty of Dave's Point. The pier is only a mile from the hospital and is perfect. We feel fortunate.

*****

Linda is wrong about her last prediction but refuses to admit it. Trey has moved into a different level of consciousness, emotionally unstable. He laughs, then breaks down and cries for no reason. Mona continues to strap Trey to the tilt table as he laughs uncontrollably and turns every shade of purple. She teases him as his head dangles and his long hair falls into his face. She fondly directs a fan towards him, trying to cool his high body temperature.

Marco finds pleasure in making Trey laugh, reminding him of experiences before his accident. "Remember when you purposely dropped your hammer from the second floor of the framing job? It almost hit Robbie, my superintendent." Trey breaks into laughter and strains as the emotion takes over. The laughing creates a small vacation, a blessed relief from stress that has shoved its way into Trey's brain. The laughing is contagious, and nurses begin smiling. It's uncontrollable. He listens intently for the following reason to laugh, and then like a light bulb, he starts sobbing instantly.

I'm happy he's awake. Or is he? Studying Trey's face, I wonder who is in there and what he's thinking. His eyes are raw, blind, and without direction. He is a ghost as he lies contently in his bed. He can only listen and laugh as he stares blankly towards the white wall, no matter what is happening in his room. Doctors come and go, asking him to focus on a pen or move a limb, but all he can do is chuckle. His body remains limp with paralysis in his left leg, and his right elbow is bent and held tightly against his body in a locked position. His body has no evident feel as he is poked and jabbed by medical instruments. His neck is weak, and his head dangles uncontrollably, while his hands and wrists are stiff. His shoulders cave into his chest, and his once-tan skin is pale and lifeless. It seems the only thing left intact is his hearing and, somehow, through my eyes, his brain seems sharp.

*****

I follow Marco down a long sandy path to a nearby bar called Turgos. The bar is small and sits right on the pier's edge in Dave's Point. The view outside the bar is of the white-tipped seagulls that own the sky. Their wings flap in the salty air as they fly towards unused bait that fishermen are throwing into the water across the harbour. We enjoy watching them against the cool breeze and clean air.

Looking around for a seat by the window, we struggle past the lines of dirty sailors seated at the bar. Everyone knows each other as they wait for their favourite cocktail. Our friend and local bartender, Jamie, greets us with big hugs and smiles. We've known her since Trey first came here. I wait as she mixes my favourite Lemon Drop martini before I order.

"How is Trey doing?" She asks as I take a sip.

"Better than expected and still gets a kick out of himself. The doctors are concerned about his vision and don't know how much he will progress." She looks fondly at me with her curly red hair. She is from Wisconsin, and her accent reflects that. "I bought some equipment that I hope will help his brain, but I'm struggling with attaching the electrodes to his scalp. Sometimes neurofeedback, which is direct training of brain function, lifts his spirits or puts him to sleep. I learned the technique from a doctor who has a clinic in Pasadena. I even got Dr Striker to approve its use in the hospital. Isn't that a small feat?" She smiles and then rushes to another regular waiting for his third drink. Spending time in Turgos is easy as the jukebox music sounds throughout the area.

Marco and I start arguing as the sun begins to set and the seagulls disappear. The vodka gently fogs our minds, and the stress becomes overwhelming. Questions about Trey's recovery lack answers as we try to find something positive to talk about. We only cope with the pressure by throwing blame at each other as the anger grows thicker. Finally, the napkin lands in the food, and we storm out. Jamie has seen this all too often as she feels the pain we are experiencing. She walks over to the jukebox and drops another quarter in as sadness fills her mind.

The old Airstream eagerly awaits us after a long silent walk home. Marco turns on the television as I slide in between our cold sheets and pray to God that things will change.

*****

Mona doesn't usually work with Trey on Sundays when the floor is quiet, and the nurses can't wait for the day to end, but today, she straps him onto the tilt table and then commands him, "Lift your head." Showing by example, she moves his head up and away from his chest. "Lift your head, lift your head." She forces his head up. She's impatient and relentless as she attaches electrodes from her electric stimulation device to the back of his neck and then stands back and commands, "Lift your head!" She turns the knob clockwise, increasing the frequency. His head slowly begins to rise as his muscles contract, and he yells out with agony. His stifled groans turn to screams. He fights to form words to tell her to stop, but it is no use. Then he goes quiet, just panting. She demands his cooperation, but he just plain can't. He has wet and teary eyes and his face glowing red as he tries to do what his therapist asks. His legs begin to shake; his face closed in a scowl, his skin goes white and clammy. Every few minutes, he screams as she increases his standing time, knowing how essential it is that he keep his bones strong. It has a raw quality, the realness of a person consumed by pain that knows no limit. I should be there at his side, at least, then, he would know someone cares. But instead, I stand outside his room, unable to bear it.

After eight consecutive months of constant work, he succeeds and lifts his head. His neck is strong enough to hold his head up now. He is finally healthy enough to sit in a wheelchair in the hallway and away from his stale bed. We have weathered the storm as Trey overcomes the emotional instability. Although his speech is unrecognizable, he demonstrates incredible humour, and permission to take him outside is fully granted by the hospital staff.

The ocean's air is fresh, and spring's sunshine on his face makes him smile. The sound of a neighbourhood trash truck is familiar as if we remember it from so long ago. Marco's joking is becoming therapeutic, and he gets a kick out of imitating the crows and making Trey laugh. I continue with the brain machines inside but find more peace outside as another day passes.

*****

I feel the warm air and cool breeze as I sit outside the hospital with Trey in his Gerry chair. I am depressed today because the reality that I've lost my son is becoming more real. The days of thinking he will snap out of this are coming to an end, and I've resigned to the idea that he won't. I've seen how helpless he is. Will he always need me? It makes my heart jump as I sit and think about his future. I suddenly feel lost and hopeless. He indeed destroyed his life and messed up his brain. It's hard to know just how much will come back, if anything at all. I don't know if he will ever live on his own again or if he will rely on the hospital staff to care for him. I'm not sure if I can spend the rest of my life driving to Dave's Point from Rancho and then back again.

I'm mad this accident has stopped my life to a near standstill. I'm angry I have sacrificed so much. I love him so much, yet I know how he was before this happened. He didn't give a crap about anything. "An eye for an eye," he once said to me as I stood at his bedroom door and watched him jam the needle filled with heroin into his arm. I couldn't reach him in time as he nodded off into his favourite place, nothingness. As I slammed his door behind me, tears fell from my eyes, and I cried, "I hate you" under my breath while feeling helpless and as alone as he was.

I'm sorry I have abandoned my other children that I love so much, and I feel jealous of others who have not had to go through this. This accident has destroyed our family structure, and I want my life back. I miss Russell, Cameron, and Madison. I miss seeing them happy. I miss being at home with them. I cried when Russell told me he was giving up his career at the fire department. He said he couldn't be away from home now that

219

Marco and I were tied up at the beach every weekend. Russell couldn't keep his mind off Trey. He was sad this happened to Trey and wanted to return to the family business to be close to Cameron and Madison.

I miss being successful. Will I ever be successful again? Do I have time to feel good? Can I help my son? Trey sits in his little world, talking in his indecipherable garble to the black crow on the line. I want to grab him by the neck and shake him. I'm sad. A part of me is mad, angry that this has happened. Should I have dropped him off after his accident and never returned? Could I have done that? I'm scared to know about his future. I'm afraid to be informed about his vision because I already know. He's blind. I wonder how he will live without his sight.

I dream that I could turn back the hands of time and redo everything I did in the past. I wish I had seen the warning signs sooner. I could have acted differently. Maybe I'm the one to blame. I question if I was inadequate as a mother. I slowly take Trey back to his room, feeling empty inside.

Chapter 33

FIVE MONTHS HAVE FLOWN BY, AND NOW WE must leave our perfect location. "We're getting complaints from other campers demanding to know why they haven't had the same courtesy extended to them." The county worker was polite as she said the words she had jotted down at the meeting earlier that morning. *We've overstayed our welcome at the Inn on the Harbor!* By now, we're familiar with Dave's Point, and we both know that our options are running thin.

"I will worry about this tomorrow." I agonize as I drive over to the hospital while Marco naps in the motorhome. With a smile and a drink waiting for me upon my return, he's excited to give me some good news.

"Guess who I just talked to this morning? I called Dave's Point boat storage and talked to the manager. For a short time, we can keep the motorhome there." His eyes are bright and thrilled with his news. I'm relieved but tired of staying in such cramped quarters. Our motorhome has served us well through these trials, but I can't stand it anymore and need more space.

"I want to buy a new motorhome. Who knows how long Trey will be in the hospital? We can trade this one in on a new one. It would lift our spirits. What do you think?" Marco breaks down and agrees, knowing he can't live this way either. I can't wait to get home and start looking for our next escape.

*****

The Internet cursor blinks as I begin typing into the search line. "Rancho motorhome for sale by owner." The return results come back quickly.

"Nearly new Monaco Motorhome, low mileage, leather, three slides, surround-sound entertainment system." It sounds perfect. I call the number on the screen to make an appointment to see it.

"One o'clock is perfect. I'll see you then."

The drive is slow, and the summer heat is starting to get to me. Over the bare hill, I see it sitting there in all its glory. The RV is like a dream. I shake the owner's hand. He opens the door, and I walk into a more relaxed place. The double-front slides are open, and the seating area is enormous. I notice the leather couches are in near-perfect condition, as the owner points out a few more features.

"The entertainment centre is already hooked up to a satellite signal. It has eight overhead surround-sound speakers." He hits the remote control and turns the volume up. "The kitchen has real tile flooring, and the dinette has four upholstered chairs, no ordinary built-in dinette. The countertops are granite, and the entire coach is cherry wood." The owner narrates as I walk through the motorhome, explaining the various upgrades.

"I even had a customized king-sized bed ordered to fit in the back bedroom." He boasts.

I can't wait to tell Marco what I have found as I speed home. Marco succeeds in selling our old motorhome, so I'm happy to move forward with the purchase.

Our new deluxe recreational vehicle is moved into the boat storage yard at Dave's Point harbour and sits among mostly old boats and trailers. The excellent location is near a grassy hill bordering the nearby restaurant row—the restaurants on the waterfront range from mom-and-pop cafés to more elegant five-star dining. The spot is a mere stone's throw away from our favourite local hangout, Turgos, and just a block from the sandy beach. We feel like royalty in our new coach.

*****

After parking on the hospital's basement level, we enter an empty service elevator that shoots directly to the sixth floor, the only tier that permits therapy dogs. Pinot is greeted enthusiastically by the hospital staff and knows where to find Trey as she rushes past the other patients' rooms. She is too small to jump onto Trey's raised hospital bed, so we lift her fifty-pound body onto the mattress, where she instinctively knows what to do. She gives Trey kisses by licking his face. I reach down and pet her, then kiss Trey on the forehead. She's grown close to him over the past year, knowing something must be wrong. Many weekends by Trey's side make her almost human-like. Her understanding and kind nature make her one of a kind.

We realize lunchtime is near as we walk to the car. We decided to treat Pinot to lunch, so we headed over to our favourite Deli on the pier named Pierside Delicatessen. Today, the boardwalk is alive, with joggers and bicycle enthusiasts out to enjoy the Southern California weather.

"What type of dog is that?" The jogger runs down the boardwalk in the warm ocean breeze.

"She's a Catahoula-Pit bull mix." I notice him slowly go by, twisting his head to get a better look at her. He swerves, just barely missing the curbside.

Another passerby stops us and inquires, "Is your dog a pit bull?"

"She is half Louisiana herding dog and the other half pit bull." Marco is proud of his little girl as he shows her off to people on the boardwalk as she prances about showing off her personality and beautiful coat.

We stop off at the Deli, where Gina, our server, welcomes us. She knows what our order is and orders it while we wait at our outside patio table; A hamburger patty and fries for Pinot, a chef salad for me, and a Philly cheesesteak sandwich for Marco. Pinot's tail doesn't stop wagging as she licks her plate clean, being sure not to miss the smeared catsup left behind.

We finally finish lunch, leave, and walk Pinot back to the car. We park the car in the hospital's parking lot and see Pinot's tail wagging. She's anxious to get back to Trey. She's aware that Trey can't react to her, so she waits to be lifted onto his bed, where she finds peace with a full belly of food and sleep at his side.

*****

"Doesn't anyone hear the sounds Trey is making, or is it just me?" I ask Sonny, the speech director, as I struggle to understand why she doesn't want to work with him. I dodge the look on Sonny's face as I say, "Don't get mad at me for hanging around, okay? I'm not giving up, and I've got loads of time."

" Say "A". Acting just like a speech pathologist; I sit directly in front of Trey.

"AW." Trey tries to imitate me but can't make eye contact.

"No, say A," I repeat, showing a little bit of frustration.

Again, he says, "AW."

"Okay, good. Now, say A." I refuse to give up while Sonny watches and her ego inflates.

"You know, Mrs Morelli, he doesn't have any ability to swallow." Sonny volunteers her expert opinion as I roll my eyes. She plops an ice chip on his tongue, and it slowly melts and drips out of his mouth.

"Okay, but do you hear the sounds that he is trying to make?" I'm becoming more frustrated. She's annoyed by my question.

"That's just yelling. I can't work with Trey until he stops that!" Her eyes are on fire as she turns and walks out of the room.

Disgusted and in disbelief, I go to the kitchen and grab a Styrofoam cup filled with ice. The first attempt is sloppy. I place an ice chip in Trey's mouth, and it melts, and drool runs down his chin. I ask the nurse for a towel and then make another attempt. It melts again. I know he can do this. I know it. "Trey, keep this ice chip in your mouth," I demand. It melts.

"Say A," I repeat.

"Aw." He yells.

"Say A." The frustration is evident as it builds. "Say A." I get an "Aw." I'm discouraged as I search the kitchen for a tongue depressor. No luck. I feel like screaming. *Does anyone have a stupid tongue depressor?* Suddenly I hear a faint "A." *Did I hear him say "A?"* I wait. Another "A." Oh my God. I rush into his small hospital room. "Did you say A?" He breaks into laughter.

*****

The September 2006 boycotted team meeting surprises us when I find a note on Trey's table in his room. "The administrators have decided to give you permission to take Trey out for the day." The letter has a waiver beside it. "South Beach Hospital Sub-Acute Department relinquishes all responsibility for Trey Morelli while he is not on hospital grounds." I sign it with excitement and leave it at the nurses' station.

It's a beautiful Saturday morning. We leave the hospital carrying Trey's backpack filled with items he'll need for his first outing away from the flat sixth floor. In the sack, we find gauze pads, sterile water, a suction device to clear his airway, a small bag of liquid food, and a syringe. I'm comfortable caring for him for the day and am eager to use my brain machine on him in the motorhome. Marco has parked the motorhome in a day-use parking lot along Coast Highway in front of the grand Pacific Ocean. It's Labor Day, and the beach is crowded with many families as our group begins to arrive. The excitement of having Trey with us for the day is beyond belief.

The lifeguards' station is a half-mile away down a long stretch of sand. Marco and I walk along the water's edge, dodging the waves and holding hands, to pick up the beach wheelchair loaned to us for the day. We can't wait to sit Trey in it and watch his expression change.

The chair is a comfortable ride for Trey in a reclined position with its sizeable cushy balloon tires and tall padded back. It glides through the sand easily as he leans his head on the headrest. Russell can't wait to get going as he grabs the handlebars and pushes Trey along the graceful arc of sand, glittering under the summer sun. The waves roll in with a soothing sound; the salty water caresses Trey's lips. Waves' spray makes them both laugh as Russell pushes him faster. Soon the laughter takes over as everyone watches on. Trey grins from ear to ear.

Cameron, Alexander, and Russell sit back, talking, with a beer in their hand as Marco barbecues hamburgers. Madison and I cut up vegetables in the motorhome while Trey peacefully sleeps under an umbrella with Pinot beside him. The sun has caressed his face making his pale face pink.

As time elapses, I sit here amongst the saline ocean shore, reflecting on my life and what has brought me here. I notice the water crashes violently against the golden sand as the amber sun glistens elegantly in the pale blue sky and begins to sink behind the horizon. As clouds start to form, we realize it's time to return Trey to the hospital, but know this is only the beginning. Marco and I will continue to pack Trey's belongings every Saturday morning and take him away from the hospital. He needs to feel normal and accepted; this is the only way to progress.

Marco and I slowly put some of our belongings into the car as we pack up to go back to our spot in the boatyard and wonder what tomorrow might bring.

Chapter 34

AN OLDER MAN WAVES, TRYING TO GET MY attention as I pull the car into the parking lot at the hospital. "Is that your son I see you with?" There was a kindness in his smile, a gentleness. Yet, most of all, he looked as though he just wanted to help.

I am pleased to see he wears a name tag on his long white jacket as he walks towards me. His movement is unhurried, choreographed, and deliberate. He has a non-threatening face as he reaches for my hand.

"Yes." I extend my arm and, without fear, shake his hand.

"I would like to introduce myself. I'm Dr Brown. I work here at South Beach hospital as an anesthesiologist. I've wanted to talk to you but didn't want to interrupt you and your son. He continued to speak with sincerity in his heart. "My mother had a stroke years ago. After a few years passed, the doctors deemed nothing further could help her, so I brought her home. Have you heard of Hyperbaric Oxygen?"

******

Through the beautiful hills of Viejo and a few miles east of the beach sits a hyperbaric- oxygen clinic located in a shopping mall filled with empty stores. The clinic is impeccable and houses life-size cylinders holding oxygen tanks that are pressurized and controlled. Working towards the best possible recovery for Trey, Marco, and I read the benefits of HBOT. "It enhances the body's natural healing process and delivers 100% oxygen to the brain via a face mask." One of the pamphlets left on the table near the door at the clinic is in my hand. I wonder if Dr Striker will consent to this.

The employees at South Beach Hospital realize now that Marco and I aren't planning on going anywhere until Trey leaves the hospital. We've made it clear we will keep our promise to Trey and won't listen to any bad advice given to us. We return to the hospital, where we find Mona and explain the benefits of the pressurized air. We are pleased she agrees that it's worth a shot. We speak to Dr Striker about it. He's sceptical. "I guess it can't hurt." He permits us to take Trey three times a week.

While driving back and forth to the clinic every other day, I feel excited and hopeful we have found a remedy for Trey, and I look forward to returning to my old life.

We pass the now familiar neighbourhood in Viejo as I begin noticing how affectionate Marco has become towards Trey, who sits shotgun in the front seat. He's sitting in the place that used to be mine. Marco's firm yet gentle hand rests on Trey's knee as I look on from the backseat trying not to watch. But as I do, I remember how it felt and how he caressed my thigh long before Trey's accident. I long for that touch. I see the fondness for Trey in Marco's eyes as I stare into them in the rearview mirror. For a moment, I look away to hide the tears that are beginning to form because I know he wouldn't understand.

I realize not only my relationship with my children has changed, but so has my marriage to my husband. I was always home with dinner waiting, but that has changed. What has happened to me? I feel like such a failure as envy begins to build. I'm jealous that my son has taken my place in the front seat? I try to look away, but the stark reality hits me square in the face. I cry inside as I watch, wishing I hadn't noticed it from the beginning. Marco and I tried hard to hold it together, but the stress has gotten the best of both of us. We argue more frequently, and Marco's stress level is high. He's torn between work and Trey. The only thing I have to talk about is Trey and his slow but steady progress. The time wears on, and we are both tired. I can't get it out of my mind as I struggle to sleep once we get home.

*****

The morning is met with new promise with the orange and red colours of the sun as it pokes its head over the mountains. The brilliant light of hope shines in the mysteriousness of life. All that keeps us alive is hope. It keeps us secure and helps us get through our most challenging days. Hope leaves a smile on our faces even when things look down. It's a promise that success is just around the corner. Hope is when a person glances past the loss of a loved one and beyond negative words. There is hope in my heart, knowing it's all I have, and I plan to spread its positivity to the families on the sixth floor, to the ones who lost their hope years ago. I put up signs in Trey's room— "HOPE." I tell the nurses about hope and the dreams I have for Trey. As I pass by patients, I smile, knowing they will be alright. I visit with their families. It becomes a habit, and I'm obsessed with thoughts and positive feelings.

Carrying a handmade sign that reads "Keep Hope Alive," I pass Candy in the hallway as I enter Trey's room. *Hmmm, where should I hang this?* I look around the room. Finding a small tack, I brought in my purse; I picked the sign up, and by using my thumb, I forced it into the thin drywall behind the television that's hanging from the ceiling. You can see the sign peeking out just under the screen from Trey's bed. That's perfect. I read and reread it.

"Candy, look at this beautiful sign I made for Trey's room this morning." I point to it. "Oh, gorgeous!" She admires the work I've done. Little do I know, Candy comes from a family of well-known artists and has a very artistic side to her soul.

"I'm going to make a few more for the other patients' rooms." Pride consumes me as my eyes well up with tears.

While I continue to admire my new sign, a note drops on the table in Trey's room. The letter addressed to me is from the director. "We have to meet today," It says. A shiver runs down my spine as the fear grows. A rush of blood runs through my veins. Trey's not ready for discharge, and they know it. As I enter Joe's office, the door closes behind me. "Mrs Morelli," he begins. "Please have a seat." He points at the chair in front of his desk. Two seconds pass when he calmly looks up at me. "Please stop speaking of hope to the families." I look into his hard-pressed eyes and remember all the times that I sat in front of the high school principal when the kids did something wrong.

"Why? That's all we have." I continue to glare.

"You are promoting false hope on the floor. There's little hope for most of the patients here. They are terminal and wait- ing for peace. You continually put me in a bad position. You've

231

encouraged the families to believe their family members may survive, and when they don't, the families come to me for an answer." I stare into his eyes as my mind races with questions. *How dare you take away the only thing we have. Who are you? Who appointed you God? How dare you say you know which patients lack hope?* I storm out of his office. My heart overflows as I look at Trey. Hope. That's all I have, and I will fight for it.

*****

Symphonic music fills Trey's brain as I place surround-sound earphones over his ears, and the black Sony CD player starts. The violin music begins to move through his head, back and forth, as both brain hemispheres synchronize and work together. Trey slumps in his bed as Mozart Divertimento #1 continues to play. With his head tilted down, his bright eyes stare straight ahead as he struggles to hear each note. There is a twinkle of light in each eye as if a match has lit. I watch with amazement as I see him lying there in peace. The music soothes him to sleep. The fifteen-minute session ends as I remove the earphones and watch him peacefully nap.

As I look at the instructions for this new listening program, I feel inspired that I have found something that might help him to recover faster. As I wonder what the program offers and feels like, I place the earphones on my ears. The music begins, and I drift away as I sit in the oversized hospital chair. Somewhere between the higher frequencies and the lower ones, I have fallen asleep, and I hear the music intensify with bursting sound. My breathing is constant, and I feel relaxed. Then, I realize fifteen minutes have passed. What has happened?

With the binder in my hand, I slowly leave the hospital, anticipating Trey's next session.

As I enter the road on the right marked "Deer Highway", I feel peaceful and quiet, yet I am in stop-and-go traffic. The commuters are rushing in their minds to get home, but they only inch along with everyone else. There's something about the vibrations in the music that leaves me feeling so heavenly. I reach into my binder and fumble to find the first session CD. I'm excited to place it into the CD player in my car's Bose listening system; I press "Play." The music doesn't sound the same, so I turn it off and sit in silence, only imagining the violin in my mind.

Following the winding road, I notice the beautiful tall pine trees that dot the mountains and then in the distance; I see a deer standing in a meadow. It looks so graceful as the sun begins to set behind the hills. Headlights start to flicker as I follow the car in front of me on the steep two-lane highway, with no desire to pass. I don't feel hurried as I head home for the first time.

Slowly entering a curve of the road, I feel the car start to pull to the left and realize I must have a flat tire. I struggle to access a nearby turnout lane and manoeuvre the car over and stop, not knowing what to do next. I don't have any cell phone reception and don't trust myself to change the tire. After inspecting my now flat tire, I returned to the car's front seat with the doors locked uptight.

There is barely enough light for even the shadows as the sun drains away. Whether I like it or not, the darkness is here, and in it, everything is hidden. Even the stars and moon cower behind a dense layer of clouds rolling in from the ocean.

My ears become sharper, and my mind paranoid. Every flash of a headlight is a predator, though it isn't. My brain jumps to every sight or sound as my body prepares for flight, fright, or freeze. For the most part, I freeze. All I can do is wait and hope. So, I sit. My heart can beat all it wants, but this body won't move until daylight breaks through the canopy above. With my hands resting on the steering wheel, and my back against the seat, I remain, waiting, breathing, wondering what to do next.

It is eerie. The street should be thronged with commuters this time of night, but it is slow, and the ones here are speeding past the place where I sit. The silence presses in on me, and all I can hear is the beating of my own heart when I suddenly see a dated four-door Chrysler pull into the turnout lane behind me.

My eyes see the figure a few feet away, and his big boots make a rhythmical noise against the rocky unpaved road. He moves toward the car but pauses. My heartbeat quickens. He approaches me with locked eyes, fixed right on me, though his head keeps moving. His face is stern as he reaches my driver-side window. I don't dare roll it down.

"I am not here to hurt you; I want to change your tire. Please open your trunk." I follow his commands, open my trunk with the indoor latch, and watch him remove the jack which he places under my car. He lies on his back and begins cranking it as my vehicle rises off the ground, freeing the flat tire. Beads of sweat roll from his brow as he replaces my tire with the spare. I fumble through my wallet, looking for his reward, and then press the down button on my driver's side window. Just barely open, I hand him a twenty-dollar bill.

"No thanks, Ma'am. I want you to be safe." He left as fast as he appeared. I am thankful and, once again, homebound.

Chapter 35

STAPH FREE FINALLY!

The relocated "Infection Material" bin is in front of another patient's room. Christian has been moved into Trey's double-occupancy room in the opposite bed by the heavy door. I'm anxious to meet him as I peer into the room. The nurses say he is taller and weighs more than Trey, weighing in at just under 200 pounds. *Gosh, Trey weighed 106 pounds when he first came here.* Christian is older and closer to Trey's age, unlike Trey's past roommates, older men. I appreciate Linda for deciding to move Christian into Trey's room. They should have more in common and enjoy more of the same music. *If that even happens when people are in comas.*

Christian's father, Alberto, approaches me as I enter the room. Alberto looks to be my age and has very dark features. *He reminds me of an Italian golfer.* His brown eyes struggle to hold back tears as he begins to tell me of Christian's accident, as his son lies near him motionless. The image that escaped Alberto's dry lips was slow as if his brain needed that time to process what had happened. His eyes remained fixed on Christian. As I listen to Alberto's every word, I walk over and kiss Trey's forehead, noticing his grin, which is always present. I understand how hard it is for Alberto to relive the memory. The thought is an old familiar path.

"After Christian's accident, his brain began to bleed. Surgically opened to relieve the pressure, the surgeons removed a portion of his skull on the left side of his head. That portion of Christian's skull is stored in his stomach and will be left there until the bleeding is totally under control." Alberto points to a large scar where the doctors removed the skull. "He is required to wear a plastic helmet to protect that area until the doctors can return the skull to where it was detached. That should be in approximately six months." *Oh, God.* Alberto holds Christian's small, atrophied hand and offers encouraging words. "You'll be alright, Christian. I will be here with you."

The nurses tell me Alberto's been supportive of Christian and is willing to do anything he must to help his son.

"We moved Christian here because it's closer to home. We live only twenty minutes south of here. It's an easy drive." I try to hide my envy as I think about driving Deer Highway and know how lucky he is that he doesn't have to. As I fill with jealousy, I glance over at Christian, and the sight of him reminds me of just how lucky I am.

Christian is motionless while he stares into the ceiling. His eyes are open but fail to work together and cross at times, and at other times they look off in different directions. His face is pale and swollen, while the left side of his head is concave. Christian's lips lack the strength to hold back any saliva that drains out of the corner of his mouth onto the towel sitting on his chest. His lungs are congested, and they rattle with every breath.

Christian appears to react to Alberto's voice but not with recognition. When Alberto speaks, he occasionally winces a smile caused by uncontrollable muscle twitching. Christian is in a persistent vegetative state due to severe damage to the brain and has little-to-no chance of recovery. *Or at least that is what the doctors are telling Alberto.*

*****

As I think about my day, the drive along the boat-filled harbour back to our Monaco is bumper-to-bumper traffic. The sadness that surrounds the sixth floor envelops me, but I choose not to become overcome. Instead, I look forward to a freshly iced vodka cranberry that I know Marco has waiting for me.

The restaurants on the pier are buzzing with tourists and locals who are accustomed to early night drinks and dinner.

"I met Trey's new roommate, Christian, and his dad today." I enter the motor home and see Marco is busy dreaming of the boat he has held in his imagination since he was a young boy on the East Coast.

"Oh?" Marco looks up, unwilling to leave his fantasy.

"Christian's dad seems nice and can't wait to meet you." I grab my drink and rush to get ready to leave for dinner.

Boats from all walks of life fill the storage area. From small rowboats to large fishing vessels, they sit in their rented spaces awaiting their owners, some of whom haven't been there for months or even years. Some boats are clean and well cared for; others are old with cracked paint and rust-covered metal around their hulls. The lucky ones have their trailer sitting in their leased space as they sit lounging in the nearby harbour.

As we stroll down the pier to Turgos, I see the parking lot and note it's alive and crowded tonight. Many patrons celebrate their favourite football team and anticipate Super Bowl Sunday, just around the corner. To me, it's just a reminder we've been here for a year and eight months. The thought seems somewhat depressing.

We don't wait long for our table in the corner, as a reserved sign sits on it. Patty-melts with extra onions soon fill our stomachs after we down libations and feel warm inside. Two hours pass as Marco, and I sit quietly at our table for two. This night we hold our tongues, preventing an argument from forming. The corner of a crowded Turgos is where we talk about how well Marco's business has done in the last year. After many days on the job and after hours he has taught our sons the company business, he feels rewarded. Russell and Cameron have taken much of the responsibility of running the company efficiently, as Madison rules the office with the superior skills she's learned in college. We're fortunate Marco's business is healthy and lucky to find new friendships that keep our minds off the sadness that surrounds the hospital.

We appreciate the dry winter night as we walk towards the motor home, when suddenly a boat appears in the parking lot, glistening in the moonlight. "That's what I'd like to own!" Marco points with excitement. "Let's look at it." He tugs my arm. "I'd love to have a fishing boat just like this one!" His dream comes alive.

The boat is a World Cat with a catamaran hull, a pleasant and smooth ride. Outfitted with a bait tank, a crow's nest optimal for spotting fish, and two diesel engines on the back, it is near perfection. As if divine intervention takes over, we spot a "For Sale" sign on the back.

I retrieve a pen and napkin from my purse, jot down the number, and follow it with a call the following day. "Hello, this is Matthew. How can I help you?" Matthew answers the phone to a haggler by nature and one who loves nothing more than to get a good deal. He explains the details of the World Cat and that he doesn't use it anymore since he and his wife started their family. He is in the process of building his dream home and needs some money upfront to get it started. *Hmmm.*

"Are you interested in bartering? My husband is a custom home builder." After a firm, yes, Marco and Matthew speak of what they have to offer each other—Marco gets the boat of his dreams and Matthew a home for his family. Matthew's new home's location is close to our office, and the drawings are simple as Marco prepares to sign the contract. The boat is detailed; the title transferred to us. It's a deal made in heaven.

The vast ocean becomes our second home quickly but is a bit intimidating since neither of us has had much salt-water boating experience. A few lessons, courtesy of Matthew, and Marco is good to go. As we list to one side and I clutch the handrail in front of me, the ocean spray fills the boat. As he grabs the steering wheel, I can't help but notice the big smile on Marco's salty face, now beginning to look more like a seasoned fisherman. Our new boat offers us a break from the hospital on Sunday mornings and is a sacred haven for fishing.

*****

"Hey, Leigh, I'm hosting a prayer meeting at my house tonight and would love for you to join us for a couple of hours." Candy spots me sprinting down the hospital corridor to Trey's room.

239

"Sounds good. I'll be staying in the motor home tonight and have nothing to do since Marco is out of town on business. Madison is coming down after school to stay with me." With no intention of ever being a Buddhist, I appreciate the invitation, which offers Madison and me entertainment for the evening.

The weather is nice as Madison, and I dress for the night's event. "Should I wear my tunic?" My sarcasm makes me laugh as I remember the satin monk robe my dad used to wear when I was younger.

"Oh, Mom!" Madison tries to hide her smile.

As we approach the mobile-home park just south of Dave's Point, I notice large wrought iron gates at the entrance and stop to press in the code that Candy had given me earlier that day. The gate grunts and grinds as it opens to rows and rows of mobile homes sitting on small patches of borrowed land. At the end of the lane was a tiny house that had once been grey. There was only one narrow window beside the weathered door, but the window box under it was filled with bright orange and yellow marigolds, giving the whole place a cheerful look. After stumbling across spot #59, Candy's house, we search for a parking space.

The faint mumbles become louder as we near the place where we plan to spend a few hours that evening. As we climb the three steps to the entrance of Candy's home and knock at the door, we hear chanting, "Nam-myoho-renge-Kyo," coming from inside. Madison and I exchange side-glances. I remind myself to stay positive and to welcome any opportunity that presents itself.

An escape from reality is what I'm looking for as Candy opens the door and invites us into the house. She grabs my hand as she welcomes us into the small living room. She wears a decorated robe over her casual street clothes and no shoes. As we peer in, we see fifteen people of all ages sitting on pillows with open knees and crossed ankles, Indian-style, who begin introducing themselves. The group are gracious people who have strong beliefs and firm commitments to Buddha. Aki, a short, frail man, takes my hand and bows. Beside him is his wife, who speaks little English. Around the circle, they all stop to introduce themselves. Each of them with gentle smiles.

Buddhist sayings and small shrines decorate the tiny space. We notice scattered cushions sitting on worn, carpeted flooring. The solid cherrywood altar sits at the head of the room. Carved-out wooden scrolls indent the near-perfect wood. I think of Marco, knowing how much he'd appreciate it. There, on top of the altar, sits a picture of Trey encased in a beautiful gold handmade frame, an import from Nepal, Buddha's birthplace, and one Candy cherishes. The image of Trey is one from his youth, where his eye colour was still cinnamon brown and held a sense of innocence before the drugs took over. Trey's picture snagged off a display board Madison brought to the hospital in the early days was to the right of the statue of Buddha made out of wood, clay, and bronze. Side by side, they challenge one another for the most attention as the group waits to begin their prayers.

Candy heads the small Buddhist group in the community and has a peaceful look on her tired face as she motions the group to stand. Everyone stands and bows to Trey and Buddha before they begin. Once they are seated, they again turn their heads and start their chant. Madison and I struggle with prayer beads in our hands to imitate the words they say. "Nom-mi-ono-ben-re-Kio," they chant methodically. The verse is repeated repeatedly as Madison and I look around the room and then at each other. We begin to pick up on the routine until the group presents more extended lyrics. My jaw drops with the new verse as I try to keep up. We find it hard to keep the smile from our faces. The grins turn to giggles, then to suppressed laughter, as we hear each other mispronounce the words. Madison looks over at me as I blurt out a word by mistake. She lets out a loud and embarrassing giggle. It's a sound we feel we haven't heard in a thousand years, and it feels good. It's as if we were both in high school again. It tickles us. Fat tears roll down my newly pinked cheeks, and it is several minutes before they subside. We don't know what we find so amusing: Is it the Buddhist chants or our immaturity? In these moments of our laughter, the temperature in the house rises a couple of degrees, and we can't help but stifle a grin.

I look up to see everyone smiling at me. Aki looks over at me with questioning eyes. "My wife wants to know if you have heard of Reiki? She knows someone who can teach you if you are interested."

"Reiki? I've never heard of it, but I'd love to give it a try." *Quite honestly, I'll try anything to help Trey at this time.* Candy offers some tea and cookies before we leave. We feel we've made new friends, and it's a great release of stress for both Madison and me.

Chapter 36

"MAUREEN'S MOTHER'S FUNERAL IS LATER TODAY." My words intend to remind Marco to get into the shower and get dressed. I know it will be a quick visit to the hospital with Trey before we leave for the two-hour drive to the family home of one of my best friends. Thank God the spring showers are over, and the freeways won't be congested. We walk down the hall and see Trey sitting in his wheelchair in front of his room. Sharon is propping his arms up with pillows as she sees me coming. Dressed in the navy-blue jogging outfit, I bought last week; Trey sits in the hall. On his feet are his black thick-soled army boots that Mona says help keep his feet firmly planted on the floor. It's all about body awareness. His hair is clean and held back with a tight rubber band. He looks straight ahead and smiles when he hears my voice.

"Are you going to be here today?" Sharon strokes Trey's hair.

"No, we have to go to an F-U-N-E-R-A-L." I spell the word not wanting to upset Trey. To my surprise, Trey frowns. Quick thinking forces my lips to say, "But afterwards, we are going to

P-A-R-T-Y." I see Trey smile. I stand back, analyze what has happened, and then scream, "He can spell!" I can't control myself. Here sits a boy who barely holds his head up, but he can spell! "S-M-I-L-E," I again spell. He smiles. "M-A-D," he deepens his brows. "C-R-Y," I spell it out. He whimpers. "L-A-U-G-H, H-A-P-P-Y, S-A-D," I make things a little more complicated. He reacts appropriately by showing the correct expressions on his face, displaying that his memory is intact.

"I can't believe he can spell!" I look at Sharon in amazement, knowing that I thought the overdose wiped his brain clean.

"We have never had a patient like him before." Sharon smiles at Trey fondly.

With the weekend nurses surrounding him, we leave for the funeral knowing that he will be well cared for and entertain them while exercising his brain for the rest of the afternoon. As we leave the hospital, I think about his earlier days in school.

I pushed him to get his diploma before dropping out of high school. I was devastated when he didn't. I prayed for a brighter future for him, so after he quit, I searched for a program that Trey could take online to secure his diploma. The home school would allow him extra time in the morning to eat breakfast and do a little homework from the day before. He wouldn't have to get dressed if he didn't want to. He could take it at his own pace without any pressure.

He chose his online courses carefully, ensuring that he could pass them quickly. His dad hooked up the computer's microphone in our upstairs office. Trey needed to communicate with his instructor if he needed additional help.

"You will be comfortable up here and able to concentrate," Marco pulled the oversized leather chair closer to the computer. Even though he couldn't mingle with other students at this

school, Trey could speak to them during class using the micro-phone.

"I come from a poor family." Trey's legs stretched out across the desk as he rambled to a girl taking the same online class. "My parents deserted me, and I am broke . . ." He kicked back in the leather chair as the instructor continued lecturing the class.

"I never met my dad. He was gone before I was born." He continued to fantasize and enjoyed the girl's reactions. I stood at the bottom of the stairs struggling to hear what he said and disappointed he wasn't learning. I instinctively knew he had fallen behind in his classes. I stepped in to help.

"Why are you studying Chinese, Trey?" He threw his head back and laughed. I looked over his class list—Chinese and algebra. I know nothing about these subjects but know that they would offer him nothing.

His next class was about to begin, so I grabbed another chair and sat in on it. His male teacher was indeed Chinese and challenging to understand. I wondered how many kids would pass this class as we struggled with his first word, "Zaigian." What the hell did that mean? Trey laughed uncontrollably after noticing the look on my face.

"You have a list of ten Chinese words you need to know by next week, so you better study. You will have an exam next Wednesday." His instructor closed the online class. I looked at the list of words, and they all looked Chinese to me, so I didn't say a word.

An hour later, his class in algebra was beginning. His teacher came online, opened the course for the students, and started tutoring them on the subject. We both got lost and bored during the class.

"Are you getting anything out of these classes?" I watched the look on Trey's face.

"Not really. You know, Mom, I'm only doing this for you." He stared into my eyes.

At that time, I realized the diploma wasn't that important. I gave up the dream of Trey receiving the unique honour and decided to send him to work with Marco.

*****

Saturday flew by quickly after experiencing the loss of Maureen's mother and meeting up with some of my old friends at the burial site. The morning seemed bright as we woke and couldn't wait to get back to the hospital to spend time with Trey. We exited the elevator and entered the sixth floor. There we heard giggling coming from the nurse's station. "Do you hear that?" I whispered as I looked at Marco with a questioning expression. Trey is seated in the local station as the nurse's continue making phone calls and working on their charts.

"Leigh, Trey is funnier than ever!" Jenny looks up from her chart with a wild grin on her face. "This kid has been sitting here since eight o'clock this morning, entertaining us and making us laugh. Linda would kill me if she knew I broke the confidentiality rule by letting him in here. I probably shouldn't have." Trey listens to Jenny's every word. He suddenly stares ahead, pretending not to hear a thing. "L- A-U-G-H," Jenny spells the word. His eyes stare ahead. "S-M-I-L-E," she tries again. He doesn't move. Trey pretends to hear nothing, knowing he won't stay with the nurses. "OMG, are you deaf now?" His eyes stare ahead, knowing Jenny is playing with him. He is still while the room buzzes with the energy around him. Finally, there's a smile on his face. The nurses' laughter spreads across the sixth floor as everyone talks about Trey and his joy to the unit.

*****

Aki's wife is on the phone. "Akiri is Reiki master and wants to teach you energy healing. Should I ask her to call you?" She speaks in broken English. I'm interested in energy healing, and I will try and learn anything that would benefit Trey. After being at the hospital for two years and two months, it seems that conventional medicine only offers relief of pain using prescribed medication. Other than that, I haven't seen much more in the hospital setting since Trey got here.

Akiri is in front of the hospital, pulling a binder of information from her neatly arranged car trunk. She dresses in a bright-red, loose-fitting tunic with matching wide-legged pants that flow with the warm air that follows her. Her sleek, shiny, long black hair is arranged on her head and held with a black clip. Wrinkle-free, her face is pure white, and she wears no makeup.

After offering us a cup of warm green tea, we listen to her explain the ancient healing techniques. "Reiki is a form of relaxation which promotes healing." She looks at both Ana and me. Andrei's wife, Ana, has decided to join Trey and me at the alternative-medicine meeting in hopes of helping her husband.

The Chinese woman follows me through heavy thick wooden doors that lead into the chapel at the hospital, and there she arranges the chairs. The nostalgic feeling of the chapel takes me back in time.

"I hope you are taking those kids to church every Sunday, Marco." The call comes from Marco's mother on the East Coast

three thousand miles away. She's already met her commitment in a church that morning with the three-hour time difference between Massachusetts and California.

"Oh, I am, Momma. I know how important church is at a young age." He chokes and barely finishes his sentence. He flashes back to his youth and memories of his teacher, a chubby older nun.

She smacked his hand with a wooden ruler she carried in her long black habit's pocket. The memory hadn't surfaced in his mind in years. The best he could recall, it wasn't his fault, and he didn't deserve the punishment. It was his friend Gary's fault all along. He was the class clown and always liked the attention he received from the girls. He was the one who put the tack on Sister Margaret's chair and waited for her to sit down. Marco hadn't forgiven Gary for the many times that the staff called Marco's mother into the office, and he had to pay for things he hadn't done. It was long ago, but no, Marco hadn't forgotten.

He spent his days in Sister Margaret's class, practising coughing and saying "asshole" simultaneously with Gary. Marco sat in the back of the classroom, hidden from the nuns, as he tried to learn. Something about the nun's strict rules bothered him, though, and reminded him of his mother and her strong laws.

The gothic church that stood there for forty years was only three miles down a long narrow road from home. Marco hated arriving twenty minutes earlier than anyone else on Sunday mornings as an altar boy. Even Ray, his older brother, didn't have to, but his mother didn't care. She loved watching Marco during the 7 am Mass.

It's Sunday morning as I wake and find myself disappointed that Marco will not be a part of the Sunday morning ritual as he declares, "I'm up to my neck in yard work."

"You have time this afternoon to get the lawn mowed." I plead, knowing how hard the kids are to get to the nine o'clock Mass. I'd rather not go myself and dream of lying in bed drinking spiked coffee, but the guilt grows so strong that I know I'm going to burn in hell if I don't go.

I wake the kids early, finding resistance as I scramble to get them dressed and to church on time. "Hurry. I don't want to be late." I yell from the other side of the house while slipping on the summer dress I bought last year. "This looks fine." It clings to my hips and reminds me of how much looser it fit when I first bought it. I hear the kids fumbling for their dress clothes that are balled up in their closet, wrinkled beyond recognition. They must have forgotten to hang them up last week. As I hold the door open and the kids file out to the running car, Trey stands before me barefoot with only his socks on. "Get your shoes on!"

I glance at the clock in the family room. It strikes eight-thirty. "Where are your shoes?" He looks at me without expression; the clock continues to tick towards nine o'clock. Feeling pressured, I go in search of them myself. I look under the bed, in the closet, and on the back patio. They are nowhere. As I continue my search, I see his dirty pair of tennis shoes in the corner of his messy room. I know I will die if he wears them again this week. Yet I'm racing the clock, so I grab and toss them to him, snapping, "Put these on!" My blood pumps as I drive through the city, and he ties knots in his shoelaces.

Walking down the church aisle with my four children as the congregation smiles and approves makes it worth the effort. I wonder if anyone has noticed his sneakers as we kneel and bless ourselves. As I bow my head and close my eyes, I hear giggling coming from behind the pew. It's there I see Russell reach over and pinch Trey. Trey squeals as he returns the favour.

Then I see Cameron slide a foot across and kick Trey on his right flank. "Stop it!" I whisper as an older couple in front of us turns around to see who is making the racket. They're having tons of fun as the boys continue to punch and kick each other while the priest talks about confession and sins. I'm getting tired of this commotion. I succeed in catching their eye and mouth to them, "You are going to get it!" They stop. Mass ends. I drive home while my blood boils and dread next week. I walk into the house.

"Madison is the only one who takes church seriously." Marco glances at me as he sits on the couch, sipping his beer and watching football.

Two chairs are in the hospital's chapel centre and the others against the walls. Candy enthusiastically pushes Trey securely in his wheelchair into the chapel. Akiri acknowledges him and then begins. With a kiss to Trey's forehead, she moves his wheelchair next to me, where I sit on a folding chair in front of the altar. Akiri motions us to close our eyes. She starts by clearing the room of any negative energy. While she chants the words, "Dai-ko-Myo," I peek to see what she does while talking in tongues. She waves her hands, drawing signs in the air in each corner of the room. She stands in front of me, pressing on my shoulder with her soft hands. "Dai-ko- Myo." She draws the same signs. My face contorts as I struggle to keep a straight look.

Next, I watch her move to Trey, and then she presses on his shoulders. "Dai-ko-myo." I feel her move behind me and connect her hands to the front of my forehead. She raises her left arm and now finds Ana's forehead and whispers the same prayer. She takes a deep breath and blows air into Ana's face. The chanting turns to three distinct phrases. "Cho-ku-rei," "Hon-sha- re-sho-nen," "Sei-he-kei." She quickly kneels in front of me, and with her tongue pressed on the roof of her mouth, she blows air making weird sounds bouncing from me to Trey and then over to Ana.

Trey welcomes the break for lunch when we stop our personal healing experience and return him to his room. Akiri encourages us to eat only pure food and drink clean water as she reaches into her bag and offers us some homemade gluten-free bread. We dread returning to the chapel as we walk back slowly.

Ana is first to lie down on the provided cot. She closes her eyes while Akiri lays her soft hands on her face. She lies quietly as Akiri's light touch moves to her neck and then to the front and back of her torso. Ana begins to cry violently as the energy fills her. Her eyes remain closed, but tears pour out the corners. She weeps as her hands turn beet red.

"Please help me in this healing experience to help my Andrei. I need him so much." She has suffered so much since his accident. She cries nightly in his absence while she dreams of the man she married and the one who would share her children. "I cry for the night we ran away together. He grasped my arm with his strong hand as he led me to the airport away from my family." She thinks of her home in Romania and when she and Andrei ran off to America to make a better life for themselves. "He is the only man I could ever love, and I beg you to bring him back." Her eyes swell with emotion. She remembers how hard Andrei worked on his studies to be a registered nurse and the home he promised her once he graduated with a degree. It was all too much for her the night of his accident. She woke up by a late-night phone call telling her that Andrei had suffered an aneurysm and would not survive. "I can't live without him. Please, I beg you. I can't live without him. Please. Please. I beg you." The tears and words ring silently in my mind.

Akiri explains that the toxins Ana has stored in her body are being released, along with feelings that are no longer useful. I stand back, watching Ana's reaction, as my eyes cry for her and Andrei.

My turn begins the same, as Akiri's hands find my face, and the warm energy begins to fill my body. For a moment, I don't know how to respond, so I lie quietly on the cot until uncontrollable laughter strikes me. I don't know why I find myself laughing so hard, but all of a sudden, I can't stop. My breath comes in quick gasps between my unstoppable giggles. Tears gather in the corners of my eyes, threatening to spill over. Another way of releasing tension Akiri explains. The session ends, Akiri bows.

I'm armed with a new tool in my arsenal now and can't wait to place my beet-red hands over Trey and watch his reaction. He's asleep as I enter his room.

Chapter 37

I CLIMB THE FIVE STEPS TO THE CROW'S NEST, which hovers above the centre of the World Cat. As I slide into it, I feel the sun warming my back as I drift far from life. As the boat glides through deep-blue waters, dolphins vault high into the muggy air of mid-August. Their shiny grey skin and white stomachs fly beads of saltwater, running down and sparkling in the light. In the distance, I see a pod of blue whales encrusted with barnacles breaching in the beautiful afternoon sunlight. It's a peaceful day while the Beatles play quietly on the boat speakers and Marco masters the quiet seas.

I once heard that life has to be tough to be like God. But this tough? Instinctively, I know I have become a better person since Trey's accident. Marco and I both have. We have found the strength we need to be better parents and people. Trey survived for a reason. I think about the angel in the sky after Trey got hurt, and I know God has sent me down this path. But, why me? He's tested me and has thrown roadblocks in my way. I've learned when one door closes, another one opens.

My inner thoughts are clear as I take in the deep, blue Pacific Ocean sights. I chant the words I have come to know. Nam-myoho-renge-Kyo. I quiet my overactive mind and close my eyes. I watch the sea in my mind, lost in the rhythmic percussion of the waves. Nam- myoho-renge-Kyo, I meditate. My eyes are steady to the horizon, face aglow with the reflection of the warm sun. My lips bear a smile, just enough to show I'm enjoying my thoughts, whatever they may be. I'm content. Marco moves closer as he feels and finds my presence yet stays quiet, allowing me to remain lost in the moment a bit longer.

*****

I've become quite proficient at shaving Trey, and I remind myself to bring new razors for him weekly. His facial hair has grown thicker now, and his daily shaves are a must. His feeding tube is still in place, but he can swallow applesauce now, so feeding him has become a daily ritual, too. It reminds me of when his speech therapist announced that he had no swallowing mechanism. Trey has proved her wrong.

It's been a tough two years and four months with the long drives and endless nights, and I realize now that I can care for Trey myself. I've thought long and hard about going to the head of the department to ask for permission to bring him home for a weekend. *And why couldn't I?* Over the last few years, I've bathed him, helped him use the urinal since he is diaper-free, fed him, and worked with him on English. In my opinion, I can take care of him better than the nurses! He needs to come home for a change! So, after some negotiation with Joe and signing several waivers, we have our weekend set. Trey will remain with me after the CNAs put him in the car on Friday, and Marco will return him to the hospital Monday morning.

*****

Securely held by a seat belt, Trey slumps in his seat as he rides to the other side of Deer Highway for the first time. To the valley from the beach, I grab his arm to stop him from swaying back and forth during every turn. I chase the car in front of me while aware of Trey's weak core strength. "You'll be OK," I whisper as his chin rests on his chest. I find it hard to keep my eyes on the road as my memory flashes to Trey as a young boy and the first time he got carsick. I remembered him complaining of a stomachache on family road trips and his workdays with Marco. Now, he can't utter a sound of protest. He falls from side to side as I follow the twists and turns in the road. The ride seems longer than it has in the past, and the cars slower. Hurry, I have got to get him home. I press harder on the gas pedal.

The car's horn blows as we enter the driveway, and everyone rushes out to greet us. Huge smiles fill their faces as I see them greet Trey and me. Marco opens my car door wearing his red-and-white plaid barbecue apron and helps me out of the car after a long hello kiss. Behind him are Russell, Cameron, Alexander, and Madison. A familiar feeling fills the air as we all come together again.

Cameron grabs Trey's belongings from the trunk while Russell carefully lifts Trey from the car. Trey's like a noodle as Russell gets him into his wheelchair. "Be sure to use the belt and harness to hold him in," I remind Cameron, who is behind the wheelchair. By the time we get to our beautiful tropical backyard, Marco turns his famous barbecued chicken soaked in his recipe of barbecue sauce, salt, pepper, and beer. The fifth ingredient no one knows except Marco.

While drinking a tall glass of wine so rightly earned, I sit back and watch everyone interact. It reminds me of the kid's younger years. Suddenly, I recognize the smell of smoke. I glance up and set my eyes on something familiar. There, on the hillside, is the beginning of a fire driven by the wind towards our house. Lured by the smoke, I enter a memory from many years ago.

It was a hot afternoon as I lay lounging on the couch, waiting for the Preakness Stakes horse races to begin. The kids were quiet. Trey and Cameron had decided to hike over to the old oak tree and promised to be home within an hour. As I sat waiting, Trey came running through the front door. "The hill is on fire! The hill is on fire!" I glanced up and saw flames torching the dry brush on the hillside and heading towards our home. I ran to the phone and dialled 911. I waited. Nothing. Then, the voice came on and told me they were on their way. The next fifteen minutes were pure hell as I watched the fire advance. The boys were in the house and revved up by the approaching fire. "Did you see those flames? They're huge!" Trey was excited. Finally, the fire truck pulled into our driveway, and the firefighters quickly put the fire out.

I was relieved that everyone was safe, but then I overheard small mumblings coming from Trey's room. "I knew I'd start a fire if I used my lighter. I didn't think it would grow to be that big!" I opened the door to a couple of guilty faces and told Trey he would pay dearly.

The next day I drove him to the neighbourhood fire station and made him face the fire chief. "Tell the captain what you did

yesterday, how you started the fire near our home. Tell him how
you used a lighter to start it and that you will work at the station
daily for the next two weeks." I heard him mumble that it was
the one-arm man who created the fire. I rolled my eyes and once
again made him confess to the fireman. He did. He polished the
fire truck and mopped the station's floors daily for two weeks
after school. He never complained or said a word. Cameron sat
in his room, grounded, during that time and never complained
either.

It shines with all its glory as it grows. "OMG! The hill is on fire!" I scream. Russell and Cameron jump onto Marco's old tractor, trying to get it started in a hurry. Alexander grabs the garden hose and drags it through the dirt along the driveway. It's heavy, but he knows there's a convenient spigot at the edge of the property. Madison is on the phone with the fire department. Momentarily, Marco stands by proudly watching his kids jump into action and remembers the many times he handled these types of things alone. With Russell on the tractor, he turns the soil to bury the flames, extinguishes the fire, and then proceeds to create a firebreak if a spark decides to start up again. Alexander uses the hose to finish the job and to save our fences.

The fire department finally arrives, and the firefighters are grateful the boys knew what to do. Our neighbour was also appreciative of it before the fire jumped the road to his house.

Russell's training at the fire academy certainly paid off. Back to our beers, drinks, and dinner, I'm proud of these kids and remember Russell's many years learning the firefighter business until he abruptly quit after Trey's accident. I guess it was just as hard on him as it was on me.

That's the excitement for the weekend. I put Trey to bed next to me while Marco prepares to sleep in Trey's old bedroom. It feels good to have Trey home with all of us together. As I lie in bed next to him, I reach over to ensure that I'm not dreaming. I can hear him breathe and realize he is here beside me. It's hard to believe we've made it this far.

Chapter 38

WHILE SEARCHING THE INTERNET AND CHECKING with other medical professionals for answers about Trey's vision, I stumble across the name of a prominent ophthalmologist. There are no eye doctors on staff at the hospital on the hill, and there are no plans to hire any. I need answers to so many questions to prepare Trey for his future. I finally pick up the phone and make the call. I'm hoping to get this doctor to come to the hospital, as taking Trey to him would be more difficult. After calling and leaving a message, I hung up the phone and realized it was Saturday. The days seem to blur together now.

It's Monday morning when the return call from Dr Boutros's secretary comes. She introduces herself and, after a brief conversation regarding the ophthalmologist's credentials, I find that he is the best in his field and has extensive knowledge of brain injury and vision. "I will check with him to see if he has time to come to the hospital and will get back to you as soon as I can." She hangs up the phone while checking the doctor's schedule. After what feels like an eternity, I receive a call back from her.

Finally, the doctor will assess Trey's vision at the hospital on Monday, so I jot down the appointment on my calendar.

Linda is apologetic as she states the team doesn't have a qualified ophthalmologist on staff. She congratulates me for finding one who will work with the hospital doctors, accept Trey's insurance, and come to the hospital for a complete examination. We are ecstatic to get some answers finally.

*****

As he walks down the corridor, I notice that the doctor has a thin and frail frame. My fingers grip my note board as I watch him come towards me. My eyes rest on the tattoos that play peekaboo up his white scrub sleeves. His pierced ears have two holes with a gold stud in each. I imagine him studying in the cramped quarters of India. I'm not sure how I expect him to talk as he opens his mouth to introduce himself. His voice is baritone and songlike. He speaks eloquently with an Eastern Indian accent. "Nice to meet you; I assume you are Trey's mother?" His eyes are a dark brown, almost black, with heavy circles under them as if he hasn't slept in weeks.

He steps into Trey's room. He reaches for his ophthalmia scope from the large briefcase he is carrying. After looking into Trey's left eye and then into his right, he takes a few notes. As he examines Trey's vision closely, Trey can't help but laugh. The doctor pulls away and looks at me, puzzled.

"He is more aware than he looks." He has a surprised expression on his face. I nod as he again closely looks into the other eye.

Trey starts cracking up. His laughter radiates outward through the packed hall of nurses who had been, up until this moment, very quiet. Now they, too, begin giggling, and soon the ripples of laughter become great waves of hilarity.

"He's having a good time, isn't he?" Dr Boutros smiles as I agree with slightly turned-up lips. After a thorough oral eye exam, he points out that Trey's optic nerve is intact, a good indication that he has some vision. He explains everything in words even a child could understand, but there is still no definite answer to when his sight will improve. Before he leaves, he writes a prescription for an MRI and leaves it on Linda's desk, who will make the appointment with the imaging department.

Two nurses appear with a gurney and transfer Trey onto it. Down two flights, I follow them into the lab. There he is rolled into a cylinder while I watch from a camera outside the door. He is attentive as he follows the nurse's directions. "Don't move." The nurse leans on the large cold machine as the knocking sound begins. "Hold still, don't breathe." He lies still until the test is complete. The knocking sound takes me back to years ago.

Jerry was a tall, lean, and beautiful teammate and modest about his looks; it made me fall for him all the more. He had the kind of face that stopped you in your tracks. He was handsome, but inside he was beautiful. Our coach searched for the perfect pair to play in the greatly anticipated doubles tennis tournament and placed me on Jerry's team. I certainly was thrilled to have a partner who looked like him, and I admired his skills. It was my first year in college, and my studies were heavy. Afternoons with Jerry made it easier.

My teammate yelled, "Get ready! The ball is coming to you. Play near the net." It was a tennis match made in hell as we grunted and struggled to return each play. I stood at the net as instructed by my demanding crush as the ball whirled towards me at a fast pace. I delivered it back with a hard blow and caught the white line. Score! Good for us.

I headed to my place at the serving line, threw the ball into the air, and knew this was the point that would take Jerry and me to the top. With a heave, my racket rose over my head, and my right shoulder blew out of the socket. I collapsed in pain and could only clutch my shoulder with my left hand. I could feel the ball of my shoulder completely dangling out of sorts. Jerry ran to me.

"Leigh, get up! We are tied. Two points will win the tournament!" All I could do was lie there on the court in agony. Soon I was lifted to a standing position and escorted off the playing field. "Default," I heard as I saw Jerry disapprovingly shake his head. "Forfeit." I struggled to hold back the tears as the excruciating pain ran down my arm, and I climbed into a waiting car.

The hospital wasn't far away, but it seemed across the planet as shock increased. Soon I found myself being lifted onto a table and pushed into a cold cylinder. The knocking noise from the MRI began. Knock, knock, knock was all I heard as tears burst down my face.

"It's a rotator cuff complete tear." The doctor on staff looked at my MRI results. I knew this would end my tennis career and afternoons with Jerry at that moment.

I'm nervous as I wait for Dr Boutros's call and the results of Trey's MRI. Weeks pass by. I call. Another two weeks pass, and I call again. *When will the doctor read the MRI and tell me the results?* I scream inside.

Finally, early one morning, the call comes from Dr Boutros. "Mrs Morelli? I have read the MRI and find it inconclusive. I didn't know of the drug overdose that caused Trey's accident, so I will not treat him."

"What? What do you mean by that?" I ask the unfriendly bastard!

"I can't treat him. His optic nerve is intact, but his brain has atrophied due to many years of drug abuse."

"What the hell does that mean? You have to tell me! Am I supposed to give up?" I shout.

"I never said that." He hangs up the phone and leaves me hanging on with confusion.

I'm upset, angry, abandoned, and alone! *Why did he refuse to treat Trey? I can't understand. What type of doctor is this as- shole? Refusing service? That pig!*

The questions and answers fill my mind as I become en- raged. *Is this discrimination?* I wonder if that idiot doctor knows what it's like to lose a child? To fight for someone you love? I think of his tattoos, his piercings, and the dark circles under his eyes. Jolted and confused, I'm utterly mortified and left with a closed door and more questions than answers.

*****

Each year, the goal for the girl scouts is to sew handmade blankets to give to the patients on the sixth floor that offer more comfort, warmth, and security than what a bed sheet has to offer. They work hard to meet their goal to deliver these gifts before Christmas.

The scouts come dressed perfectly in ironed white blouses, green vests with honour patches, and skirts. They file into Trey and Christian's room.

The girls form a perfectly straight line in front of the twin electric beds, crowding each other so they will all fit in- side the small room. Their knee socks keep them warm from the storm that has rolled in over the ocean. Their ages range from eight to twelve; I note as I study each of their sweet faces. The little one at the end is the youngest and has the most freckles. On the other end of the line is the oldest of the group, who sports an awkward pair of black-rimmed glasses. She looks smart as she directs the others to approach Trey to present their custom blanket. The blanket is soft and cosy as I cover Trey and tuck it under his chin. I smile and thank them for the generous gift.

"What song do they want us to sing?" The chubby girl in the corner looks around the room.

"Frosty, the Snowman!" the little one blurts out. A nod, and they begin to sing.

Each girl practices and sings her rehearsed part. The room becomes more crowded as they sing when the nurses lean in. Trey listens intently with his head tilting down while his muddy-green eyes stare forward without a blink. No smile or reaction, just the stare.

While I watch him react, his lips form a slight smile. I know he is thinking about something other than the song. There is a devious look about him that is indescribable. Trey's blanket begins to expand. The wind under the sheet starts to form. The strong pressure starts to build and explodes. Trey passes a giant fart. The noise is an explosion, and he bursts out laughing. He holds his breath; his face turns purple. Nurses gasp as they try to hide their smiles.

The embarrassment is beyond belief as I look to see the damage done. Some girls act like they didn't hear it, others can't contain their smiles, and still, many snort. Their heavy-set group leader leaves the room before the girls can see her reaction. Her laugh echoes down the hall as Trey immaturely continues to giggle for a solid fifteen minutes. The girls file out of the room, and I thank them for coming.

*****

Trey is on a roll. He is eating solid food, becoming more assertive, and finding humour in everything he does. Trey laughs at everything: the patients, the nurses and CNAs. He doesn't care what or whom he chuckles at; he finds everything around him hilarious.

Rolling the waterproof gurney into the shower with Trey draped in a sheet concealing his nakedness, he roars while Sharon and I bathe him. He chuckles at the television during Divorce Court, the local news, and Sunday-morning services while Christian lies still. Trey listens to Christian's breathing, then laughs. He hears Christian cough, and he cracks up. Then one day, while Trey is thoroughly entertaining himself, Christian suddenly gives Trey a thumbs-up. It is an honest-to-goodness thumbs-up! The nurses fill the room with excitement.

"Trey, go ahead, laugh!" The nurses coax him. As Trey follows the nurse's commands, he bursts into a loud cackle as Christian's left thumb emerges from lying flat on the sheet to a raised fist with his thumb pointing straight up. A loud applaud is heard through the sixth floor and across the hospital.

The nurses call Alberto in a hurry. "Come to the hospital! Christian gave a thumbs up!" Linda's voice is excited as she speaks. A hopeful and excited Alberto puts down his golf clubs and rushes to the hospital to see if it's all true.

Trey's cackling is contagious; he laughs, then everyone follows. Here, in the hall, surrounded by nurses, Trey sits in his navy-blue long johns, sharing his laughter with anyone who will listen. With little trunk or neck control, he's made a joke of this entire thing, and it's benefiting everyone around him.

Then one day, Andrei grins. Andrei, paralyzed for over four years, smiles at Trey while Trey cracks himself up. The subacute unit has turned from a sterile, quiet environment into a place where nurses smile and families have hope.

*****

The stage is set for Christmas morning as I hang the stockings from the knobs on the cupboards in the motor home. It's nothing like the Christmas mornings the kids experienced in their youth, but we're all together, the motorhome is warm, and the pre-ordered food is here. We bring Trey to the motor home early, where gifts from Santa Claus waited. We sit, open presents, and eat breakfast. It's different; it's good; it's sad.

We slowly return Trey to the hospital, and as we leave, I see Candy pushing Trey's wheelchair towards the elevator to say goodbye. I stop and look. It's been hard to leave him here the last three Christmases, but I know we need to, as I drop a tear and turn to go. I swear I miss him already and know my Christmas day will drag on. The void is impossible to fill.

Chapter 39

CLOUDS ARE THICK THIS MORNING AS WE BOARD our little fishing boat and watch a dirty, salty older man get off his ship. In his calloused hands, he carries traps filled with lobsters. His weathered face is always on the lookout as he peers over at us. Legend has it that his left eye is closed with crisscrossing white scars caused by a hook to the eye.

"Do you do any shark fishing?" I shiver from the cold air.

In a raspy voice, he smiles. "Oh, that's easy. Go up five miles off the hospital, out three miles, then drink a tall cold beer. Fill the empty can with fish guts and chum, drop it down on a fishing line to the bottom of the sea. Throw out a line with a large mackerel on it, and in five minutes, you will have a good-sized shark on your rig." Marco listens while he sceptically looks at me.

We pack our windbreakers, hats, poles, and bait and grab our close friend, Brian, who lives nearby. We motor up the coast, bouncing through the strong surf and waves. After following every word, the older man mumbled, we drop the chum, throw out the mackerel on the line, and wait for the nearly impossible to happen. I stare out onto the sea, consumed with my thoughts, as I suddenly blink to see a massive shark circling our bait. After a few laps, its tiny mouth strikes at the mackerel, and the line takes off, spinning uncontrollably. Down to the depths of the blue sea, the shark goes deeper and deeper. The line on the power reel sings when the eight-foot shark flies out of the water, then lands with a splash. The display is spectacular. Down again, he goes. Marco and Brian struggle to hold the pole tight while realizing the power behind the shark might pull them into the water.

"It's got to be three hundred pounds!" Marco struggles with the idea. Jumping and diving, the shark begins to tire as Marco puts on his gloves and works to get the shark close to the boat.

"Brian, grab the gaff!" Marco points over at it. Brian excitedly grabs the long, sharp hook and reaches over the side of the boat to swipe at the shark. The shark suddenly jumps out of the water, his body twists, and he slaps Brian across the face with its massive tail, leaving Brian's nose gushing with blood. As I step closer to get a better look, I see an extensive abrasion across the entire width of his face.

"Am I alright?" The blood covered his face.

"Yeah, I guess." Marco glances at me, knowing that probably wasn't the truth.

We head back to the dock with the shark tied to the side of the boat. We crack a beer and smile, knowing the old, salty fisherman was more intelligent than we thought.

Brian isn't going to forgive the shark that quickly, and after cutting the fish into chunks, he hangs the shark's four-foot-long tail on his fence.

The hospital staff is thrilled and applauds us as we walk down the hall carrying bags of fresh shark to pass out to them.

Marco and I have a great time reliving the afternoon's event and then making a call to the newspaper's headquarters. The next morning's newspaper headline reads, "Brian got Bitch Slapped by a Shark!" Brian didn't think it was funny while waiting for antibiotics for a newly festered infection in the emergency room.

*****

The hospital staff is shocked when Ana announces she and Andrei are returning to their old country, Romania. Ana is tired of waiting for Andrei to recover and has contacted her family, who promises to help her once she is home.

She writes a list of items she needs to sell before leaving. The file contains many things she and Andrei dreamed of to make their home special. A black leather couch built for comfort was bought two weeks before Andrei's accident and sold for half the cost they paid for it. A dining-room table, chairs, and dishes are on the chopping block. She seems cold and unattached as she describes the items. She hangs the list at the nurses' station and asks the best possible price to help her get Andrei home where he belongs.

Ana is deliberate while making travel plans for the over-sixteen-hour flight and wonders how she will do this alone. There are no tears as she walks blankly down the hallway and slowly packs Andrei's belongings, which consist mainly of scrubs and pyjamas. She is spiritless, and we know her communication with us will cease once she leaves and tries to forget about her time in the United States. Ana has shown strength very few people have. The young woman stood by her husband's side through the toughest of all times. The darkness of the cold room surrounded her daily as she listened to her husband's beating heart, often wishing it wasn't. She will board the plane and try to forget what happened on the sixth floor and the night she never dreamed could happen.

*****

Mona is in a hurry today but stops in the hall to ask if we have dinner plans tonight. She wants to meet us at Sonny's for dinner, which is a stone's throw away from where the motor home is parked. Sonny's, an authentic Italian restaurant in the heart of San Clemente, is busy seven days a week.

With its checkerboard tablecloths and sawdust floors, the sound of mandolins and castanets take front and centre as the trio of Italian musicians begins to play. Marco and I have been here many times. Our favourite server waves to us to come to the front of the line. She then leads us to our perfect spot in the corner of the open-air restaurant. Our favourite red wine and warm Italian bread wait for us as we take our seats. "Three of us will be dining tonight." Marco wants to make sure she adds another chair and place setting. She nods and then mentions how busy they have been tonight.

"I haven't seen you in here in a few days." She smiles as she grabs another chair. "No, we've been trying to cook in the motor home more often." Marco takes a sip of wine from his glass. Smells of garlic and pizza bread fill the air as we wait for Mona to come in.

Mona rushes in, knowing she is late. "God, I'm sorry. I'm always late." She pulls her chair in and takes a sip from her preordered wine. "The unit has been busy since we admitted the new patient." She takes another sip. We gossip, and after some time and a few glasses of wine, she begins.

"Trey has had a good week in physical therapy. We have now progressed to heavily- assisted walking in the Lite Gait. He did four laps around the sixth floor earlier today." Mona has Trey attached to a wheel device that holds his dead bodyweight with a sling that hangs from metal bars. The gadget allows Trey to swing while attempting to walk. Mona follows closely behind and, with her hands, pushes the apparatus as she adjusts the pace. "I want to advance him as quickly as I can." She takes a breath. Her hair is pulled back with a rubber band in a sloppy ponytail. "He is trying to walk. The nurses are distracted, laugh and applaud when he passes their stations. I know they love him, but they are not helping him. Please assist me." Marco and I finished our dinner. I sense a sort of possessiveness from Mona.

"I'll talk to Linda in the morning and ask her to speak with the other nurses. Maybe that will help." I reassured her I would take care of it. We've become good friends with Mona, and I admire her knowledge. We head back to the motor home feeling good that Trey is progressing very well. I feel confident that he will be walking before leaving the hospital.

*****

"Help! Help!" Trey screams in unrecognizable words from his bed. The tiny room is dark and cold as Christian thrashes around. "Help!" Trey continues to try to get someone's attention. Hearing the pleas for help, a night nurse rushes down the hall into Christian and Trey's room. It's midnight as Christian lies in bed convulsing and shaking, and Trey lies frozen. Nurses surround Christian as they turn him onto his side to open his airway. They struggle and shove pillows under his left rib cage to ensure he won't teeter onto his back. He finally goes into a deep sleep, and they know nothing is left for them to do but monitor him for a possible next round.

Trey lies still while listening, hoping Christian won't start up again. He's not laughing this time. His face is solemn as one of the nurse's returns.

"You did good tonight; you might have saved Christian's life. You should be proud of yourself." She leans over Trey in the dead of night and places a kiss on his forehead.

My cell phone rings, waking me early in the morning. It's Jenny, the night charge nurse from the hospital. "I'm sorry to bother you, Leigh, but I need to tell you something before I leave work."

"Is everything okay with Trey?" I glanced at the clock. It's 6:43 a.m.

"Yes, he's fine. It's something he did last night. He yelled for the nurses while Christian had a seizure. If it weren't for him, Christian might have died. We are all so proud of him." Her voice cracks.

"Thank you for calling me. Hopefully, I'll see you before the shift change." I hang up the phone, reach over, and rub Marco's shoulder while snuggling against him. He's still asleep as I dream of slipping back to la-la land.

Chapter 40

THE SKY IS DARK AND LOW WITH DENSE, BLACK clouds, and the wind whips up, howling and warning into the premature twilight. The first crack of lightning lights the sky, and within seconds the rolling boom of thunder reverberates overhead. The boom rolls across the campground, announcing the start of what the looming cloud layer has promised since dawn. Our bench on the hillside under the red coral tree is vacant as we watch the storm's fury forming from inside the motor home. We are the only ones in the campground and enjoy the show that nature is beginning to put on for us.

The branches of trees sway in the strengthening gust, surrendering without a fight. Soon the rain falls, slow to start, haphazardly splattering the front windshield. Then it begins to fall in buckets, cascading like a waterfall from the heavens. A jagged bolt of white lightning splits the chilly sky on the far hill, and then it's gone. The thunder is only a second behind, while Marco and I wear matching grins and exchange tense glances. It is a storm promising nothing but pure and incredible views. The morning we'll never forget.

"Well, it doesn't look like we will be fishing today. Let's get out of here early, see Trey, and take the RV home with us. I need to have a few things checked on it sometime this week." Marco runs his strong hands through his now almost all grey curly hair.

The storm passes through quickly as we leave the hospital for home. I'm excited to spend some time with Russell, Cameron, and Madison. I've told Trey how proud I am of him and how much I love him. We exit the parking lot as I follow Marco in my car and crank up the music.

It's nice not driving the Deer Highway today, as we find ourselves too far south to make sense in using it. Instead, we will take the straighter but longer way around to Rancho on the busy California freeway. I notice how beautiful the crisp air feels on my face. My memory finds the last time I drove on this freeway was when I followed behind the ambulance on the way to the hospital years ago.

The drive is long before Marco decides to pull off at a casino for the night. I follow him into the RV park, passing by other rigs while looking for a pull-through spot. With grass on both sides of the small parking spot, we pull in and ready the motorhome for its overnight stay.

"Do we have shampoo?" Marco turns the lever to the right in the walk-in shower.

"Yes. It's on the ledge." I reach behind the pillows stacked on the bed and grab my teddy bear. Closing my eyes, I visualize Trey and begin my ritual of sending healing energy to him.

With the shower water running, I somehow turn my focus from Trey to the gambling just inside the casino doors. Breathing deeply, I see the lucky sevens light up, and I blow hot air over them. I place my hands over my eyes as I concentrate on sending Reiki to the sevens again and think of nothing else. My hands are red hot as I set them on my knees, never letting the sevens leave my mind. Suddenly the water in the shower stops running. I'm alert and realize it's time to go.

As we enter the casino, I sit at the first video machine I see but notice the energy doesn't feel right as I lose my first hundred-dollar bill. I have lost the money and Reiki, I fear. Tonight will be a short night. I sadly eye the single hundred-dollar bill stuffed into my pocket. Marco motions to me to make our way over to "high limits" with fewer people and a better selection of booze.

Once there, I sit at the first available video keno machine, close my eyes, focusing on the number seven as I drop my last hundred-dollar bill into the slot. I'm in deep concentration as I bet on all four cards and slowly drag my finger across the sevens row. The bet is steep at eight dollars per pull. Nothing. Nothing. Come on!! Then, with sheer might and the third press of the button, I hit six out of seven numbers. I am in shock as the bells and lights go off. I sit in disbelief as I shout to Marco, "I just won! I just won!" He takes me into his arms and practically shakes the life out of me with genuine excitement. After ten minutes pass and a large crowd forms behind me, I see I've won twenty-seven thousand dollars!

Three men in black suits walk up to me, check my player's club card inserted into the slot, and then escort me to a small private room where a casino teller sits. After taking the twenty-seven-thousand-dollar voucher from my hand, she grabs a stack of hundred-dollar bills and feeds them into a reading-type machine. The hundred-dollar bills shoot out of the register. "Is this the first time you have won?" There sits an Asian woman behind bars.

"Yes." I watch the remaining bills spit out. I leave the room with my massive amount of money left behind in a safety deposit box, knowing that many people in the casino witnessed my good fortune. Marco is on the phone when I approach him. He's talking with Russell telling him of my winnings. The next call goes to Cameron and finally to Madison.

"Do you want to play some more?" He sees me walk over. His face is ablaze and excited.

"No, let's go have dinner. I'm tired and hungry."

"Come on, just a little longer," he coaxes, knowing that he's hungry, too, but not for food. I sit down at the machine and place a hundred-dollar bill into the slot. I bet max on the four cards, close my eyes, see the sevens again, and push the button. Nothing. My luck has gone dry. Again, I breathe in a deep breath, place my hands over the screen, see the numbers, and then hit the button. Marco is leaning over my shoulder as the high-pitch winning alarm screams through the air again. Thirty-two thousand dollars! Another big win! Jumping up and down, I see people trying to see how much I've won this time.

The same three men in black suits escort me again to the cashier, who counts out the money and hands me 1099 after putting the cash into the same safety security box.

We leave high limits and see Russell, Cameron, Madison, and Alexander smiling ear to ear at the door. The casino manager escorts us to The Oak House, a fine steakhouse.

There we toast each other and drink champagne and high-end vodka. Hors-d'oeuvres taste fine as we wash them away with expensive wine. Steaks, lobster, shrimp, and sides coat our stomachs as we celebrate our lives. Hoping our stay at the casino will be extended, the casino's management offers us a two-bedroom suite along with our complimentary dinner. Both are on the house.

"I'm not going to stay in the suite with the temptation of gambling more." I look at Marco as we float out of the casino to our RV spot after saying goodnight to the kids. We hit the mattress and smile as we peacefully end the night. A good night's sleep is what we needed after such a magical evening.

We lazily wake Monday morning and realize Marco's workload is light as we make our way back into the casino to pick up our winnings. I stuff the stacks of money into my overnight bag, and we walk out. *Not bad for a couple who just witnessed a scene in Ocean Eleven.* I drive straight to the bank as Marco follows behind in our motor home. We couldn't believe our luck! It felt like a beautiful dream that finally came true. Too much for us to take in. Too much to imagine. While insurance was paying for Trey's care at the hospital, we spent money on gas, food, travelling, and equipment I purchased to help with his recovery. The extra cash would help with all the therapies I was doing for Trey and everything I planned to do in the future.

*****

Trey's bedroom in Rancho had been collecting dust, and his door remained closed since his overdose. Lisa came to stay in his bed occasionally but couldn't handle the heartbreak and memories. Just a photograph was all it took for her tears to burst. She would clutch the solid wooden frame tight in her hand, able to see a lonely reflection of her face in the thin sheet of glass that covered it. The girl looked past her own sad eyes and stared upon Trey's face in the moment of absolute perfection. It was the happiest memories that hurt the worst; they were the ones that cut her the deepest. Lisa stared in at his eyes, which were glistening with the twinkle that she loved so much. They reminded her of what she had lost. Lisa clutched the frame tight, pressing it to her breasts, wishing to feel his head resting upon them one last time. At that moment, Lisa realized she no longer knew how she felt. Her body and mind were numb, yet somehow in total pain. She longed to be free of him yet wanted him back more than she'd ever wanted anything before. Other than the few times she was there, the room was empty, both the room and Lisa.

Anticipating Trey's homecoming, Marco and I know we need more space for Trey, his few belongings, and exercise equipment. One afternoon while Marco and I share a few quiet moments, he makes the decision. "I'll remodel Trey's bedroom. I can add ten feet to it before he leaves the hospital." Marco begins making plans for its immediate renovation.

Once Marco's work is complete, the room will be better. We decide to replace his king-size bed with an electric twin-size hospital bed. That will give us ample space and make my job more manageable, with the push of a button to raise and lower the head of the bed. The spinning bike isn't an option because of Trey's poor balance and weak core strength, so we redesign the bike by removing the seat. That way, Trey can remain seated in his wheelchair while he exercises. We also decided to switch out the pedals and replace them with big, black army boots once used to keep Trey's feet firmly planted on the hospital floor. We hope these modifications will keep him safe while he remains limber.

We bought large mirrors to cover the closet doors, making the already ample room seem even more substantial. Many expressive paintings hung in groups are on the almond-coloured wall. The bed is dressed in the most beautiful bamboo sheets to welcome Trey home with softness and warmth. The girl scouts' handmade blanket is draped over a nearby chair, offering cosiness and security.

A large flat-screen television faces his bed, and Alexander perfects the surround sound to suit Trey's listening needs. Wood shutters block out all light from the room for possible napping. We installed a personal heater/air conditioner, as Trey's body usually runs cooler than Marco's and mine.

Trey's room is well situated as it sits in its own wing and has easy access to the garage. Russell has built a well-made ramp to make it easier to get Trey's wheelchair into the room from outside and through the sliding glass door where the car is typically parked.

A handicap-accessible shower is added, with custom tile surrounding the floors and walls. An ivory toilet hangs from the wall, making it easier to mop excess water into the drain after Trey's shower. An overhead fan blows warm air over the shower area to chase away any chance of chills.

I'm fortunate I found a red Dodge van that has a built-in electric ramp in the back for easy access in and out. We've installed an aftermarket safety system into the car's floor and onto Trey's wheelchair. The system locks automatically in between the two backseats, and the quick release makes it easy to push Trey up the ramp and into the van where he can ride securely in his wheelchair. It's a step down from the luxury cars I've been accustomed to, but it will make my life easier.

Our efforts to make him comfortable once he gets home are apparent. There is a nostalgic feeling in my heart as I remember bringing him home from the hospital as an infant and the excitement of knowing things would get easier.

Chapter 41

THE NURSES MUMBLE THAT AN INPATIENT DRUG-and-alcohol rehabilitation centre will replace the sixth-floor subacute unit. We've seen signs that this could be true as we watch the people with addiction problems hang outside the hospital doors.

The patient's families should start looking for new accommodations for their loved ones, Deb Dunne warns me. The subacute unit has been losing money for years and is in trouble. Medi-Cal and Medicare pay for the patients here, and these entities pay less than the big private insurance companies who cover many of the population with addiction. The decision for the future of the sixth floor is coming and slated for September.

It will soon be time for Trey to leave the hospital, although, at this point, he doesn't have to. I am ready for him to come home, though, and everyone has done all they could do to help him, I believe. No one thought he would leave the hospital, but Trey has proved everyone wrong. I have settled into accepting things as they come.

Deb has been looking into other hospitals where Trey can move to more acute physical therapy. The patients who can tolerate intensive treatment are eligible for six-week inpatient rehab. According to Deb, Trey is the only one on the floor who can. *I'm not sure I'm willing to send him away again.* She's been in contact with three prominent hospitals and has planned for Marco and me to tour their facilities.

In this setting, acute rehabilitation hospitals typically are crowded, and their waiting lists are long. I dread the thought of putting Trey into another hospital and taking on more driving, but I feel I have to do what's best for Trey.

At first, I find it hard to pinpoint why I feel so unsettled as Marco, and I make the trek to visit the first hospital on the list. *Maybe because I read that the nurses there reportedly see ghosts during their shifts as they pass out their scheduled meds?* The temperature is colder than seasonable, and the streets quieter as we pull into the Ranch Amigo's rehabilitation parking lot. I stop to listen as I hear a weird noise as Marco and I enter the hospital. *Was that a scream, or was it just my imagination?* I see its grounds and floors are cold and vacant as I look around. The hospital is supposedly haunted, initially built as an asylum, but I never dreamed it would affect me this way.

I reach and open the massive double doors by their round chrome handles. I pull my eyes from the highly polished linoleum floor to catch a glimpse of the hallway when a draft of air hits my face. It's cold and smells of bleach. Ahead of me are white walls, decorated with old black-and-white photographs of hospital staff—most likely, of staff that are either deceased or in some retirement home. The strangest thing about this place is that there is no energy, no patients working out or talking. I pass different doors with hand sanitiser dispensers every few seconds, but still no liveliness.

How could this benefit Trey? No energy, no therapy. The tour lasts a solid hour, and as we leave, we know this will not be the place for Trey.

I am starting to feel down but don't know why as I toured the second hospital in the heart of Fullerton. Nowhere is the chronic underfunding more evident than in the hallway where I wait. The hallways see patients crammed in corridors, some being tended to by strained relatives and some sitting alone. They sit in their chairs, eyes avoiding the naked fluorescent tubes that flicker above them. *Are they here for rehabilitation? How could people get better by sitting around all day?*

For a brief moment, I think about the exorbitant private fees. As I look around, I see cheap prints that are tasteless, lacking vibrancy on the walls. They appear sun-bleached in this window-less hall. I notice its rehab equipment is dated, and the exercise room is empty. The embarrassed administrator approaches me and points out that the hospital is about to be remodeled and that some patients will need to move to another location. I can't take the chance Trey could be moved further away. This hospital is already more than an hour from home.

Casa Alexandria is the third and most impressive hospital we tour. It's a decent forty-five-minute drive from home, and the hospital is clean. The journey begins with the inpatient unit and ends with the sizeable outpatient rehabilitation centre, where they offer daily services of three different modalities: speech, occupational, and physical therapy.

The atmosphere is entirely different from what we'd seen elsewhere on the private ward. The air has an aromatic scent, and the seats and tables are plush. Every surface is dustless. The nurses are not hurried during their rounds from room to room. There are vases of flowers and beautiful framed art pieces on the walls. In the corridor is a water dispenser and, in most rooms, there is the noise of a television. This ward makes a little more sense, but we learn that Trey is not eligible for their inpatient program because of his extended residency at South Beach Hospital. We are disappointed but half-heartedly relieved.

We cross the parking lot to the sizeable outpatient rehabilitation centre where Trey could receive the therapy he needs. Plans could include bringing him here three days a week for six weeks. We could opt for more services if he's progressing at a decent pace under the insurance company's guidelines. The hitch—he'll be placed on a waiting list until a spot opens up once he comes home for good.

*****

Trey's speech is still difficult to understand but is slowly picking up. He is more articulate when speaking spontaneously and harder to know when he premeditates. He yells out a word or small phrase every so often, and the words are said perfectly. He shows some frustration but gets a kick out of himself when his words don't come out the way he wants them to. He struggles with simple vowels and "r" sounds, but his critical thinking is excellent.

Trey's vision is there at times. I know he can see, but recent tests point to ocular motor delay. His eye movements are weak, and his muscles need strengthening before he'll use his eyes again. I've used the brain-machine for years and hope it's generating new nerve growth. Trey can identify blinking lights; that's encouraging, as I remember the idiot Dr Boutros.

His occupational therapist, David, and I are working hard on his upper-body strength as Trey continues to make gains. It appears the paralysis on his right side has disappeared because he can now raise his arms over his head. In hopes of helping Trey's tight muscles regain function, Dr Postigo, a prominent neurologist on staff, injects Botox into his stiff wrists and is thrilled with the progress Trey is making. His biceps are finally showing some strength, and he can wiggle his fingers on command. It's amazing how the small things matter so much.

Some obsessive behaviour is beginning to show. Trey stays in constant and steady thought when he isn't working with his therapists, and it seems as though there is another world that he exists in. I have become aware of him whispering as if he is speaking to an imaginary friend.

Physically, he is here, but the rest of him is somewhere else. In that place, he is peaceful. It's a place where no success for acceptance is required, and no one is listening for the stress in his speech. He seems content to be there, but it's distressing to me.

Trey is obsessed with practising his math skills, which come out in a garbled mess. Deb is burned out after spending hours with him. He loves listening to addition/subtraction rap/rock CDs while participating. They are helping, and, most importantly, they are exercising the left side of his brain, where we believe much of the injury is.

Mona continues to work diligently on Trey, whether on his core strengthening or walking. She is focused and is wholly committed to his recovery.

The establishment overrules the hospital's rigid mandatory feeding tubes and trachs rules. Trey's nurse removes his trach and the feeding tube as the day of bringing him home comes closer. He will finally be free of the life-saving devices he needed for many years.

The days have grown shorter as our patience grows longer. He continues to improve, but it's all so slow. As the days go by, I know that his accident happened by divine intervention. God's plans for Trey and me were like blueprints for a contractor, an x-ray for a doctor. I'm confident that if this hadn't happened to Trey, he'd be dead or homeless by now, and he would have never successfully beaten his addiction. *Did he ever want to is the real question?*

We're thankful to the people involved with Trey's recovery process, from the people who helped us with the motor-home locations to the servers at the restaurants to the nurses. I thank God that I found South Beach Hospital, but now it's time to say goodbye.

Chapter 42

THE SADNESS ECHOES DOWN THE LONG STERILE hospital hallway while we slowly pack Trey's belongings and begin to say goodbye to the people we've met. The nurses take pictures with Trey, never wanting to lose the memory of what occurred on the sixth floor while he was there. They cared for him for three years and four months, but now it's time to let him go.

Deb packs bags full of Trey's belongings as she remembers meeting him the first day. Tears fill her eyes as she recalls the many days of math and laughter. Marco's hammer to spur old memories is packed between the girl- scout blanket and the CDs that the CNAs have copied for Trey. Pictures of Halloweens and Christmases in the hospital's activity room are duplicated and put into a book. Going-away cards are opened and read to Trey by some of the nurses. Greeting cards come from as far away as the restaurants we frequented during our extended stay at the Pacific Ocean. The sixth floor is grim and quiet.

Then a frequent visitor who worked in administration comes to say goodbye. She cries as she tells me her story and says farewell. She's coincidentally the mother of one of Trey's long-time friends who suffered a heroin overdose that ended his life at age twenty-eight. She explains that she came in on many late nights to seek comfort and take shelter in Trey while looking for acceptance that her son is indeed gone. She glances toward the picture window as she continues. "Trey willingly sat quietly in the dead of night while lending me his ear as I prayed to God to help me find peace." She struggles to hold back her tears. She leaves Trey with a kiss to the forehead and a whisper, "Thank you for keeping me company all those nights when Brad couldn't. Thank you for letting me cry on your shoulder. Thank you for always being there for me. I will never forget you. I love you."

I climb into the backseat of the car, where I see Trey sitting and then Marco begins backing out of the driveway behind the hospital. The hospital's parking lot is where we watched crows fly, garbage trucks dump their trash, and where I practised my brain machines on Trey so many times. It seems the entire hospital staff stands on the curb and waves goodbye. My tears fall as I see faces I will never forget. Memories that will not go ignored.

Their eyes are filled with tears as well. I leaned out the window. "We'll be back to visit." I wave as I see Mona put her sunglasses on, trying to hide her glistening eyes. Candy turns her back so I can't see her face, while Dr Striker shakes his head in disbelief as we honk and speed off. We enter the on-ramp to Deer Highway as I feel happiness and sadness concurrently and wonder what we will face once Trey is permanently home.

*****

The chill in the air confirms the end of summer, and Trey is home now. It's much easier on us all. I'm glad his hospital days are over, but I miss the people who work there in a weird sort of way.

Our boat is home and sits in our driveway, waiting for its turn to get back on the open seas. Every time I look at it, I remember the many times it saved my sanity when things seemed so down. The teddy bear I clutched to my chest sits on the bed in the motor home. It holds a special place in my heart, and I feel fond of it just looking at it. We clean the RV before it is closed up for storage.

It feels like a new life, and I'm ready for the change. The house seems alive now that Trey is home, and I can hear his every move on the baby monitors I have placed in different rooms. Just the hum of his television over the speaker gives me peace, knowing he has survived the most challenging part of his recovery and that brighter days are ahead. Marco and I talk many times about getting back to normal, and this is our chance, and we seize the opportunity.

We're fortunate to live in California for all the programs to people in our position. Trey qualifies for In Home Support Services which opens up an opportunity for us. The state will pay me for caring for him at home. I can take that money and put it towards the many therapies that I have in mind for him. I enjoy watching him progress. I practice the many modalities I've learned since Trey's accident and spend significant time studying the many English language sounds in his room. I work on keeping his muscles robust and enjoy taking him outside to enjoy the sunshine while working in my garden. Where has the time gone?

*****

After many hours of research, I find an article about horseback riding and its many benefits for people with brain injury. It shows tremendous results, not only for balance but also for social interaction. Studies show the back-and-forth movement of the horse's gait benefits the rider's brain vestibular system, that is, the rider's balance. My search continues.

A brief Internet inquiry leads me to a therapeutic horseback-riding facility in Bonsall, about an hour's drive south. The reviews are outstanding. Hundreds of people, ranging from young children to retired individuals who require the vestibular practice, come from far and wide to this horse ranch. I'm encouraged.

When I suggest horseback riding to Trey, he laughs, then stubbornly refuses to go. "Trey, you've got to give horseback riding a chance. It's going to be good for your brain." I watch for his reaction.

"Horses stink!" He doesn't want to be associated with being a cowboy. I walk away and realize I must brainstorm ways to convince him to go. I called the centre and set up a meeting with Director Cassidy. She runs the ranch at Therapeutic Horsemanship, so I decide to bring him there to see how it goes.

Trey and Madison are with me as I drive to the facility. We exit the highway and squint, trying to read the road sign covered with overgrown trees. We look for the entrance to the driveway and see the hand-painted sign reading "HORSES THAT-A-WAY." We enter the driveway and slowly creep along a wooden bridge that gives passage over a creek fifteen feet below.

Green trees hover until we reach the clearing, opening an impressive twenty acres filled with horse arenas. We drive the

289

dirt road leading us around the impeccable horse corrals and grounds to the main building where a handful of girls are talking out front.

All of the girls are pretty, and their ages range from the early twenties to the late thirties. The exception is Cassidy, who stands out with her long blondish-white hair pulled in a ponytail underneath a sizeable, brimmed cowboy hat. She is in her mid-sixties with blue eyes and a warm smile. She sincerely looks the part of a full-fledged cowgirl.

*****

There's a spot along the dirt road to park the van where we have enough room to lower the rear ramp. As we approach the group of girls, we see smiles. Cassidy steps out from the group, extends her hand, and then discusses Trey's ability to ride. She's not concerned about his lack of strength or his dysfunctional hands. He's adamant against riding the beast but perks up significantly when he hears the girls will walk the horse beside him while he rides. We mention Trey loves Nirvana, which leads Cassidy to an idea. She suggests we play the Nirvana CD on the outside speakers in the arena while he rides. I conveniently have his favourite CD in the car.

Trey agrees. Madison takes hold of the wheelchair's handles, and with a running start, pushes him up the steep ramp until they reach the platform at the top. From there, Madison slowly stands Trey—he is more than capable of bearing his weight—and begins moving his legs backwards, one by one, with her foot. She carefully moves him until his rear is even with the horse's back. She lays him onto the horse while the girls help swing his legs over the horse's sides. Once he is lazily sitting on the horse's back surrounded by the six girls, he slumps over—his core is weak. In a flash, the girls are everywhere; some hold his hands, others have his feet, one girl leads the horse, and one follows.

Trey's horse, Harry, is led over to the arena, and the music is on. The speakers blare as the excitement builds. I look over at Madison; we both have the same look on our faces. The glimpse of hope.

The music soars through the air, taking with it the souls of everyone at the ranch. Harry is slow at first, showing signs of excellent training. He is cautious and aware of Trey on his back and the girls by his sides, but something clicks as he looks over the crowd. He hears the punk sound over the loudspeakers, and his head extends forward with his ears flat back. Puffs of moisture escape from his nostrils as Harry begins to pick up the pace. His heart keeps time with the drums, pumping the music through his veins as he loses himself in the arena and to Nirvana. He steps gently, aware of not moving too quickly, while Trey's smile burns a hole into our hearts.

I glance over at Madison and remember the day she began looking for work after completing her business degree at college.

The call caught Marco off guard in his office. He began answering questions from the company where Madison had an employment interview. "Yes. She's an excellent secretary although she only works part-time. Yep, always on time, works hard, knows the computer, and types fast." He stopped and thought. Hmmm. What can I say that would make them think twice about hiring her? Oh, okay. "She's already promised to work for me full time after the summer's end. Sorry. She made the decision last night."

Madison is confused about why she hasn't received a return call from the company. She was so sure she aced the interview.

She waited. No call. She hesitated but then decided to call them. The corporation's receptionist explained they were impressed with her skills but were looking for a full-time employee. She argued that she could work full time but then found out about the conversation between her dad and the interviewer. Madison was furious as she rushed into Marco's office.

"How dare you? I need a job! I need to work and make some money! That's why you sent me to college!" Her brown eyes glared at her father.

He listened intently then explained. "Here's my proposal. I will gainfully employ you to work in my office and help your mother with Trey. I can't risk the chance of her getting injured. Your mother needs help lifting him and pushing him into the car, and he weighs twice what she does. If you can be in the office in the morning until she is ready to leave, you can help her get Trey up and then go to his appointment with her. It would be helpful for both of us.

Madison listened and carefully considered his offer but then reflected on her hopes of being a high-powered professional. Madison knew her heart couldn't ditch out on Trey and take the chance I could get hurt, so she put her dreams aside and agreed to his proposal.

My memory ends when I hear Trey's laughter in the arena. Harry is on a roll but is conscious of Trey on his back as the song ends. We giggle. Trey thinks only of horseback riding, and the girls he knows will be there for him from that day forward. The three of us drive down the freeway twice a week for a thirty-minute horse ride. Trey's progress is remarkable in just six months. His shoulders sit properly and erect when seated on his riding companion. He is sitting straighter more after he first started at the ranch. His hands are looser as he tries to grip the reins. His legs are more relaxed by Harry's side, and his balance seems better. His communication skills seem to improve as he engages with the girls surrounding him as much as possible. He laughs and plays with the ranch hands as if he is one of them.

*****

Suddenly, Harry is no longer Trey's riding companion and pastured. Trey thinks he is at the glue factory. As Trey sits on Flicka, his new therapy horse, the girls urge the horse to progress from walking to trotting on the trail, to challenge Trey's reaction time in keeping himself balanced. The experienced girls run beside Trey, making sure he doesn't fall. He loves it.

The specially trained horses at the ranch handle all types of disabled people. There's no concern about them bucking or harming their riders. The farm proves to be a sanctuary for families. It calls to many children with different problems. Some of them can't sit upright, so they lay flat across the horse's back during their lesson. As I watch, one of the waiting mothers approaches me. She shares her story.

"While my husband and I were packing one day for a vacation, being sure to watch our twins, one wandered away. It was quite some time before we realized she was missing. We panicked and searched for her, but once our little Aly found the small pond, the water closed in around her. It filled her with panic. I'm sure she held her breath for as long as she could; her thrashing arms failed to catch our attention. She felt nothing as her heart beat rapidly. When my husband and I realized we had been watching the same child, it was too late as Aly lay motionless in the pond. We struggled to pull her to the shore.

We pounded her frail body, forcing her to take a breath. Our attempts left us empty. There was nothing. We pounded and struggled to remember the method of CPR, being so desperate to save her. I screamed, "C'mon Aly, C'mon. Take a breath, sweet baby, take a breath!" as my husband continued to force her to breathe. Her eyes remained closed, her face pallid, her lips blue. She was gone, we feared until she started choking, vomiting, and spitting water from her mouth. "She is breathing!" I screamed as I crushed my other daughter's hand in mine. We knew she had been without air for some time as we took her to the closest hospital. The prognosis was dim, and we knew that there would be severe consequences of brain injury. We thanked God she was alive but had no idea what her future would be, while we promised that we would always care for her." Her voice carried shame. There beside her was one of her twins at age five, Aly, on the horse. The mother's eyes welled with tears.

A friendly Asian woman parks her car beside the corral and flashes a calm smile. She gets out of her car and then lifts her four-year-old son into a wheelchair. He is limp and lifeless. He is dressed in tattered pyjamas as if she is too tired to clothe him. She is too familiar with that kind of tiredness that needs a good night's sleep and another type that requires so much more. I offer to help as I notice an emptiness in her heart where nothingness has taken over and holds her soul captive. She has a heavy feeling, and she can do nothing to get out from under it. That same hole in her heart makes her feel the need to wipe away any nonexistent tears she wants to form but can't. She has used them all up.

She begins to explain why she feels the way she does. "I left him unattended while he was sitting in a clip-on chair at our dining-room table during breakfast one morning, two years ago.

When he leaned back, he fell out of the chair backwards, landing on the back of his head, two feet down, and leaving him with an injury to his brain." She bites her lips as the dam of tears are held back. She's guilt-ridden and barely alive. She's another example that illustrates that everyone has a problem, some have bigger ones than others, but we all have one.

The girls lead Flicka with Trey on his back into a small corral where the horse's gait plays a role in activating the area of the brain that controls the sense of touch (tactile), sense of balance (vestibular), and understanding of where the body is in space (proprioceptive). All of which are important to Trey's recovery.

As Trey's lesson ends and we begin to leave the ranch, I pass the Asian woman pushing her son in his specially designed wheelchair to the waiting horse. It's his turn to work with Flicka. He won't sit up or enjoy the girls surrounding him and the familiar smell of the ranch. He'll only lie peacefully across the horse's back while his mother prays to God he will recover.

*****

Thoughts constantly invade my mind about giving Trey the most normal life he can have. *How can Marco and I help Trey make the best of what he has? How can horseback riding only two times a week help him in his quest to recover?* I sit day after day searching for the answer as I watch him slowly regain the things he has lost.

Chapter 43

DIRECTOR OF SPEECH-LANGUAGE PATHOLOGY at reuter's wonders if she can help Trey as we enter the office that specializes in speech, occupational, and physical therapies. Through the examination, Trey is uneasy as Debra gives commands rather than requests. He is highly uncomfortable. As I sit in on the testing, I find afterwards that she will schedule two sessions but warns me not to get my hopes up. "Few patients benefit from speech therapy with this type of disorder." *A negative attitude is not the way to start a new therapy relationship.* The woman is ordinary, wears drab clothing, and is plain-speaking but direct. "Trey's speech is slurred and is not understandable to the average listener." *No kidding, Debra! Even I know that!* She hands me the date of his first appointment.

We arrive right at his scheduled time —11:00 a.m.—and we go to a nearby cubby for his lesson. Debra begins slowly and is called out of her office just as she starts. She leaves us waiting for most of the session. "I'm sorry, I will issue you a date for a make-up lesson." *Does she think I have that much time? Does that idiot think it's easy to get Trey ready and out the door on time?* She walks out of the office, leaving me with cuss words at the tip of my tongue.

"Are there any other speech therapists that can work with Trey?" I look at the girl at the appointment desk.

"Debra is the head of the speech department, and you need to go through her to make any changes to Trey's schedule. You could, of course, go directly to Kyle, who runs the centre." She points to the office behind her. I notice the sign on the door reads "Kyle-Director."

"Can I get Kyle's direct line?" I ask.

"Call the office and ask for Kyle. You will be connected to him if he is in." She smiles as I wonder if other people feel the same as I do about Debra.

I rush to get home and make the call. "Is this Kyle?" I ask the man who picks up the phone.

"Yes. How can I help you?" His voice is pleasant but is powerful and in command.

"I'm Trey Morelli's mother and want to know if I can change therapists for him. Debra's too busy. I need someone to help Trey and am not sure she can." I use a direct manner but am not too pushy.

"Okay. Let me check Shelly's schedule and see if we can fit Trey in there." He places me on hold. "She has a cancellation tomorrow. Does that work for you? It's at 10:00 a.m." He offers the time slot.

"Yes. Thank you. We'll be there tomorrow." I'm pleased I made the time to call him today.

*****

The door swings open precisely at 10:00 a.m., and after looking around, Shelly comes over to Trey and me to introduce herself. She smiles, and instantly we know we like her because she makes us feel welcome. Trey's eyes beam as she speaks and leads us back to her small office. I can tell they will get along just fine. Shelly goes to work instantly. She opens her book and begins with breathing exercises.

"Can you take a deep breath and hold it?" She notices that he can't, as she watches him struggle. "That's okay. Most people can't." She moves on to separation of movement. "Can you stick out your tongue?" Shelly reaches for her tongue depressor. Trey barely sticks his tongue between his lips. "Oh, good. That's great!" She makes Trey feel successful. She seems to be all about simplicity, making things easy for her patients, helping them relax, and being happy with what they have. "Okay, you can pull it in," her voice directs him. His tongue remains there between his lips. "Okay, that's good." Her voice begins to crack, and a smile appears on her face. "My! You have a long tongue!" She smiles as Trey breaks into laughter, remembering he's heard that before.

Shelly drills him on articulation as she moves close with the tongue depressor. He senses she's close and smiles widely. "Say *ah*."

"Aaaahhhh." Trey intentionally breathes deeply. She drills him solidly for six straight weeks, is never late, and is always on time. Trey's desire to recover, combined with Shelly's knowledge of speech pathology, make for the right combination. They work together three times a week, establishing successful goals for Medicare.

As the lessons go on, so does Trey's infatuation for Shelly. She makes speech therapy fun and teases Trey day in and day out. Although Trey doesn't see it that way, they act like friends. He finds her humour mesmerizing. Trey procrastinates, daydreams, projects fantastical futures of him and her. In his mind, they are runaway lovers; in hers, he's just another therapy hour. They laugh, they joke, and Trey's brain shuts down at the thought of her. Simple ideas barely form in his mind before his fantasies of her take over. His infatuation grows for Shelly as his obsession for her becomes obvious.

*****

Casa Alexandria is world-renowned for spinal cord- and brain-injury rehabilitation. After waiting for nine months, an opening becomes available for Trey. Speech, occupational, and physical therapies are offered back-to-back under one roof, making it convenient for Trey to receive three modalities in one visit. The problem is that Medicare won't pay for double sessions of speech, one at Casa Alexandria, the other with Shelly, so I have to decide which will benefit Trey the most. The scheduling is difficult as I look at my calendar and realize Trey benefits from Shelly in more than one way. He likes her, enjoys working hard with her, and could plateau if I change his routine. A forty-five-minute drive to physical and occupational therapy three times a week isn't difficult, while I can continue to take him to speech locally on his off days. After deciding this is best and leaving Madison to tend to her office work, we hit the road again.

The gymnasium is immense, with five large, raised, padded mats in a single room. Over fifty patients lie on tables while their therapists instruct them on what to do to recover.

Trey's core strength is better, but it's still weak, and he struggles to sit up entirely on his own while seated on the mat. His spatial awareness is nonexistent as he fights to keep his feet on the floor. He can't distinguish right from left and doesn't know where his body parts are or what they are doing. He holds his arm up but is unaware that he is doing it. His claims of pain are difficult to deal with because he has no idea where the pain is. When he says it's in his foot, it could be in his back. It's hard to know. His hearing and sense of smell are sharper than usual because his vision is poor. He uses his hearing to focus on the other patients' conversations surrounding him, making it harder for him to do what his therapist asks. I can't assist because I don't have the strength to help. His female therapist looks concerned and motions for help from other therapists after realizing that she, too, is useless in trying to move Trey's dead weight around.

Rudy sees her frustration and joins in with Trey on the mat. As Rudy does this, I notice he has no traces of boyhood. I take in his muscles, the clean-shaven square jaw, and tune into his voice. It is as deep as any man. He smiles with ease and makes fluid arm movements to exaggerate his buoyant speech. He can't be much over twenty-five. He has a look about him, the dark hair and glasses—almost nerdy but strong.

Grabbing Trey from behind, he pulls Trey's shoulders back and signals the other therapist to hold Trey's feet to the floor. Trey cringes as Rudy forces and holds his head back.

Day in and day out, we alternate driving to Reuter's Therapy Center with Shelly and Casa Alexandria. At Casa Alexandria, the therapists are cold and unconvincing that they care. I wonder how many others sit in this same position as the therapist in charge comes to speak to me.

"Rudy is a strong physical therapist and can work with your schedule," she explains to Trey after speaking with the person who changed the program. Her words find Trey unhappy as a frown forms on his face.

"Go along with it. It's only for four more weeks," I whisper to Trey, who hates working with male therapists but unwillingly agrees. Another appointment with Rudy is set for tomorrow and will involve aqua therapy.

*****

Madison is bored at work and needs a break. This time last year, she began working, enthusiastic and looking to expand her knowledge in construction. Now every morning is spent doing the necessary preparation on autopilot while her brain prepares for any other possible scenario that might come up. She is constantly trying to find solutions to make Marco's business more robust. After telling Madison about my experience at the gym, she wanted to be involved, so she cancelled work for the following day. The bonus is she can help Rudy get Trey into the pool for aqua therapy.

We arrive at 10:00 a.m. sharp with Trey dressed in his blue-and-white board shorts. His legs are thin and white, showing signs that he's not walking enough. We meander into the pool area, where Rudy meets us and tells Madison he wants to get Trey into the pool by himself. He looks like a professional swimmer in his speedo and rash guard.

The pool water surface is perfectly flat and glassy; Madison and I sit poolside. Rudy's water shoes slap the white tile as he uses the automatic lift to lower Trey into the heated chlorinated pool water. Rudy muscles Trey to the edge and struggles to get him to float while fighting with him in the humid area.

Other therapists move past them, trapped in their heads, just as Rudy is, as he fights to find a way to use this time to benefit Trey. He is appeasing, frustrated, and sometimes forceful while working with Trey. The thirty-minute session seems an eternity as Trey's body relaxes and floats on the surface of the water. Rudy holds Trey's head above the water, hoping it doesn't bob beneath. He doesn't seem concerned about a bit of water getting into Trey's ears but is worried about it going over his head. After only thirty seconds more, Trey begins to sink, and Rudy's legs tire and struggle to bring him back toward the choppy surface. Rudy deems the session is over as he peers over at Madison and me with an exhausted look on his face.

Jack in the Box for lunch is Trey's reward while reflecting on his day.

How'd you like the water?" I ask while noticing Trey is quiet. "Is working with Rudy bothering you?" He makes no facial expression. He's slow as he struggles with his speech to tell me what is wrong. After multiple attempts at guessing his words, I finally get it.

"I'm not working out with Rudy anymore." His words squeeze together, no breath between them.

"Why?" I remember doing this before.

"Rudy tried to dunk me." Trey's speech slurs as he tries to convince us it really happened. Madison and I shake our heads.

"No, he didn't. We were watching." I speak to him in disapproval.

Trey insists. "He did! He did!" He's determined to make me believe he is speaking truthfully.

"Why would he do that, Trey?" I'm disappointed he would lie as I think about how hard Rudy tried to make the aqua therapy successful. From what he says next, I can tell he is thinking deeply, already with a strategy.

"Because he's jealous of my package," Trey spits out enough words for me to understand while he keeps a straight face. He's as serious as he can be as he thinks about his half-hour session. He honestly believes Rudy is so jealous that he tried to drown him. Madison and I look at each other in bewilderment while trying to hide our smiles that Trey thinks this is true.

The stint at Casa Alexandria ends after six weeks, and we have no plans to return. Trey lacks the desire to go back, and, truthfully, I didn't see any progress anyway. We leave there with a promise that a new Rifton Lite Gait will be delivered within a few weeks so we can work on Trey's walking at home. While I think about how he dangled in one at the hospital under Mona's watch, I wonder how it will help.

Chapter 44

I CONTINUE TO SEE SIGNS OF RECOVERY, ALTHOUGH progress is slow. Trey grows stronger by the day, but his balance and vision are still significant problems. A strange case of psychosis has slowly increased. He obsesses over visions of fairies instead of working out or solving mathematical problems as he did in the hospital. The emergence is slow and hard to understand. *Is it his medications or some side effect from his brain injury?* He claims the fairies named Angie and Wendy are taking over. It seems he can barely think, and if he tries, the result is scrambled logic. He speaks to them in whispers both day and night, and I find him constantly accusing them of improper sexual activity. When asked to describe the fairies, he swears they are not in his head but are here. He has clear images of them of nut-brown miniature people with silver wings. He can see, in his mind, of course, the flowing dark locks of hair and their bright black eyes. He recalls the black jumpsuits and their tiny boots, but when he opens his mouth to explain it, desperation is all that comes out. His psychosis has elevated to new heights, and now he's refusing to eat. I can't understand it. My worry grows as I report it to his psychiatrist.

"Is he drinking plenty of fluids?" Dr Gee looks up from her chart.

"Yes. Trey will drink anything but will not eat. I have been buying protein shakes to ensure he's getting some nourishment. It's been six months since he last ate, and I'm worried sick."

"That's a good plan. As long as Trey isn't starving, he should be all right now. His weight seems average." *How can it be? He's six feet tall and only one hundred and twenty pounds!* "Make sure you give him a healthy shake at least three times a day. I'm sure the voices will subside after I write a new prescription and increase the dosage."

When I returned home from the store, the ingredients I bought hit the Magic Bullet, which sits on the kitchen's centre island. The blender mixing mixes up the healthiest shake I can create as I add the ingredients. His taste buds pop as he sips the thick juice through a wide plastic straw.

The voices in his head are driving him crazy. He cries in indecipherable English, trying to make them stop. Trey sobs as if his brain is has been shredded from inside. Emotional pain flows out of his every pore. From his mouth comes a cry so raw; his eyes bleed a thick flow of tears. He talks in his sleep and shouts in gibberish. His tangled words are a mess.

He's created more visions in his mind. This time, it's a friend he knew back before his accident. He's a guy he did plenty of drugs with, the son of the woman who visited Trey at night while Trey was in the hospital and a more significant threat than the fairies. "Bradley is making me use drugs." Trey's body winces and squirms, not unlike withdrawal symptoms, as if forced to use drugs. His stomach aches as he grunts and groans feeling the need to vomit.

I scream, "No! He's not; he's not here. He's all in your mind!" He cries for an unusual amount of time. My tears fall as quickly as his, but only out of genuine frustration. I keep asking myself. *What is causing this?*

I can't take it anymore. I'm at my wit's end and argue until I'm sick. *Sick of all this. Sick of life.*

He cries. "Make Bradley stop giving me drugs." He begs. He pleads. Lost for words, I cradle him in my arms and don't know what to do. "Angie is trying to kill Wendy." He weeps. "Wendy died last night." He's confused and worried. I don't know if this is just part of recovery and increases his thought processes or medication. All I know is he has episodes daily, and all of them are so real they are terrifying Trey. No matter what I say, he believes these people in his head are trying to hurt him. I fill my days trying to distract him, but to no avail. As I worry about his mental health, the days pass slowly, and I lose my mind. There's no rhyme or reason to his thinking; there's no consoling him, no matter what I do.

*****

The phone rings. Shelly wants to talk to me after Trey's speech lesson. It's important.

Her words ring in my mind as I enter the medical office building, and I can't wait for Trey's speech lesson to end.

"Trey told me he's not eating because he doesn't have to. All he needs to do is imagine it. Isn't that a scene in the movie *Hook*?" She surmises and continues, "Wendy is a character in *Hook*. I believe he's combining his real life with his daydreams."

I telephone his psychiatrist for help. I share with her my belief that Wendy, Angie, and his refusal to eat are all residual

306

effects from obsessing over *Hook* while he lived in the hospital. I remember it like it was yesterday.

Candy sees me walking down the hallway at the hospital. "Oh, Leigh. Trey is so funny and loves watching Hook. *Deb found the movie in the social room and put it on his DVD player in his room. He lit up when he heard it for the first time. We've been playing it for him ever since."*

"Oh? How long does he watch it?" My concern builds.

"He stays in bed for the entire time. Sometimes he's there for three hours."

"Is he still sitting in the hallway in the afternoons when I'm not here?" My eyes are turning the colour of rage.

She begins to look nervous. "Yes. The CNAs put it on for him as soon as he's finished his lunch. Trey has seen the movie many times and seems to know some of the words. When the children sing, he looks like he wants to join in." I feel blood rush to my head. I walk out of the room and head straight to Joe's office. As I knock on the door, Joe opens it and motions me to enter.

"I thought I made it clear that I don't want Trey spending too much time in his room. It's easier for the staff to leave him in bed to watch television and ignore him. He needs to be more engaged and stimulated in his surroundings. Would you mind asking Deb to remove the movie, Hook, from his room and ask her not to play it for him anymore? It's starting to harm his therapies, so please do as I ask." Joe looks stunned. I'm not sure he understands my motives, but honestly, I don't care. I know what's best for Trey, and lying in bed all day is unhealthy.

"Don't argue with him about the voices; just reason with him," his psychiatrist lectures me. The advice doesn't sound that easy. "I will see you next week." She hangs up the phone.

The following week is brutal after my conversation with the doctor. The only two modalities he's involved in, horseback riding and speech, are put on hold as he becomes more delusional. The calls for help continue. "Bradley is trying to kill Angie. Wendy made Angie use drugs last night. I don't want to use drugs, but they are making me." His words are cluttered, indecipherable, and, as I try to figure out what he is trying to say, five, ten, fifteen minutes pass by. He wants to curl up and die. He needs protection from everything around him, but he still has to live with his thoughts, with the sad memories swirling around in his head. His eyes, already red and puffy from crying, are squeezed shut to push out more tears. He lets his head fall to his chest. No matter what he does, there is nowhere he can hide from the visions, threats, and his crazy imagination. I call the psychiatrist again, panicked and exhausted.

"I need assistance. I'm scared, worried; I feel drained." Thoughts of finding him a new home cross my mind but fade just as fast. Nine months of insane behaviour pass as I try to find ways to distract him, but it's no use. He refuses to eat, so I continue to develop concoctions to keep him at a healthy weight. I'm tired and stressed that this would never end. Is he mentally ill? A referral is written from his psychiatrist to see a neurologist.

Chapter 45

WE PULL INTO THE PARKING LOT BEHIND THE
new neurologist's office and notice how flat the area is. Industrial
buildings surround her office, and the entrance is in the back lot.
The office doors are heavy as I hold the doorway open with my
right leg while shoving Trey through the opening. *Why are all
these people staring at me in the waiting room while I struggle
to open the door? Can't one of these idiots get up and help me?*

Dr Canelo is an intelligent young neurologist who deals
mainly with patients affected by multiple sclerosis. I peer into
the office to see her standing behind the receptionist's desk. She
has a nonthreatening face and a cheery disposition as she speaks
to her assistant. We waited in the room next door and were offered some water by the receptionist. Trey is seated in his wheelchair and is in a mellow mood.

We are finally called into one of the smaller offices and
wait until Dr Canelo comes in. She is pleasant and introduces
herself as she watches Trey closely. Her movements are calm
and deliberate. Her voice is soft, and she speaks without jargon.

She understands what is going on and periodically stops to address me directly to explain her opinion. She laughs as she notices Trey's awareness and offers her hand to him. He doesn't see it. She takes his hand and detects how much spasticity there is in it as his hand tightens. "What can I do for him today?" She wheels the computer screen closer to her.

"Trey hears voices, and he's scared of them. He's also refusing to eat. I have offered him meals many times, but he will not take in any food."

"Oh? Is that right, Trey?" She directs her attention towards him and waits for his reaction. There's nothing as he stares ahead. She assesses Trey and then makes changes to his prescriptions. I question her decisions as I remember the words said by the neurologists I met in ICU.

"There is no brain activity, and he will never come out of this coma. His brain is dead, and now all that exists is scar tissue. He's in a deep sleep state, and there's nothing we can do for him except to keep him comfortable."

We leave with the new prescriptions. As I read the writing, I noticed the doctor had prescribed baclofen for the spasticity in his hands and some clozapine for the psychosis. I remember the baclofen pump that Christian had surgically placed into his stomach and how it malfunctioned and needed replacing. I'm not sure how I feel about the new medications, but helping him is necessary for his severe delusions.

I patiently sat with Madison and Trey in the waiting room at Trey's second visit two weeks later. Finally, a nurse guides us into a smaller space, where Trey transfers onto a paper-lined table. Dr Canelo carries a set of fifteen tiny needles in her hand. They look like slivers as she begins inserting them into his feet, along his spine, and into his hands. She places two needles into his temples, then waits twenty minutes and removes them. We reschedule him for next week. Within three treatments, the voices begin to decrease. After the fourth, the scary sounds are gone. Dr Canelo specializes in acupuncture and has practised the ancient art for years. I'm grateful I've found her.

"Has Trey ever had a brain MRI?" She prescribes it on her pad and hands it to me as I shake my head, no, and question why not. I then think of Dr Boutros, who only ordered Trey's optic nerve imagery.

*****

The drive to the Imaging Center is short, and I'm aware of how quiet he is. There's no constant conversation between Wendy and him as we pull into the parking lot. I push his wheelchair into the office, where a technician comes around the corner to take the paperwork from me. After entering the information into his computer, the technician pushes a gurney over and then helps me place Trey onto a table. The table and Trey roll into a cylinder. The noise and the knocking are horrific as I watch Trey jump at each loud sound. I recall that he didn't jump at all the last time he had an x-ray under Dr Boutros's direction. Trey just laid there. *That's progress and proof he is aware of his surroundings!* The technician motions me to pick up the nearby microphone to speak to Trey to keep him calm. "Don't move, honey. The MRI is almost finished." My voice soothes him, and finally, the test is complete.

The MRI reveals Trey stroked in the watershed region of his brain, between his occipital lobe and parietal lobe. There is also damage to his cerebellum, which explains his balance problems. The loss is bilateral on both sides of the brain.

Dr Canelo explains, "Trey is fortunate his frontal lobe was left intact. The frontal lobe is typically the first to be taken out after an anoxic event. Trey's wasn't, which is a miracle in itself. The frontal lobe controls emotions and personality." She looks over at Trey. "See? That's why he's smiling. When it's damaged, there is a cascading event, which leads to aggression and anger. He's lucky he still has his funny personality. I have high hopes for a full recovery."

Constant and significant repetition is the only way the brain can repair itself. He will need to relearn everything he once knew. While his brain starved of blood and oxygen, it began dying, leaving behind a river of dead tissue. It will take time for his mind to create new pathways to help his vision, speech, and motor function.

I'm relieved to know what happened in those many minutes during Trey's overdose. I think of the psychologist who advised me to take care of myself because it would take time for Trey to heal. *Thank God I have.*

*****

The constant whispering is gone, and now Trey can return to horseback riding and speech therapy. His speech is slightly better now but still challenging to understand. While I search for progress, I notice his reaction time is getting faster. He can carry on limited conversations, and he regularly asks questions, which gears towards himself and the little world surrounding him. There are times when I feel like I'm dealing with an only child— a self-centred child and, for him, the world that matters stops at the tip of his nose. I'm beginning to think he is emotionally blind and can't empathize with other people's thoughts or feelings. He interacts, of course, laughs and jokes and makes friendly gestures from time to time. He is entirely alone and seems to enjoy his solitude. I liken him to a baby whose only concern is for himself to be fed and clean; no worries about the people surrounding him. As long as the world revolves around him, he's okay, and I know the brain injury is causing this.

His motivation remains high. His vision is unchanged, although he says his right eye is more vital than his left, and then he changes his mind. "I can't see shit." There is still hope his eyesight will improve, though; finding the place to start is the hard part. It's all about delayed motor function.

Time has passed quickly since our fourth visit with Dr Canelo. Trey seems more content and happier now. He is finally at peace, and it shows on his face.

*****

The rich aroma of the dish Marco and I are preparing is undeniable. We throw mounds of fire-roasted tomatoes into the saucepan coupled with garlic and salt. It simmers as we add a dash of wine and toast each other for a job well done. We can't resist the delightful sensations that swim in the kitchen air as we think of dipping our forks into the little white pockets of pasta filled with fresh portabella mushrooms.

Trey's stomach snarls and howls, and from it comes the not-so-subtle undertone of hunger pains. It comes in waves, and it seems as though his stomach has been slowly shrinking. He clutches his empty tummy, pulling it, in an attempt to silence it, but to no avail. It grows louder. It's leaving him feeling drained and empty. He knows it is time for him to eat, so he calls out loud as he hears me chopping and throwing ingredients into the blender for his nightly smoothie.

"Ma." His eyes look straight ahead. I leave the open kitchen and all its amazing smells to see what he wants, and in a difficult-to-understand voice, he asks for something I can't understand. "Paas." I try to understand him. His speech distorts as he tries again. "Paas." It goes on as he tries, and I sense frustration beginning to build.

"Don't give up, honey. Keep trying." I continue to encourage him. After over ten minutes of back-and-forth guessing, I finally stumbled upon the word. "Pasta?"

"Ya!"

"Would you like some?" He hesitates and struggles with his imagination for a moment, and then a "Yes!" leaves his lips.

"Trey wants pasta!" Tears fill my eyes. Marco is pleased. It has been a long twelve months since Trey chewed anything or used his teeth. I quickly pour ravioli into a bowl covered in marinara sauce, afraid he'll change his mind. I sit down next to him and promptly give him a small bite.

"Umm!" That's all he manages to say as I fill his empty stomach.

Chapter 46

THE SHOWER ROUTINE ALWAYS BEGINS WHEN I place the soap and shampoo on the ledge in the shower. Months ago, Marco turned the shower area into a total spa experience with two shower heads that fill the large room with steam. The plush towels hang close to the shower area if it's necessary to wipe the soap from Trey's eyes. A large armoire, designed to resist water damage, stands near the sink and holds many of Trey's items. The small decorative tiles on the floor and walls make for a designer bathroom, fit for any home style. I reach down to clean between his legs with a bar of soap.

"You pinched my left nut!" I decipher his words as he jokingly makes accusations. He tries to conceal his smile.

"I did not!" I admit I enjoyed the inappropriate conversation that we couldn't have held not long ago.

I continue to wash his hair and run the razor down his face. The razor struggles to cut through the wire strands that have grown overnight. A few tiny dark hairs creep from his ears. I grab a washcloth to wash them away, knowing there's only one way to defeat the busy mess, and that's with nose hair clippers. *When did my boy become a man?* The buzzer sounds as I clean up the hair in his nose and ears. A few strands of grey hair have crept in along his temple and sideburns; his hair on top has thinned. *I think of Cameron, who claims that you can see through the hair on the top of his head!*

Battle wounds mark his body from his accident. There's a hole above his belly button where the feeding tube lived for three and a half years. Above that, another three-inch scar exists for the colon screw-up in the ICU. Still, above that, in his neck is the brutal scar left by the trach so carelessly placed while he struggled and stormed in the first few days after his accident. It was done so recklessly—because of the dim prognosis. Memories of the hospital invade my mind.

He lay naked under the white sheet that surrounded his body. The nurse rushed into the room and, without hesitation, removed the covering and exposed his thin frame. As I watched, I felt embarrassment creep into my being. I wanted so badly to look away, but the nurse continued to speak to me while she worked. "He has many bedsores." She pointed to his butt, where the pressure sores were prevalent. She grabbed a pan of water and sponge as she ran her hand onto his face and along his body. She worked the dry shampoo into his long stringy hair as she pointed to the towel on the chair. I handed it to her. She worked so fast that she hadn't realized I had never seen Trey naked before. Not like this anyway. Had she worked in that unit for so long that she became numb to patient privacy? Who else has been in the room during Trey's bed bath? As I left the bedroom, the questions filled my head, stunned by the image still in my mind.

I thoroughly rinse down below, trying my hardest to be gentle. "Be careful; that's not Marco's!" He giggles. I can't contain

316

the smiles and laughter as I turn the shower off. Trey excels in so many ways and is a joy to be around, making everything a pleasure. *He's that rosebud that is slowly opening.* The simple task of showering him has turned into a half-hour of laughing and joking as his humour runs rampant.

*****

The magic of acupuncture is impressive. I remember what I witnessed in Dr Canelo's office, and I'm anxious to find another doctor to accelerate Trey's healing. Dr Canelo's time limits her duties at the office and treating multiple sclerosis.

The Chinese doctor sits at his Asian-inspired desk as he drinks from a cup of cooled green tea. I notice how thin he is. Ancient herbs adorn his office, lining the shelves and pamphlets describing their benefits. The phone is as quiet as the office while waiting for the doctor to finish his paperwork. The office is Dr Ling's clinic, where he practices the ancient art of acupuncture.

He finally waves us in, and I push Trey past the swinging doors. He motions us to go through the door at the end of the hall on the right. After struggling to get past the door, we find a bed lined with sheet paper. Madison muscles Trey onto the table. There we wait for the doctor. I watch the doctor as he tries to figure out what kind of healing Trey needs. He leaves the room and reappears with a tongue depressor and over seventy-five needles in his tiny hands. He asks Trey to stick out his tongue, and while examining it, he mentions the thick white coating on Trey's tongue. Dr Ling explains that the tongue is a window into Trey's body and directs him to place the needles. He begins to insert them into Trey's body one by one. "Do they hurt?" His Chinese accent disguises his words as he looks at Trey and me.

317

I see no expression on Trey's face, so I assume the answer is no, as Dr Ling continues. Once the needles are in place, he begins twisting them one by one.

Then he reaches over to the table next to the bed and grabs an instrument that looks like a pair of small tongs. He clamps it to one of the needles and turns on the electricity. He leaves us for thirty minutes, then returns. While removing the tiny needles, he asks if we will be back next week.

Eight weeks pass as Trey is treated to an afternoon of thin needles three times a week. The doctor gives us herbs Trey is to take while he is at home, and the days he is in the office, he is to sip on green tea. I worry the voices in Trey's head are returning when I hear Trey repeat the words, *Leslie Chow*, over and over. Something about those words makes Trey stop to laugh, and then he continues whispering the words *Leslie Chow, Leslie Chow*.

"Who the hell is Leslie Chow?" I look over at Madison.

"He's the naked Chinese guy in the trunk of the car in *The Hangover*." She remembers the movie, which makes her smile. "I bet Trey thinks the doctor is Leslie Chow!" We both laugh and then hear Trey break into a roar.

"Is that what you think? That the doctor is Leslie Chow?" He smiles as he remembers the movie. It's morning as we prepare to go to Trey's appointment. He stops cold faced.

"I'm not going."

"Why? You've been doing so well. Why don't you want to go? Do the needles hurt?" I'm trying to understand what his problem is without losing my temper.

"Leslie Chow doesn't like me," he struggles to form the words.

"Why do you think that?" I'm confused. The Chinese doctor has always treated Trey with nothing less than total respect.

"He gave me a sign." Trey is confident in what he says.

"What kind of sign?" I think he's kidding.

"He stuck a needle in my middle finger. I can get a hint."

"That's ridiculous!" I shake my head as I question myself. *Should I force him to go? Is he getting benefits from it?* I look at the calendar. It's been eight weeks. *What has he achieved since we started seeing Dr Ling?* These questions I can't answer with certainty.

Chapter 47

"WALK ON, FLICKA," TREY COMMANDS HIS HORSE as he starts to move. The smell of the ranch is familiar after a long hiatus, and many of the faces are recognizable. Some of the same volunteers remain here while others are gone.

The ranch has grown with its towering trees offering shade to victims of the summer heat. Artisans built heavily crafted ramps to help visitors get onto their horses. Straps hang from carport-like structures, lifting Trey and others up and onto their horses quickly.

Trey loves the ride. While watching him ride down the path armed with girls all around him, A caregiver approaches me.

"I've been watching your son and know a doctor who can help him. He's excellent in the field of physical therapy. My patient was electrocuted and searched all of Southern California for someone to help in his recovery. He stumbled upon a highly educated doctor in the county of San Diego. While the doctor couldn't help my client because of some of the client's serious anger issues, he has helped others." As she speaks, her patient on one of the horses from the ranch approaches us with white knuckles from clenching the animal's lead too tightly. He grits his teeth to remain silent. His hunched back exudes animosity that is acid burning. His face is red with suppressed rage. We surmise that if we gaze upon him for any time, he will mentally snap, so we look away and allow him space to pass. I remembered my conversation with Dr Canelo about the frontal lobe and anger.

The caregiver writes down the name and number of the doctor as she keeps an eye on her client.

*****

We pass through the hills in Singing Brook, lined with palm trees that sway in the early morning breezes. We then move into the city of Hidden Valley, where the traffic backs up, freeways connect, and then we finally arrive in Arrington. It's a small town compared to many of the other cities we've encountered. It exudes health-conscious yuppies where high-quality health food and Panera Bread are in demand. The three-story office building sits next to an empty Sony building that once housed over two hundred employees. Due to the failing economy, many people lost their jobs.

Madison, Trey, and I pull into the small parking lot below the upstairs office of the physical therapist, Nathan. He sees us from his office window and runs down two flights of stairs to greet us.

The building houses empty elevators at each end and another in the middle. The staircases wind up to each floor, old and used by the employees. Nathan enjoys jogging and practices physical therapy as an occupation. Many years of school rewarded him with a degree in medicine. He lives close by and sprints here every morning in time to prepare the gym. His thriftiness is evident. He's proud he saves money on gasoline. He does some note writing, which he sends to Medicare, and he prepares to greet many clients who seek his help.

His office is merely a fifty-minute ride south into San Diego County, where the breezes blow, and the smell of the ocean is close. The office has four rooms, two of which he rents out to other professionals, one he made into a makeshift gymnasium, and the last is a place for the reception. Duct tape and different Home Depot items hang on walls and achieve the results he wants every day. He wears only his ankle-high socks, gym shorts, and a Nike tank top as he begins his evaluation. His notes are detailed and written with much thought as he scribbles on his notepad and measures different parts of Trey's body. He starts by measuring Trey's arms, then his legs, and eventually his calves. He moves to the circumference of his head, writing notes as he goes. Madison and I are impressed by his knowledge of the body.

*****

I'm excited to open Trey's initial evaluation I received in the mail this morning. It begins,

"Trey presents with two essential attributes for a high level of recovery. The first is the fact that he is fully oriented, alert, and engaged." *These words I don't believe because I wonder how oriented Trey is.* "The second is his clear high degree of motivation. He wants to work. Motivation is probably the most important factor for an extraordinary outcome, given the proper structure. As stated in history, another factor, which is greatly in Trey's favour, is his large and supportive family. As stated, Trey's case's systemic involvement and complexity are required three times per week for ninety-minute sessions. Furthermore, Trey must have the proper upper-extremity orthotics. In my judgment, without these tools, it would be nearly impossible for there to be a meaningful rehabilitation of the hands. Without these orthotics, it would likely condemn him to a lifetime of expensive Botox injections instead of eventually weaning him from this intervention. Note the planning for this type of neurological patient is viewed three years from the current status. This assessment is honest and reasonable, and while it may seem costly, it is a minimal cost compared to the long-term medical costs of a patient who never fully rehabilitates and ultimately becomes a dependent of the state."

I read and reread the evaluation and realized it's another commitment I must make for Trey's future.

*****

Nathan's first observation is Trey's weak abdominal muscles. Nathan begins with core strengthening: sit-ups. Although Trey can barely lift his head while lying flat on his stomach, Nathan starts every session by getting Trey on his back on the floor. He recruits Madison, who holds Trey's feet on the ground while his knees remain bent. Nathan kneels behind Trey, shoving him physically into a sitting position on the floor and then lets him fall back. Again, he shoves him up into a seated position and allows him to fall back. The act is sloppy at first, but Trey begins to get the hang of it with time. He assists Nathan by using his abdominal muscles and pulling his belly to his spine. Nathan lets him rest when his hair is saturated, and the salty sweat drops run into his mouth. It never ceases to amaze me that the muscles worked so hard only seconds ago now struggle to hold him up. Nathan works just as hard, and while Trey rests, Nathan staggers over to his desk to note the accomplishments that Trey has made.

While creating something and then implementing it, Nathan always uses his imagination to get results. A makeshift balance cage made of pipes, bungee cords, and carabiners are standing alone in the back part of his gym. Trey is in the centre of this gadget with a belt strap holding him tight, as Nathan and Madison stand on either side of him. Gently, Nathan pushes him to the left; Trey's feet stay firmly planted to the floor as his body falls to the side. Madison shoves back to the right towards Nathan. They test Trey, back and forth, trying to get him to react and use his muscles to resist. Trey gains more balance as he tries to correct his position. He falls to the side, swinging recklessly, hanging by the bungee cords as Nathan grabs the ropes to slow him down. "He's beginning to correct his balance. That's a good sign." Nathan wants to be sure I understand that he knows what he's doing.

Trey moves onto the treadmill for the second half of his ninety-minute therapy lesson as Nathan grabs for his duct tape. He guides Trey onto the treadmill while Madison places his feet, making sure they are both planted firmly on the belt. Nathan duct tapes Trey's hands, wrists, and lower arms to the front bars using large amounts of tape. He grabs the stop button on a strap and moves in behind Trey. The specifically designed treadmill moves slow as it starts. Nathan concentrates on weight shifting as he guides Trey's hips with his hands. Madison and I are seated on the gym's floor at Trey's feet on either side of the treadmill. We help guide his feet, ensuring that they don't step too far to the side. As Trey's legs decide not to move, his feet stay planted on the treadmill's belt. "Stop, stop, stop! He's not stepping," Nathan pushes the stop button. He cuts Trey free from the tape and ends the lesson. With no hair left on his lower arms, Trey complains of the slight redness that the duct tape has caused. *I remember when the doctor at the hospital told me that Trey would never straighten his right arm again.*

"We will try again in a little bit after Trey rests." Nathan calmly assesses Trey's energy. For months this is the routine we are on. The slow drive to Nathan's office, a ninety-minute session, and then home again. This routine is relentless. The only thing that makes the drive bearable is that Madison and I are planning her up-and-coming wedding slated to be in approximately a year. I dwell on wedding plans for Madison and Alexander on our way to our home.

Chapter 48

IT'S MONDAY MORNING, AND THE RAIN HAS been falling during our drive to Arrington. It will be another gym day, with streets wet and the air filled with moisture. Nathan wants to get Trey off the treadmill and walk. His new goal for Trey is stepping out of the office, to the elevator, and out to the car. Walking to the car and riding home in the passenger's seat will improve Trey's confidence. The task takes up half the session. Things start clicking for Trey. He walks with Nathan, who assists him down to the vehicle in forty-five minutes, then again in forty minutes, and then in thirty.

Nathan's therapy-oriented mind is continuously setting new and challenging goals for Trey. A long stretch of asphalt directly outside the office gives way to a new idea. Nathan walks Trey out of the office and down the narrow hallway to eighteen indoor commercial stairs, which takes roughly twenty minutes to complete. Once outside, he guides Trey across the parking lot, where another set of uphill stairs leads to the street. A half-mile later, he presents him with a new test. Madison and I follow behind Nathan and Trey in the van if Trey gets tired and needs a ride back to the office.

Madison cranks up the radio that plays "I Would Walk One Thousand Miles." Both Trey and Nathan burst out laughing when they heard the song. It fits as we watch Trey take one step after the other. Although the traffic is light, the road is central for the surrounding offices. People walk, run, and jog on their lunch break. Trey begins to build an enthusiastic audience. "Keep up the good work! Way to go, you've got this!" It's fresh and inspirational to see people showing so much encouragement for Trey, but he is oblivious to the comments as he struggles to walk.

With Trey's stamina increasing, Nathan needs to find something more challenging. He knows Trey can handle it. Outside there are twenty-five stairs up to the street and twenty-five stairs down to the parking lot. Trey bends too far forward and struggles to find the next stair as he attempts the task. Nathan has a tight grasp on the handrail as his other arm wraps around Trey's waist, preventing him from falling. Trey can't judge on his own where to place his foot, so Madison sits stair-by-stair, putting Trey's foot firmly on the next. Lift foot, place foot, move. Lift foot, place foot, move. Sweat appears on both Nathan and Trey as they climb up and down the stairs. Trey works out until his skin takes on a glossy shine, and the salty drops invade his eyes. As he keeps moving, the sweat is a welcome addition, cooling and helping him feel like he's worked hard.

*****

Alexander and Madison's marriage has been inevitable since they first met. They are inseparable. Over the years, they

327

have remained devoted to one another. Through sickness and family tragedies, they've supported each other.

"I can't believe how fast this year has gone." I look at Madison on our way back to Los Angeles to pick up her preordered gown.

"I know, and I'm getting nervous about my wedding." She bites her nails. After parking the car in a three-dollar-an-hour parking lot, we start down the long dirty street. The area is scary, with tall buildings that seem to be waiting for an earthquake to strike in the middle of a busy workday. *I'm glad I left Trey home with Marco.* We see shop windows boarded and front doors locked. The Garment District in Los Angeles I know well from working after graduation from college. It's the place to buy high-dollar clothing cheap.

"Hurry, let's make this quick. I want to avoid the traffic on the way home and don't like this area. It gives me the creeps." I rush to the boutique's front door as I reflect back in time.

He was watching from a seat outside a coffee shop as I hurried up the long street of towering buildings. "I've got to get to work on time," I muttered and rushed as I felt a strange feeling come over me. As I felt the chill in the air, I noticed a man following behind me. His expression was absent. His gaze was unwavering and shameless. His grey eyes behind silver glasses did not travel up to my face or down to my high heels, but they followed me as if they focused on something a couple of feet further away. He made no move of recognition, no raised hand or friendly nod. I moved more quickly to the street corner, then melted into the streets of the Los Angeles crowds. I entered the building, glad to be away from him. Then my work phone rang.

"You look so pretty in your yellow dress." His voice was raspy and creepy. "Are you staying late tonight?" I slammed

down the phone and held my breath. I suddenly wished my car were closer and not parked in the underground garage four blocks away. The phone rang again. I stood and knew I didn't want to answer it but had to.

"Will you wear that dress for me again?" His voice was deeper and scarier. I grabbed my face and looked out the window. There I saw him sitting across the street on a bench gazing up towards the window. The phone booth was within his reach. Then there was a knock on the door. Sheer panic froze me. I looked out the window; he was gone. I didn't know what to do, so I called 911.

The police showed up reasonably soon after I called and listened to my quivering voice. There was no one behind the door. My eyes bled tears as I spoke to them and begged for a ride to my car. They obliged. I gave up on my dream of a modelling career and never wanted to return to the garment district again.

"We need to ring in." Madison presses the buzzer on the wall. The girl at the front desk waves us in and scampers off to retrieve the gown from the back room. The day blurs together as we pay for the dress and leave the dirty downtown area to return home.

*****

Wedding bells are ringing in Trey's mind as he tells me that he and Shelly will get married, and he wants me to plan the wedding. "You like Shelly, right?" Now that Wendy and Angie are out of the picture, Trey can safely wed Shelly without feeling threatened. "We've decided to get married in Paris. Do you like Paris?" He struggles with the words and his thoughts.

I remember the psychiatrist's instructions not to argue with him, so I agree. "Yes. I love Shelly. She will be a wonderful wife." My conversation with Shelly just a week ago reminds me that she's married and currently pregnant.

"When are you going to call her?" He's anxious to get the wedding planning started.

"I called her. She's at school." I lie through my teeth.

"Call Shelly!" He demands.

"You call her, and she's YOUR girlfriend!" I try to find an easy way out of this and can't believe I'm arguing with a madman.

"She'll listen to you, Mom. She likes you. She will listen to you." He pleads for me to make the call. *How do I handle this? I don't want to hurt him. Do I state the truth? Do I play along and hope it goes away?*

I sit at my desk in the kitchen and try to find a way out of this. "Call her!" he shouts from his room.

"I did!" I yell back.

"Call her!" he yells again. I slowly get up and walk into his room. I sit beside him and try to find words that he will believe.

"Shelly is nice, and I know you love her, but she is married to Justin, honey." He interrupts me before I can finish my sentence.

"No!" He's enraged.

"Trey, she's pregnant. She told me herself." I can't get through to him.

"She's lying. She's lying to you! She's not married! Call Shelly!" He continues to scream.

I lie again. "I did. Shelly wasn't home. She's at school." I wonder how long this will last as I recall the many months of dealing with his past psychosis. I struggle with ending this delusional thinking but don't want to shatter his dreams. Maybe I should talk to Shelly and ask her to tame down the innocent flirting.

The realization that physical therapy isn't enough three times a week has hit me. I know I need to find someone who will come to the house on Trey's off days. I'm standing in the kitchen when Russell walks in.

"Do you know anyone who might work with Trey here?" Since he graduated, Russell has stayed in touch with many high school friends. I see a sadness cross his face as he flips his phone open and scrolls down to find Chase's phone number. Russell seems to be the one who has had the most challenging time accepting Trey's disabilities.

Chase is a bodybuilder who has completed a class in kinesiology and is looking for new clientele. We set the date, and Chase will come up in the morning.

He dedicates himself to working out, and his muscular body shows the person-hours that he has put into it. He has a chiselled and sculptured chest, and his skin glows healthily. His abdominals are near perfection, and his shoulders are square and burly. In his high school years, he made a few dollars piercing friends, and in exchange, he got tattoos that cover his strong arms and chest. Chase's kind nature combined with his strength are the right combination for helping Trey with his many physical problems.

*****

Once here, Chase decides to work Trey's left hip first. That hip has been tight and knotted since his accident. I remember the doctor's words just as if they were said yesterday.

"Unfortunately, Trey's paralysis is universal. His left leg has no feeling, and he will never move it again. His right arm

is also paralyzed and locked into a position where he will never be able to straighten it again. Mrs Morelli, no matter what you do, you will never change these things. Time will not heal. It's as simple as that."

According to Nathan, this is an excellent place to begin since his tight hip makes it awkward for Trey to stand or walk normally. Chase pulls and stretches his left quad while Trey dreams of running for the hills. Once there's more flexibility, Chase focuses on core strength, working Trey's abdominal muscles that have come a long way since he first met Nathan. Chase fumbles around but finally gets into a routine. He stretches Trey's hands, arms, and legs before starting any strength-building activities. It's hard on Trey, and I hear him grunt and groan through the tiny speakers spread throughout the house. He never complains, though. He's focused and dedicated to his independence.

Chase reaches into the drawer in Trey's nightstand and grabs the muscle-stimulator device, and then attaches the electrodes to Trey's leg, forcing his foot to flex forward as it pulsates. I'm reminded of Mona in the unit at the beach.

"The 'stim' machine is the only tool I have that helps stimulate muscle mass when you have a patient who can't cooperate," Mona says as she attaches the electrodes to Trey's neck. She turns the dial and increases the intensity until it's evident that Trey feels it. He jolts and cries as his neck muscles force his head to lift, then the power slows down, and there's a relief that crosses his expression. Not a minute later, the frequency rises, and Trey's neck begins to lift his head again. "He'll eventually do this on his own without any stim, but until then, it is an important tool to have."

332

During the following year, Chase begins attending seminars and looking for ways to help Trey. He dedicates himself and is resourceful. One of the more significant benefits I have witnessed is that it allows Trey to socialize with someone outside our family. They are friends, and that is one of the most critical components.

Chapter 49

I APPROACHED THE BIGGEST TREE IN THE backyard, remembering how small it was when we first bought this home. The pleasant wind was like the music of old memories to me as I touched the tree, opened my photo album and went back in time.

Russell is in a hurry to get into his own home and start a family. He's busy courting the women in his life and is very picky about who he chooses to be in his company. He watches closely for his opportunity to buy a home while the economy is down, so we go in search of his dream. I drive Russell down the narrow road to a house with a "For Sale" sign in front of it. It is an older home in a nice neighbourhood, as we judge the neighbours who live there and then deem it clean enough to inspect.

I fumble for my key, open the door, and we walk in. The home is tri-level and in surprisingly good condition. The paint on the house was fresh, and the owners installed a new carpet. Someone lost her home to the bank, and it's an opportune time to seize on that moment.

I point out the many features the home has to offer. "The house is in a wonderful neighbourhood close to excellent schools and new shopping centres. The backyard is large with a pool and would be perfect for your future family." I point outside. I reach into my purse and eye my unused real estate license. In my heyday, I made significant money buying land and selling it to developers.

"We should write an offer on it." I struggle to find a pen in my purse. "This one won't last due to the low price and poor economy," I smirk as I remind myself of an average realtor. The offer was written, accepted, and escrow closed quickly.

I sit back and dwell on the picture I have in my hand of Russell standing in front of his newly bought home, grinning from ear to ear, with his small dog standing between his legs.

The next photo I flip to and hold close to my heart is Cameron, standing with Casey and their new baby girl. It's been nine years since Trey's accident, and they've been busy. The photo represents the day that Cameron's first child was born.

The cold hospital hallway fills quickly with the whole Morelli clan waiting to see the new member of our family. The clock races as I dream of meeting my new granddaughter but find myself distracted by the memory of many stressful days spent in the hospital at Trey's side.

Cameron quickly alerts us that Casey is in extreme pain. With each contraction comes a pain that controls Casey's whole body. She can think about nothing else. She hears screaming coming from other rooms, yet she makes no sound. When the pain passes, it is only for a minute while she breathes with closed eyes, unwilling to re-engage with life. The doctor is telling her that it is time, time to push. With a guttural grunt, she does and has to stop. The cord wraps around the baby's neck. Cameron is scared as he stares into Casey's bloodshot eyes. She can feel the baby crowning as the doctor reaches in and tries to untangle it. Without any further effort, the baby slides into the hands of the doctor. There is joy and relief, a girl of their dreams.

Cameron is a proud first-time father as he holds his new little girl in his hands while tears drip from his eyes. What a beautiful day for Marco and me as we gaze into our granddaughter, Catie's, eyes. It's a precious time in Cameron's life.

I sit and feel so blessed to have had the experiences that God has given me. I turn the page of the photo album, and there is a picture of Madison and Alexander at their wedding. I remember it like it was yesterday.

The clock strikes 5:00 p.m. as Marco walks his stunning daughter towards the altar set up on the west side of our driveway. It's in front of the coral trees with their large beautiful red flowers this time of year. Decorated palms wave in the afternoon breeze as Marco and Madison approach my brother, who has studied for months to be the perfect officiant. Marco gives Madison to Alexander; a small tear forms in Marco's eyes and mine as he glances at me. He always knew there'd be a day when he would leave her hand and place it into the palm of the man of her dreams.

Seven beautiful bridesmaids, wearing strapless solid-red gowns with matching red high heels, stand to the right of Alexander and Madison. To the left are the groomsmen. Trey sports a smile, wearing his sharp black tuxedo while sitting in his wheelchair at the end, just barely on the grass. Next to him is Cameron, who fondly makes sure that Trey is in the shade as the sun shifts and begins to fall behind the hills. Russell is there in his tuxedo, looking handsome and happy. He, too, watches out for his brothers, making sure there's room for them on the luscious lawn.

The sermon begins. "Marriage isn't a ring or a paper signed. It is not something endured but savoured. It is the union of two hearts beating as one, each that would sacrifice for the other's happiness and well-being."

With that, Brian Adam's recorded voice loudly sings, "Have you ever loved a woman" as we bathe in the warm summer breeze and stand as the newly married couple leave the altar and waltz down the aisle. Madison is radiant as she waves the flowers entwined between her fingers, holding fast in her hand. The light reflects the crimson bouquet, making her look dazzling in the spotlight. Her face shines with excitement.

I sit and ponder the pictures I see and reflect on Russell, Cameron, and Madison.

Throughout the years, they've been warriors. They've loved, and their lives are moving quickly now. Russell has taken the lead in heading the household when Marco has been away. He has looked after his brother and sister in our absence. Cameron is married to the love of his life, and they share two children. Their home is a block from Russell's. They are best of friends. Madison and Alexander choose to live on our property, close enough for Madison to keep her word for Trey. They plan to buy a perfect home in the future to accommodate their dreams of having a large family.

My love for my children would move heaven and earth. It is a love that would take on anyone, anyplace, anytime. I guess, in some ways, that makes me a warrior too.

*****

The Lite Gait ordered at Casa Alexandria is delivered so Chase can begin training Trey at home. It will assist him in helping Trey shift his weight and work on his balance while it holds

337

him safely between the rails of the walker. The armrests hold his arms as his muscles flex. The Lite Gait is lightweight; Trey raises his arms and lifts them. His feet cross and kick the bottom rails with each step. He leans towards the wheels on the left side as Chase rushes to stop it from falling over. Trey feels awkward in it and confined by all the belts and straps, which are around his wrists, ankles, and waist, but it's here, and we'll make the best of it. Chase struggles with it day in and day out. It just isn't something he can get used to, and Trey truly hates it. He feels confined, and I might sell it

After weeks of use, the final decision to sell this piece of equipment on Craigslist seems fitting as I see how crowded Trey's room is. Two wheelchairs, one for the car and one for the house, sit in one corner while the standing device is against the closet doors. Halfway out of the closet is the spinning bike, which makes the closet access nearly impossible. The folded shower chair holds a large, red exercise ball in another corner. Behind the dresser is a grab bar available for use. The room has become a therapist's dream.

*****

"For Sale . . . A nearly new XL Rifton Lite Gait. Asking price. Three thousand dollars...." The phone rings within one day. It's an older gentleman who inquires about the walker for his granddaughter. I ask him to send me an email explaining his situation.

Dear Leigh, I'm so happy I met you. You see, my granddaughter was in a horrific accident when she was just a baby. Would you mind reading the newspaper article I have attached?

I begin reading the attachment.

A bomb ripped through the house of a man who police believe may have been feuding with the Hells Angels, injuring him, a pregnant woman, and a baby, authorities said. The explosion shattered the front of the one-story, stucco-and-brick house, causing the roof to collapse. Half a block away, the force knocked out windows in places and damaged four vehicles. The owner who lives in the house was associated with the Hells Angels, but we are not sure if he was a member or not. Police were investigating reports of tension between the owner and the motorcycle gang.

Wow! I wonder if the Hells Angel article is referring to him. I ask him to continue his story.

JJB was a top lieutenant of the Hells Angels and had been a member for many years. He had a bad reputation as a Mafia-style murderer who removed anything that stood in his way. In the seventies, he became the power in Oakland beside his leader, Sonny Barger.

We worked together on the same turf as wholesalers of amphetamine known throughout the club as crank. I was hard-driving and a friend to JJB, or so I thought, until one of our dealings during a drug raid went wrong. I continued to ride with the gang but took particular notice of two items in JJB's contraband inventory, a military handbook on booby traps and an address book containing my address, phone number, and the license plate number of my car.

JJB said he considered the dispute a personal matter. He internalized it. "I should teach that son of a bitch a lesson. I should get a gun and blow his head off." Then he smiled and said, "The best thing for the fucking punk is to hit him, cripple him." JJB wanted me alive but hurt and out of the MC.

I knew the Angels were stalking me when I woke to the sound of a loud car outside my house one night and knew it was JJB. I started performing a ritual of checking for a bomb every morning and night after that.

A remote-controlled bomb planted underneath my bedroom window by JJB was amidst a tangled patch of ivy, and I missed it during my nightly search. Suddenly, dirt and ivy leaves showered the street. When it exploded, I slept in bed with my granddaughter, who was shaken hard by the force of the weapon. The bomb was built of dynamite and triggered by remote control and designed to disable, not kill, and proved efficient.

I stood in agony and semi-blindness amid the chaos. I soon recovered consciousness and found myself standing by the bed where the stucco walls had collapsed, some distance from where I had been lying. I saw a place where tables and chairs were all upside-down, amid the debris of glass and breakage. The house was almost empty, my small granddaughter white as a sheet and unconscious. The blast rattled her. I was deaf in my left ear and heard very little in the other. My neck was stiff, my hands partially paralyzed. I still had no idea of what had happened. I thought perhaps something had broken down. I couldn't understand, and then I thought of JJB.

The article and writings made me shudder, but I admit I was intrigued.

"Robert, I'm intrigued by your story. Please share if you want to." My fingers can't type any faster as my heart pounds with excitement.

Leigh, honestly, it has been hard over the years. I've never forgiven myself for the horrible things I did while with the Hells Angels. I've felt responsible for Chrissy's injury for the last twenty-three years.

I found myself feeling sorry for the old guy. His writing continued; my eyes glued to the computer's screen.

"To continue my story, I saw JJB on the freeway who shot at me. I wanted to kill that bastard more than I've ever wanted anything. I was relieved when I heard the feds finally arrested him for possessing an illegal gun, which earned him a felony and a five-year sentence. He hung himself in Sacramento County jail not long afterwards. This story is turning into a book, and I hope it makes some sense to you. Thank you for being here for Chrissy and me, as having no one to talk to anymore is depressing, and it is nice to share my concerns about my child with someone who understands my situation. Thanks so much for your ear, and please give our best to your family. Thank you for being our friend." Your friend, Robert.

As I entered the postal annexe with the Lite Gait, I could feel pain for his granddaughter. It wasn't her fault that the bomb targeted her grandfather but got her. It wasn't her fault that her grandfather made poor choices in his life.

"Hi, Randall." I see the owner of the postal annexe as I push the massive piece of equipment through the door. He looks up and smiles. The words of Robert's story continue to pound into my brain. *Hells Angels? Murder? Death? My insides are in chaos and a mess. It is bothering me. The story hurt me. My stomach aches and feels wrong, so invalid.* I continue to try to process what I read. *Was he real and telling the truth? Was he using me? Can I trust him?* Then I thought of his granddaughter. This piece of equipment could enhance her life.

Randall looks at me, smiles, and hands me the invoice for shipping fees. It reads *Four hundred dollars! OMG!* I'm shocked, lost for words, and the feeling of giving turns to anxiety. *I could have donated it for free.*

I leave the postal annexe. The process is bittersweet. I'm happy to help her, but the cost drives a hole in my wallet. I go home feeling slightly down and reach out to Robert telling him it has shipped.

As I read his words and visualize what happened back then, I become afraid. I don't know what to believe or not to believe. I feel threatened. I can't do this. Thoughts of violence run rampant through my mind, and protective instincts to guard Trey invade me. *What if the Hells Angels are still out to get him? What if we get tangled in a mess? Can I risk the chance of inviting something into my life that's so negative? Can I possibly be friends with someone like him?* I lie in bed, trying to sleep as I stress over the questions I have in my mind. *Does Robert want to be friends?* Madison said his granddaughter called earlier to talk to Trey. *What else does he think I have to offer?* I roll out of bed the following day, walk over to my computer, and turn it off. I never hear from Robert again.

Chapter 50

BEADS OF SWEAT DRIPS PAST MADISON'S shoulders and continues towards her pregnant and large stomach. Her belly has expanded to prove that another being resides within her. Two heartbeats within one body are music to my ears. Her back aches as her entire weight rely upon it. Madison awkwardly climbs into the van, being far into her first pregnancy.

"How much longer are you going to be able to help me with Trey?" I'm concerned about the baby as I watch her struggle to navigate her growing body into the tight-fitting car.

"Mom, I'm not sick; I'm pregnant!" Madison snaps with hormonal dignity. She's been my rock since Trey's injury and has always been ready to offer her help in any way she can. She has handled her pregnancy with pride and never complains. The new baby has given us a lot to talk and think about as we take Trey from therapy to therapy. My ego swells as I watch her and dream about my up-and-coming grandchild. *I can't believe this will be our third. (Cameron has two already.)*

Nathan flies into walking backwards with a vengeance while Trey's fan club grows.

Clusters of people form behind Nathan and Trey as they make their way down the street. They cheer as Trey crosses the road going further than he did a few days ago. He takes it well but doesn't enjoy being in the limelight as the crowd claps and whistles. It takes me back to the hospital.

The nurses on the sixth floor fixated on Trey and his accomplishments. They watched quietly as he slowly made his way, dangling in the Lite Gait, to their stations. They could not control their emotions as they watched the thin boy take on the challenges his therapist demanded. One step was one more accomplishment. Slow but steady, as he focused on just one muscle at a time, one more time, only one more time. He inspired the nurses with his eyes that told what words could never say. The nurses felt transfixed at the moment as they watched him trying to walk around the ward, ignoring the praise the nurses offered. They were lost and speechless by his mere presence. They were motivated to give of themselves, though they feared the inevitable. He would leave soon. But for this moment and this moment only, they basked in the present. These were memories the nurses would treasure forever.

Madison and I bring an exhausted Trey home, where he works out with Chase the next day. Then we hit the road back to Arrington the following morning—many days spent in the gym where Madison and Nathan laugh over political news and Nathan's personal life. Trey is excelling. I'm proud as I watch him work towards success. I'm happy with his progress and have dreams of his full recovery.

*****

Subway for lunch is a quick go-to on our way home from Arrington; it's close to the halfway mark to our house. Madison routinely steps out of the car to get in line at the Subway counter as I wait in the car with Trey. The wait is never long, and the sandwich maker knows our order before Madison gets out of the vehicle. Day in and day out, the routine remains the same. It's one hour to Arrington, thirty minutes to Subway, and thirty minutes home. We continue every other day with the drive, the workout, and the pleasure of watching Trey's commitment to independence.

Madison watches the Subway girl finish making our sandwiches as she remembers when the doctor said Trey would never eat again. She looks at the foot-long sandwich and smiles. *Boy, they certainly didn't get that one right!* Dr Striker's face rushes through her mind.

The steamy summer heat becomes far less bearable as the day grows longer. My eyes start to drift as I suddenly spot Madison's phone on the front seat with her money shoved into a side pocket. *She'll need it to pay for the food. Should I leave Trey for just one moment? I would never forgive myself if something happened to him, but I reluctantly go.* I can feel my hair stick to the sweat on my face as I enter the sandwich shop and hand Madison her phone.

After a brief absence, we return to the car when I realize I accidentally locked Trey in the vehicle with the keys in the ignition. It's dead of summer and hot as hell as summer degrees hit over one hundred and five.

Shear panic runs through my bones. I begin moving around the car as if there's a tornado inside me. "Run and get something that we can break the windows with." I look at Madison while beads of sweat run down my face. My eyes are wild, and when I try to calm down, I explode into motion again. Suddenly I start yelling, "Madison, is he all right?" I'm peering into the car and see nothing. No sound. No Trey. The windows are tinted, the glare of the sun upon them. My words squeeze together, and some are missing. My sentences break apart, and my thoughts seem to jump from one thing to another, "Break the window! Jimmy the back door! Call the police!" All of my fears go unchecked by my brain. I'm in some kind of mental breakdown, unable to analyze things or assess risk. Finally, Madison's words make sense as she notices I have my phone and wallet in my hand.

"Mom, calm down, call AAA. Trey is fine." Now she is in front of me, as she grabs my phone and makes the call. I need to calm down. I beg Trey to say something while I peer into the tinted windows. No reaction. He's exhausted, burned out, and listening to his favourite music. I knock on the back window while trying to get his attention. "Trey, can you hear me?" I suddenly know what it's like to be an irresponsible parent who has left a child in a car on a hot day. My panic grows.

Ten minutes later, we see the AAA truck come around the corner and pull into the parking lot. I sigh with relief. The truck's driver slowly moves as he approaches us, not in a hurry. He is unsuspecting and unaware that Trey is locked in a car for what seems like an eternity. As he begins to fill out the paperwork on his hand-carried board, I notice he's casual as he asks me for my AAA card. I look at him. I stop. Then with a loud yell, I cry, "My son is in the car!!!" The graceful look on his face turns to worry as he jimmies the door open and frees Trey, who sits comfortably in the air-conditioned car. I can't forget how irresponsible I've been as I pull out of the parking lot and onto the freeway. Thank God for AAA!

*****

As the days linger, I have become aware that Trey is evolving, and this morning for the first time in many years, he asked me how I slept last night. I flipped and was thrilled that it was not only about him for the first time. This evolution is progress, slow but steady progress, which is why I continue down this road. He is opening up like a tight-budded flower, and it is truly amazing to watch. He is becoming more aware of his surroundings, and when he asked if it snowed last night, I replied, "Why, do you want to go sledding?" His response delighted me.

"No, we just need rain." His gaze was unbroken.

Trey feels successful as he struggles to accomplish things asked of him. He is motivated. All he lives for is independence and taking care of himself while not asking for anything in return. We are fortunate that frustration only appears occasionally. I've seen him cry only once since his accident, when Wendy, one of the voices in his head, died. The lack of tears reminds me of the day my mother died.

The clock chimes five o'clock as Madison and I load Trey into the van, knowing this may be the last time we see my mother alive. She has fought a long and hard battle with Parkinson's disease for twenty years of her life. She is a fighter, I have thought, as I have painfully watched her slow decline. After hearing the rattle in her chest, I know her days are few, and I realize the end is near.

347

The last ride is long because hundreds of residents search for an autistic boy lost in a nearby rural neighbourhood. Because of the search, the only paved road to my mother's house is not useable. The feeling of loss consumes me. I glance to the left and see cars going down a dirt road. I hesitate, then glance over at Madison. "Follow them!" Madison's blood rushes as she points in their direction. We "off-road" the van, kicking up dirt and zigzagging down the dusty road. Finally, we are on a paved street, and I see my mom's house in the distance. Her home is a half-block away now. She's fine. I know she'll be fine. She has to be. My brain is numb and won't accept that the end is near. She needs me to be there right now, and then I can go home.

The summer's air is hot, or maybe I'm just moving too fast as I enter the house. I'm in overdrive as I feel a sense of urgency. I rush to my mom's side as Madison brings Trey in from the car. Madison notices my mother's shallow breathing. Death is coming to her with the slow rattling gasps. Her erratic breathing stops for a time, only to reemerge. I leave her side for a brief pause while speaking to my dad, who stands in the kitchen. He is heartbroken.

"Mom, hurry!" Madison sounds desperate as I come around the corner. I kneel beside my mother's bed and place her cold hand in mine. She gurgles, struggling to breathe as all of her organs begin to shut down. She signals me to lean in during one of her few coherent moments.

"I'm saving you a place next to me in heaven." Her earthly tether separates, and her soul is bound for the Lord. Her eyes close forever, leaving me empty and in denial. Madison responds with tears gushing down her face. Too much for both of us to process. Too much for anyone. I look up to see Trey absorbed in his music.

"Nonnie went to heaven to be with God." I wanted the news to be gentle as I searched for his reaction. There's nothing, only a slight acknowledgement with a turned-down mouth. The devotion I felt as I held her in my arms for the last time was overwhelming. Madison remained confined to her thoughts and tears as she tried to comfort and console me. What will I do without my best friend? How can I survive? I sit in the darkness feeling only emptiness as the coroner removes her body, and once again, I feel swallowed up with heartbreak.

Chapter 51

NATHAN BEGINS SHOWING SIGNS OF STRESS during our scheduled sessions and regularly complains that Medicare isn't paying for his services. His wife frequently calls, facing the inevitable hang-up. He can't stay focused while the other professionals leave his offices without paying their rent. He's barely in business as he hangs on and seeks help from those around him.

I'm nervous Trey will lose the best care since his accident. I begin making calls trying to get answers from Medicare. With each request, I meet a dead end. Nathan lacks no other choice but to close his doors.

Feeling helpless and fearing the worst, I receive a call from Shelly. She, too, has bad news for me. She's pregnant again and has decided not to work outside her home. *It's hard to be happy for someone when your problems consume you.* Shelly dreams of her new family. She no longer has time for Trey, so I must let him know and dread his reaction.

"Shelly isn't able to work with you any longer. She is pregnant and retiring." I wouldn't say I like the sound of the words and the reaction on Trey's face.

"She's lying to you!" He's indignant, and there's no changing his already made up mind. *He'll figure it out when she stops coming.*

"She's going to have MY baby! We need to plan the wedding!" The fantasy comes alive in his mind, and his eyes sparkle. I hope and pray we don't have to do this again. I'm tired and burned out trying to convince him of things that he won't accept, so I walk away, shaking my head. *Will he ever be normal again? Was he crazy from the beginning?* Then I start wondering what normal is? All I know is I need a vacation away from therapy and the monotony of my everyday life.

*****

Retirement was never an option for my parents' friends, Davy and Gina. They worked so hard that there were days they never saw one another. They pinched every penny with dreams of travelling once they reached that golden age. But then bad luck came their way. Their daughter had a brain injury in a car accident. After that, everything she had learned since birth was gone. So, at age twenty-five, she needed every type of therapy available, and nothing was free. Davy and Gina's savings started to disappear. Their friends were generous, but the bills kept rolling in, and one of them had to be home with their daughter at all times. They sold their house, moved into a first-floor apartment, and watched their spending closely. What could they do? Give their daughter up to the state? Brain-damaged or not, their girl was the joy of their lives, so they gave up on their dreams of travel.

Steve and Susan worked their entire lives making sure that a small portion of their paycheck automatically was deposited into their vacation savings account. They planned, dreamed, and made notes of the places they wanted to visit once they retired. Each day at work took them closer to their dreams. They'd done it right as their day approached. Then all of a sudden, Susan's knees began to ache. Each moment the pain increased. It reduced her knees to painful twists of hardened skin and muscle. The bones were beginning to cripple beyond repair. As time passed, Steve realized their vacation dreams would never become a reality. Susan was too disabled to go.

As I watch the people around me, I realize I don't want to be like them. I don't want to save up for a rainy day. I want to be the one that tells of the most incredible journeys. I want the lines around my eyes to know of laughter, of warm smiles and affection, and my forehead to tell of worries, past and present. I want them to learn of the trials I've endured, but mostly, I want them to know of a woman who has lived life to the fullest and has seen it all.

*****

Large floor-to-ceiling glass panels slide open, offering 270-degree views of the ocean, city, and mountains in our expansive condo for the week on the Bahia de Banderas. After a short plane trip to Puerto Vallarta, Alexander kicks up the music on the surround-sound stereo as we unpack our bags. He searches for something in English but finds only Spanish channels. Madison and I blend margaritas and mix up guacamole while we imagine mariachis playing right here in our condo for the week.

"This is the place I've only dreamed of," I said as I looked over at Madison, who was stunned by the beautiful ocean views. The golden beach stretches out into the distance in the shape of a horseshoe bending around the coastline and dotted with families enjoying the universal gift of warmth. This place is heaven on earth and something we all need so desperately. We are away from the schedules and daily routines of life as we appreciate the beauty of the ocean and enjoy our eight-month-old granddaughter.

The warm breezes coming from the Pacific Ocean make the giant palm trees sway as our minds and bodies begin to relax. We look over our balcony from the fourth floor of the condominium complex, where an infinity pool awaits. Guards protect it from unwanted intruders, and it seems exceptionally refreshing.

All of our bedrooms open to overlooking the Pacific Ocean. Our sliding-glass window stays open as we drift into la-la land for the night. Trey snores as he sleeps in his private room in a king-sized bed. His speaker sits on his nightstand, ensuring that I can hear him if he needs me.

The cobblestone street is wet with the night's rain and is made slippery by the humidity and high temperatures. Marco's tennis shoes slip on large pebbles pounded smooth by the Pacific Ocean long ago. As always, we have to take our chance with the traffic and walk in the middle of the street—a better choice, we feel, than tripping over the worn and broken pavement on the narrow sidewalks. The crooked road leads us to the food tour, where Marco dreads pushing Trey through the sleepy Mexican village for the afternoon.

An eighteen-year-old Mexican boy for hire wears a wide-brimmed sombrero waits for Trey. He greets us, taking the handlebars of the wheelchair.

"Como se llama." The words roughly come from Trey's mouth.

"He speaks Español?" The boy questions his hearing as he looks at me in amazement.

"Si." Trey beams as he speaks better in Spanish than he does in English. I remember it all too well.

Marco was holding three small work bags bought earlier that day. His eyes gleamed as he thought about what was about to be proposed. Marco remembered his young age when he took his first job working with his dad. Somehow, he knew that it wasn't his father who needed him to go but his mother who wanted him out of the house at a young age. Marc was small when he began learning the construction trade, maybe too young because, after all, how many three-year-olds can hold a heavy hammer?

His memory took him back to the cold winter weather and his father's thirst for success. He remembered his dad's constant whistling that buried itself into his brain while he waited for his dad to end his day. He didn't know if it was stress or hyperactivity, but he knew it bugged him as he watched his dad gather his belongings.

The smile on Marco's face showed pride as he put each workbag around his sons' tiny waists. His dreams of them starting in the family business of building houses were only beginning as he made his announcement. "I've decided to take one of my boys to work with me each day during the summer break. I want them to learn from me and have the same dreams I have." Marco burst with satisfaction as he smiled down at his boys' young faces.

"Don't you think they are a little young? My God, it seems Cameron just got out of diapers." I wasn't ready to share my boys during their short summer break.

"I was already working with my dad when I was only three, so no, I don't think so. My God, Leigh, Russell is almost seven, and he doesn't know a thing about construction." I stood back and shook my head.

Every morning before the sun was up, Marco assembled his crew, himself, and one of his sons. They sat down to a full breakfast and then headed out the door onto the lonely highway.

Trey was the only one who didn't have an interest in going. He always complained that it made his stomach sick, but he had no choice. Russell and Cameron couldn't wait for their turn, and Madison didn't understand why she couldn't go.

Surrounded by Marco's employees who typically ate burritos for lunch and spoke only Spanish, Trey began to pick up a few words. I was proud he showed interest in learning a second language. He soon became proficient in a few chosen Spanish words.

It was early one morning when the telephone rang. It was Jayne, my Colorado Boulevard buddy, who had something important to tell me. She was almost weird at first as she spoke her carefully planned words. "Leigh, I'm sorry, but my housekeeper doesn't want to babysit your kids anymore." Her maid was making a little extra money babysitting the neighbourhood kids, and she had watched mine a few days earlier.

"Why?" I was confused but knew my kids weren't angels.

"Well, um, Trey called her an "asshole" in Spanish!" I sensed a strange pleasure in Jayne's voice.

"He what? I will talk to him about it. Maybe she misunderstood him." I hung up the phone and instinctively knew where he had learned it.

Trey and his newfound wheelchair friend spent much of the day speaking broken Spanish and English. A few words here, a laugh, and then a few more. They laugh between themselves as Marco and I drink margaritas and taste some of the best Mexican food we've ever had. We're enjoying everything, from the goat tacos to the fresh milk from a cut coconut.

The city is beautiful as the bells of Our Lady of Guadalupe ring, and we realize travelling with Trey is more comfortable than we could ever imagine.

Chapter 52

I GAZE OUT THE WINDOW AS WORD SPREADS throughout the small community. Another death from a heroin overdose claimed one of Trey's old friends, Mike. The words ring close to home and whisper through the swaying trees, making me feel overwhelmed and saddened. Heaviness fills my heart. I slowly make my way toward and into Trey's room.

"Remember your friend, Mike, from high school?" I face Trey. "He died of a drug overdose last night." I search for a response as I watch his reaction. Trey seems annoyed, but his memory is sharp.

"He was younger than me, but I remember him telling me he was a junkie." He stops, looks away in thought, and then makes eye contact and continues. "You know, Mom, I had a "ruler" back then. It only took a few stupid choices, and then I was hers. I didn't care about anything as she controlled every part of me and drew me in. I started to visit her more often because I'd go crazy, feel weak, and my stomach would ache if I didn't. So, I'd struggle to go back to her. When I finally did, everything was good again. She was all I needed. I would do anything for her—lie, steal, cheat. She changed me into somebody that sickens people, but I couldn't help but love her."

He continued. "I never did drugs with Mike because heroin is a drug you do alone. You feel repelled when you first shoot up, but you try it again. It clings to you like a devoted lover. The rush of the hit and how it makes you feel makes you want more. It traps you. I can't remember much more than that." He's blocked it out, most of it. He doesn't recall the many times that he got stoned with Mike, nor does he seem to care much about it.

His one-sided conversation continues. "I quit drugs cold turkey. Not many people can say that," he boasts, as I remember the drives to and from his doctor's office, the many written and failed prescriptions. He's blocked that out too. Trey wants to believe he beat it on his own, but I remember back to the sixth floor, where they prescribed him methadone to ease his withdrawals.

"I fucked myself up, you know." He's brutally honest. "I would do things differently in life if I had it to do over again. I'd never do drugs. I might smoke pot, but I'd never do narcotics again. I'm happy I'm alive and want to stay that way. I might even try to get my diploma someday." He's direct as he speaks, and I'm amazed at how well I can understand him now.

"You know, pot is a gateway drug." He hears me and throws his head back, and laughs. "Do you remember Lisa?" The question seems silly as I look for a loving reaction.

"Yes, but I don't remember living with her."

"Do you remember dying?" The question was difficult for me to ask.

"I didn't die. I'm still here." He smiles.

"Did you see God when you died?" I think about my question as I realize it is something everyone wonders.

"No, but I never thought much about God before. Now, I know there is a God." He's sure about his answer.

"Do you believe in the afterlife?" I thought about the many times he said he would never grow old.

"Yes. You never die." He's tired and strains to remember his life before, during, and after drugs.

*****

The thought of Trey getting his diploma is more than I can comprehend. I remember his high school days when he had no goals or drive, and now after so many years, he's found interest in a rolled-up piece of paper. I need to find out where we can help achieve his goal.

I find myself seated at Trey's doctor's appointment, waiting for the nurse to call his name. We enter the small cubicle, and I begin joking with his doctor. His doctor shot Botox into my forehead in exchange for gambling secrets the last time I was here, so we've become excellent friends.

"Trey has expressed a desire in getting his diploma." I look intently into his doctor's eyes and wait for a reaction. He smiles.

"I think he should. He has experienced more in life than most people my age. I have a friend who heads the education department here in the city who might help. Let me make a few phone calls to see what we need to do."

With Trey's physical limitations, he is eligible for special services and can study online courses. *I can't help but remember the challenging Chinese class he took the last time he sat at my desk upstairs.* During his test, he qualifies for a scribe or a live reader. He will be eligible for the audio-cassette editions, large-print books, talking calculator, private room, and extended time. We have looked into tutors from the high school, and many have expressed interest in working with Trey. A tutor can work with him in the privacy of our own home and make sure that he passes all of the exams required for his diploma. I move the computer downstairs to the kitchen. The hard work begins next week, and I will be beside him until he succeeds.

*****

It was late afternoon when I opened my laptop and decided to catch up on some billing.

In my inbox is an email from Madison giving me the latest gossip and asking me what I am doing this afternoon. As I finish my response to her, an email from an old friend from high school hits my inbox.

From: Diane Smith
To: Leigh Morelli
Subject: Mary's Memorial

Hi Leigh, Here's a blast from the past!!! It's Diane from high school. How are you?
Diane is online! I jump onto my newfound toy—Skype messaging---and see she's available. I quickly type a message.
Leigh: *Hey, how are you?*
Diane: *I'm great! How have you been all these years?*
Leigh: *Busy. What's new?*
Diane: *I'm not sure if you've heard, but Mary died last week from an apparent drug overdose. I'm putting plans together for*

a memorial and trying to reach out to her old friends as possible. She was such a great person. Her family loved her so much. I want this gathering to be extraordinary for such a big heart! Do you think you can make it?"
I pause and then tell Diane I'll get back to her.

I'd been in contact with Mary throughout the years. She married and gave birth to a little girl named Kelly. Mary had been switching jobs but had stayed within the pharmaceutical business to supply herself with drugs. She called me during one of her drunken blurs to see if I could take her daughter off her hands. She was arrested for a second DUI and didn't know if the court would allow her to keep her three-year-old daughter in the car. With four kids of my own and not fully understanding the situation, I declined as I tried to convince her to seek help. I thought about my conversation with Philip, who was twenty years sober. *There are thousands and thousands of people who need help and only a handful who want it.*

I knew she was putting her husband through hell and felt sorry for her little girl. She was going downhill quickly and taking her family with her. Now Diane wanted to celebrate her life? My fingers rapidly found Diane's message and pressed, "reply."

Leigh: *I'm struggling a little bit with Mary's death. We both know she fought with alcoholism for many years, and because of that, I had to back away. Maybe I should have stayed and tried to help her, but I decided on how I wanted my children raised. I feel sorry that she is gone, but I feel worse for William and Kelly and what they went through. I know firsthand.*

My middle son, at age twenty-one, overdosed and was pronounced dead at the ER. He'd been dead for over twelve minutes. "Pull the plug and move on," his doctor told me. He suffered a massive cardiac arrest and was comatose. I called a priest in who gave him last rites while I sobbed. The doctors told me that he would live out the rest of his life in a persistent-vegetative state if he survived. I refused to listen and have spent the last thirteen years fighting for him. I drove to the hospital every day for three and a half years to be by his side. I have stood up in front of twenty-five doctors and told them to fuck off as they casually said to me that my son would never leave the hospital. I have spent hours in hospitals. I have held doctors accountable in court. I have stood up for my son's rights with insurance companies. I've learned acupuncture, neurofeedback, Reiki and have practised all of them on him. I've been there and done that and continue to fight for him. Marco and I are his only advocates. He walks, talks, and eats when no one believed he ever would. I wouldn't change a thing that my family and I have done for Trey. He will achieve independence, and then I'll have my life back.

Now I stand here and don't judge Mary. I understand drug and alcohol addiction very well, but how can you memorialize a person's life when they spent years and years of selfish be-haviour? The survivors like William and Kelly are the ones who you should commend. All the years of pain and suffering they went through are a sin. William and Kelly did when most people don't have the time or love to stand by their loved ones. That is rare in this world. I wish the best for Mary's family and hope that you can give them my condolences.
Leigh

My eyes settled on the text as my chest constricted, my breathing became more challenging. I took a long deep breath and then sighed. My dry face must have been an insult to Diane, who cried at the news of Mary's passing. They say to love the addict and hate the addiction, but all I can do is remember who she was before she met her ruler. I hold in my mind Mary, but while my body grows older, my heart fills with rejection for addiction. I suppose I'm hardened by repeat exposure, just as the nurses were on the sixth floor.

The years have taken a toll on me. No longer is it a young girl looking back at me in the reflection of a mirror, but a tired, older woman. The smooth skin that once covered my face is uneven and rough. I am now a grandmother and look the part. As the years go by, the girl I was is disappearing from my memory, as if she never really existed at all. I look back on what I remember with her mother's eyes, old eyes, eyes that have seen so much. I see that earlier version of me with affection and accept the dumb mistakes. It amazes me how the small choices have created the person I am today.

Ageing has embedded me further into the love of my soul mate and best friend, Marco.

Growing up is a part of being a parent, and so is putting your children's needs first. Wisdom and experience help you give back and guide the younger generation. So, while being young is exciting, ageing is an opportunity for ongoing growth and knowledge and acceptance of the blessings given. With age comes a slowing. The feelings are all there, but the dial gets turned down, and the small pleasures of life take a more prominent role. You savour peaceful times and learn to cherish your loved ones.

EPILOGUE

IT'S BEEN TWENTY-THREE YEARS SINCE TREY got out of the grasps of drugs. I sit here, as I have so many times before, at the head of our massive dining-room table before God and my family. I see the Christmas tree aglow to my right and remember the many years I spent decorating it. I see Madison and Alexander with their three beautiful children before me, who have all grown into a healthy and prosperous family. I notice the candle's glow as I see Cameron whisper to Casey. They, too, have three gorgeous and respectful children. I can't believe Catie will be turning twenty next year. Russell finds extreme happiness with his beautiful daughter, Leah, his spitting image. He and Cameron have taken complete control of the family business, and together they have made it very strong. Across the table is my beloved Marco, who has proved to be a robust support system and an excellent husband. God only knows I wouldn't be here if it weren't for his love and devotion. To my left, sits Trey who is beaming. Over the past few years, his vision has improved where he only needs glasses to see clearly.

In my memory is my proudest moment.

The high school's football field seemed more extensive than I remembered. As I entered the neighbourhood school, I remembered hallways and offices that I'd visited so many times in the past. I thought about Russell and his escapades with the PA system, Cameron swooning over his high school sweetheart, Madison's run-ins with the security guard, and how out of place Trey seemed. As I moved through the crowds, I noticed the American flag in the sky above me. It flew with pride and honour.

As the field buzzed with excited chatter, I was aware of the nonexistence of colour in the sea of black caps and gowns. The moment of truth, the stepping-stone into the real world was upon them. Graduation was what they'd prepared for most of their lives. It was finally time for them to step out into the bright light, shake the hand of the administrator, and grab their ticket to freedom. The piece of paper that would remind them forever that they'd accomplished something.

Not Trey, though. He'd already experienced all life had to give. He'd worked hard to get back to where he started. He'd learned to appreciate the small accomplishments that took a lifetime to complete. He'd experienced life, sometimes in its most raw form. He was here, not because someone forced him but because he desired to be.

After I was seated towards the front, I began to scan the area for Trey, not far from the podium. I strained over the crowd and then spotted Trey near the stage. I saw him signalling for someone to come to him. There were only two more names to be called before his, and I felt the excitement build.

The principal called another name before him, and I saw a younger girl approach the podium and take the microphone. She began, *"Never be like a flag, dependent on the capricious breeze for its direction. Be the captain of your ship; chart a course and navigate with determination in choppy waters. You alone are the master of your destiny and responsible for keeping your humanity in the harshness of life. Do that; no matter what happens, you will be proud of who you are."* *She turned and smiled at Trey. As I watched, I saw him look toward the flag as though he had taken the speech personally. I saw his eyes were wet, as a proud smile formed on his face.*

All at once, his name sounded through the air as his walker came forward. He struggled to stand. His legs were weak as he pushed his wheelchair aside. He had long since forgotten what it felt like to have joints that moved freely. His memories both warmed and haunted him, sometimes drawing a smile and other times a tear. And time was the thief he always suspected her of being. The students that surrounded him seemed to respect that he had come this far. They didn't know him from their classes, but somehow, they were drawn to him and his accomplishments.

As Trey wrestled his walker with a shuffling gait across the stage, I felt the urge to help him but knew he must do this alone. He took three more steps, waited, and then pushed forward. The students watched as he walked three more.

I felt a hand press onto my shoulder and turned to see that Russell, Cameron, and Madison had made their way behind me. I smiled at Marco and once again was proud to be their mother. Madison bent down and whispered to me. "He can make it, Mom. I'm so proud of him."

I felt the love and hope the other kids in the audience felt. Their enthusiasm raged as Trey took one more step, just one more, to the podium. Tears of pride filled my eyes as I grabbed for Marco's hand. I sat without a word and watched him receive his diploma. I saw the students' faces around me and heard people clapping and cheering and then saw them rising to a standing ovation. Trey's proud smile was infectious as I saw his eyes go in search of me. As our eyes met, no words needed to be said. I knew how he felt. I felt the same.

I am proud of the man who never gave up, the man I always believed in, and the man who proved everyone wrong. He is a determined man, a proud man, a confident man. Now, I sit back and see him engage with the world around him, loving life, and happy to be alive. A different path might have held less pain but not more love.

Trey sits back and lets the happiness soak right into his bones. He wants the feeling to last forever. He closes his eyes and savours every moment. For the first time, his body and mind are relaxed. At this moment, there are no expectations made of him, no deadlines and no schedules to meet. He is in; he's made it; he has found himself.

Acknowledgement

It would be thoughtless if I did not thank the many people who helped me survive Travis's early days, the empty nights without him, the hospital and life after his overdose.

I thought about you, my husband, Marc, and gratitude filled my heart just a moment ago. So before another minute passes, I want to thank you. You have been my rock, and I don't know how I could have survived this without you. You held me up when things looked down, cried with me while you held me in your arms and believed in me when all of my belief was gone. Without your strength, patience and love, I would never have survived.

To my beautiful and talented daughter, Mekenzi, thank you for keeping me grounded throughout the years and teaching me to see life through clear eyes. The last sixteen years have been a long haul for you and me, and there are many thank yous that I owe you. You are a bright, insightful co-editor who helped me unravel many emotional problems and storylines. I thank you for all those brainstorming sessions over a glass of wine and those last-minute read-throughs. You stood beside me through the roughest times. I love your insistence that I complete the book and the assurance that it will be successful. Thank you for holding my hand when I felt so helpless and for the times you offered me a hug when I couldn't hold back the stream of tears. I would never be able to come this far without you here beside me.

To my sons, Rustin and Claitn, who stood strong in Marc's and my absence, keeping the business growing and holding Travis close to your hearts and in your thoughts. You are warriors in everything you do, and I'm proud to be called your mom.

Thank you to everyone at South Coast Medical Center who cared for Travis on the sixth floor. It was a labour of love for all of you, and I appreciate it more than you know.

I want to thank those who took the time to laugh with Travis and make him feel successful and loved. You are the special people who can take credit for keeping him motivated.